ANNALS of DYSLEXIA

Annals of Dyslexia is listed in *Current Contents/Social and Behavioral Sciences* (CC/S&BS), the Social Sciences Citation Index© (SSCI™), and *Chicorel Abstracts to Reading and Learning Disabilities*. Microfilm and photocopies are available from University Microfilms International.

Annotated and Indexed by the ERIC Clearinghouse on Handicapped and Gifted Children for publication in the monthly print index *Current Index to Journals in Education* (CIJE) and the quarterly index, *Exceptional Child Education Resources* (ECER).

The Orton Dyslexia Society
Chester Building/Suite 382
8600 LaSalle Road
Baltimore, MD 21204-6020

Printed in the United States of America

Notice

Members of The Orton Dyslexia Society receive ANNALS OF DYSLEXIA without charge. Additional copies of this issue are available from The Orton Dyslexia Society at $13.00 each for members and $16.00 each for nonmembers plus 20% for postage and handling. Send orders prepaid to the address above.

Cover design: Joseph M. Dieter Jr.
Compositor: Brushwood Graphics, Inc.
Printer: Port City Press

ISSN 0736-9387

ANNALS OF DYSLEXIA

Volume XXXXI   1991

Contents

FOREWORD

Once again The Orton Dyslexia Society is privileged to present a series of papers by distinguished researchers and practitioners in the field of dyslexia. Each year our Associate Editors and members of the Editorial Advisory Board review an increasing number of submissions. This reflects both a growing interest in all aspects of dyslexia and a recognition of the position that *Annals of Dyslexia* has achieved in this field.

Publication of *Annals of Dyslexia* is a year-round task, with much of the work being done by volunteer readers. The Society's annual national conference continues to be a primary source for much of the contents, but each year we receive more unsolicited manuscripts than in the previous year. We welcome this trend for it substantiates our view that more and more scholars are turning their attention to the issues of language learning disorders.

The 1991 *Annals of Dyslexia* marks my eighth year as Managing Editor. Over the course of these years I have had the pleasure of meeting and working with many of the finest workers and writers concerned with dyslexia. I have had the support of knowledgeable and skilled professionals who have given their time to review the works submitted to this journal; and I have had at my right hand one of the very best copyeditors and proofreaders, Myra K. Hicks. To her and to all who continue to make *Annals* possible each year, I again express my gratitude.

If you are interested in submitting a paper to be considered for publication in the 1992 *Annals of Dyslexia,* please request a copy of Information for Contributors from the Society and follow it carefully when preparing your paper. In addition to this style guide, we suggest that prospective authors familiarize themselves with and adhere to the principles of good writing found in *The Elements of Style* by William Strunk and E. B. White, available in paperback at most bookstores. Our goal, as befits an organization devoted to language usage, is to have *Annals* reflect the highest standards of clear, concise, comprehensible writing.

All papers in the current issue, as well as previous issues (including those from *Bulletin of the Orton Society*) are available from The Orton Dyslexia Society, Chester Building/Suite 382, 8600 LaSalle Road, Baltimore, Maryland 21204-6020. Cost, including postage and handling for reprints and photocopies is $3.00. An index of past papers covering the years 1957–86 may be purchased for $2.00.

Rosemary F. Bowler
Managing Editor

The Samuel T. Orton Award for 1990
Presented by The Orton Dyslexia Society to
Diana H. King

Presentation by Shirley Kokesh

We are here to celebrate the evolution of a dream. Forty years ago, Diana Hanbury King, a vibrant University of London graduate, who read voraciously and wrote eloquently, discovered that intelligence and motivation were not sufficient for the world of language to unfold for many children. When her passion for the written word was not enough to enable her to teach reading to a young nephew living in Africa, she began her "walkabout" in the world of dyslexia. Driven by the mystery of the "why not?," she set in motion a perpetual search for answers, a search that thrives today.

While teaching the first form in The Ruzawi School in Southern Rhodesia, Diana developed some permanent convictions about teaching children. "When a child is not learning, the teacher is not teaching," she observed. Thus, when she found one child who was unable to learn to read, she changed her strategies. "Spell the word out loud and see if that helps you to remember it;" "write the word many times until you know it," she would advise her students. She lived Montessori's maxim that if, indeed, you observe the child, he will teach you all you ever need to know. Since the children she taught in Africa never learned to print, Diana has always believed that cursive writing is both viable and desirable as a beginning skill, and if we would but remove the "fence posts" we ask children to use as a tool, they could prove it. As her career began with limited teaching materials, she has often declared that if you can engage children with paper and pencils, you can call yourself Teacher.

The fact that Diana is being honored here in Washington, D.C. is quite fitting. It was here at the Sidwell Friends School that she first learned about the Orton-Gillingham approach. As a fifth grade teacher and a tutor in the Language Training Department, she mastered the multisensory, sequential program under the direction of her mentor, Helene Durbrow. In those few years, she had the occasional opportunity to work under the scrutiny of Anna Gillingham as well. She absorbed the tenets of the successful "Problem Prevention Program," where the children identified as having difficulty with language skills were placed together in one of the four first-grade classes. They were taught phonics and cursive writing from the start. The class was kept together through the primary grades and by the fourth grade the children were on a par with their nondyslexic peers. Only the extreme cases required more intense remediation. In the early 50s, Helene and Diana witnessed a successful program in which dyslexics never had to experience failure. Even more profoundly, they did not need a law or child advocate to ensure the children's right to appropriate teaching.

At the age of 28, Diana launched the initial phase of her legacy. Combining interests in both camp directing and teaching, she purchased property in an isolated area of western Pennsylvania and founded Camp Dunnabeck. Modeled after Helene Durbrow's Camp Mansfield, the eight-week tutorial program for dyslexic students was created on that site. It contained a lodge, eight cabins, and a barn. When I joined the staff several years later, we had about 32 campers, seven tutors, a riding instructor, and an artist in residence.

Diana became my mentor. Gifted teaching was only one of her innumerable talents. From George Washington University, she had earned a Masters Degree in Comparative Germanic Philology. She spoke Italian with the art instructor, French and German with well-travelled tutors, and taught Latin to anyone who was willing to learn. No one could keep up with her schedule including six or seven tutoring students, five hours of Senior Study Hall, the inspection of cabins and fingernails, the counseling of the boys found sitting on "bad boy's rock" outside her cabin, and ending with a trail ride in the moonlight or the exploring of an unmarked, unlit cavern after a three-mile hike. I have seen her nurse sick children and an ailing horse in the same hour, make breakfast for the entire camp when it was too foggy for the cook to climb the Summit, and look into the sky to determine whether a sudden thunderstorm would occur in the middle of the evening activities. Vigor and intensity have always characterized Diana's behavior. Camp Dunnabeck became synonymous with phenomenal growth in language skills, self-esteem, and study habits for both the students and the staff.

While the summers were spent in Farmington, Diana worked the remaining part of each year at the Potomac School in Maryland. There she taught English to grades eight and nine and tutored middle and upper school students who were dyslexic. She ran a complex lighting system for the school's elaborate dramatic presentations, learned to scuba dive, and conducted workshops during the formative years of what is now The Orton Dyslexia Society.

After eleven years of that rigorous routine, Kurt Goldman, an appreciative parent, supported Diana's dream of one day creating a year-round program. Together they founded The Kildonan School, located in Solebury, Pennsylvania. To my knowledge, it was the first school in the country to serve only the dyslexic child and to provide daily individual tutoring in Orton-Gillingham language skills as part of the student's regular curriculum. Even today, there are only about ten such boarding schools.

The Kildonan School is now 22 years old. For the past eleven years it has been on a 450-acre campus in Amenia, New York. Like the original Camp Dunnabeck, it is surrounded by the grandeur of hills, and insulated from malls and mobs. Diana's courage, vision, and unique teaching abilities, have made what was once a mere whisper in the air a reality.

As a member of the Board of Directors for The Orton Dyslexia Society and the Capital District Council, and as a member of the Advisory Council for the New Community School, her expertise in identifying problems and developing solutions has enabled the plight of the dyslexic to be diminished in great measure. Diana's five publications devoted to writing skills have enabled literally thousands of teachers and children to profit from her years of experience and her clear thinking. Through her unexcelled energy, her commanding presentations, and her sincere dedication to teaching, she has eliminated illiteracy within some of the brightest minds in this country. There is no greater service to democracy than educating our children; no more demanding job than teaching them to read with accuracy and inspiring them to read with insight. Diana Hanbury King has earned her place in the Orton constellation. With the love of every child who can read because of you, Diana, I present the 1990 Samuel T. Orton Award.

The citation:

Samuel T. Orton Award Citation for Diana H. King

Diana Hanbury King is a dynamic presence. As a tutor, she penetrates the entangled language of a dyslexic, organizes and encourages it, and dares it to flow. As a teacher and administrator, she is generous with her expertise, exacting in her expectations, and bold in protecting the student's right to an optimum education. She has the energetic spirit and inspired vision essential to found and direct both Camp Dunnabeck and The Kildonan School and has enhanced beyond measure the quality of life for a myriad of dyslexic students and their families. On behalf of the positive force her gifted teaching has set forth in serving this Society, we are proud to present the 1990 Samuel T. Orton Award to Diana Hanbury King.

Response
by Diana H. King

I have been attending these meetings for almost 40 years now, and have listened to many award acceptance speeches, often critically, never dreaming that my day would come.

It is unfortunate that Regina Cicci received the award last year because hers was the best such speech we have ever heard. She expressed clearly and beautifully what The Orton Dyslexia Society has meant to all of us. Regina's is a tough act to follow.

In her opening remarks, she referred to this audience as a captive one. I want to talk about a different sort of captive audience.

Every Monday and Wednesday I walk through a metal detector so sensitive that I have to remove not just my ring and bracelet, but my watch and shoes as well. I pick up my ID, sign in, and pass through seven locked doors before I enter my classroom. Since last spring, I have spent close to three hundred hours in this maximum security prison with this truly captive audience. How did I get there? Well, Roger Saunders passed on to me a letter from an inmate, and Bob Hall gave me some books. Why do I go? I think I can best answer that question by telling you about an inmate whom I will call Jose . . . not his real name.

On the first day, faced with a class of half a dozen men, who seemed to know the sounds of the consonants but not much else, I groped for something that would work, and showed them how an *e* on the end of a word makes a vowel say its name. I had them read words . . . *safe, joke, home, name*. . . . When it was Jose's turn his voice became increasingly high pitched and tense. I said, "You're doing fine . . . just relax."

He said, "You don't understand. I want to say something."

We looked at him and listened. He said, "I have never been able to read words before. Always, the teacher said to me, 'just concentrate and try harder . . . you can do it,' and, always, I just got a headache." Another man remarked, "I have been looking for a class like this for three years now."

Well, six months later, Jose can read. Last week he came to class waving duplicate copies of a ticket he had received for some minor infraction. He insisted on reading all of it aloud, and with very little help decoded *vi o la tion, mis be ha vior* and *reg u la tion*.

In New York State, there are 56,000 inmates. Sixty percent of them are illiterate. Wilson Anderson tells me that 80 percent of all adult illiterates are dyslexic. New York's rate of recidivism is 41.2 percent, but among those who have passed the GED since being sentenced, the rate of return to prison is estimated at 17.1 percent. There are perhaps better ways of solving our crime problem than building more jails.

But it is not necessary to be in jail to be a captive . . . to be emotionally crippled by frustration and failure. Every year at Dunnabeck in the summer and at Kildonan in the fall we see ten- and twelve-year-olds who cannot write the letters of the alphabet and fifteen- and sixteen-year-olds who do not know vowel sounds, have never read a book, and cannot write a simple paragraph.

Years ago we used to believe that the need for special programs and schools would diminish, that dyslexic students would be diagnosed before they had a chance to fail, that they would be taught by the multisensory alphabetic approach through which they can learn and that this would happen in public schools throughout the land.

I have a grandson, probably dyslexic, and "at risk." Guess how he is being taught to read. Well, he is learning to read the names of the colors. And yesterday a former student told me about his dyslexic daughter in fourth grade. She has difficulty in copying from the board . . . her teacher cannot understand why. The love of this child's life is singing in the chorus. A while ago her teacher said to her, "If you go on getting D's in spelling, you won't be allowed to sing in the chorus." Fortunately her father knew exactly what to do and to say. But things like this should not be happening to children.

As I said earlier, I have been coming to these meetings for a long time. I attended my first, brought by Helene Durbrow, in 1950 or 51. Some of us remember these gatherings of fewer than a hundred people . . . now the Society's membership has grown to over 9,000. But clearly it is not enough.

Ten years ago in Boston, I had the honor of presenting this award to my mentor, Helene Durbrow. Now that it is my turn, I have had the joy of having it presented to me by a teacher with whom I started working over 30 years ago. Moreover, two of Helene's children in this audience worked with me almost that long ago. One of the advantages of this Society is that we are able to gather here and pass on what we have learned . . . so that the growth of the Society is both down in time and out into space. Anna Gillingham had a bookplate with a picture of a banyan tree sprouting roots from its branches and spreading and spreading . . . a good metaphor for the Society.

I am specially happy to be receiving this award in Washington. I taught here for many years, first at Sidwell Friends School and then at the Potomac School. But it was in Southern Rhodesia that I fell in love with teaching. I went out for an interview to this place of white Cape Dutch styled buildings set in green playing fields and shadowed by eucalyptus trees. I really wanted that job. In college I had studied the legend of Dr. Faust who sold his soul to Mephistopheles for what he wanted. I believe I would have done so too, but Mephistopheles wasn't around, so instead I made a pact with God . . . just let me have this and I will never again ask for anything for myself. And I never have . . . never needed to, because, you see, I have had the joy and the privilege of teaching all these wonderful students and of watching the pattern of their lives change as they gained the freedom that comes with confidence and skill.

Before school started in Rhodesia, I picked up a little book that purported to be a guide for the beginning teacher. It contained a lot of very British advice. On the first day, change everybody's seat. When, inevitably, some student remarks, "but I always sit here," you correct him by replying, "You mean, you always used to sit here." Having established your authority, you can then proceed to teach. But the book ended with a quotation from the greatest teacher of us all, "I am come that they might have life and that they might have it more abundantly." And it is this, surely, that best expresses our mission as teachers and as members of The Orton Dyslexia Society.

I am grateful to the Society for this award, of course, and for much else. For the many friendships, the generosity . . . the colleagiality . . . for too many people to mention. But there is something else . . .

When I was at school mandatory religious services were a daily event. And we often used to sing Blake's words, written about another kind of battle, in another country and in another century:

> Bring me my bow of burning gold!
> Bring me my arrows of desire!
> Bring me my spear! O clouds unfold!
> Bring me my chariot of fire!
>
> I will not cease from mental fight,
> Nor shall my sword sleep in my hand,
> Till we have built Jerusalem
> In England's green and pleasant land.

And it is The Orton Dyslexia Society that has provided all of us with somewhere to go in that chariot of fire and with something to do with that bow, that spear, and that sword. The battle for literacy is far from won, and there are still countless captives to be freed.

Part I
The Long View

Taking stock, viewing one's field in the context of its times, is essential for healthy growth. In this first section of the 1991 *Annals of Dyslexia*, we are privileged to present four papers which, in varying ways, look at where we have been and where we may profitably travel in the last decade of this century.

In her paper based on the Samuel T. and June L. Orton Memorial Address at the Society's 41st Conference in Washington, DC., Elisabeth Wiig describes the significant changes underway in the models on which practices in education, special education, and speech-language pathology are based. "Language Learning Disabilities: Paradigms for the Nineties" presents models for collaborative language intervention and provides descriptions of several means of implementing such models.

Viewing the world of dyslexia over the past three decades, C. K. Leong, in "Developmental Dyslexia Revisited and Projected," identifies elements in research, theory, and practice in the 1960s and 1970s, showing how all later work relates to these. He discusses several key issues of the 1980s, and then looks ahead to the challenges and the potential of applying computer technology to enhance teaching and learning.

Of special interest to teachers and clinicians is Betty Sheffield's "The Structured Flexibility of Orton-Gillingham." This paper presents the philosophic and historic foundations of the multisensory teaching approaches which derive from the work of Samuel T. Orton and Anna Gillingham.

Diane J. Sawyer and Katherine Butler provide us with a major study of the language roots of reading in "Early Language Intervention: A Deterrent to Reading Disability." They examine in depth what they consider the critical components of reading: phonological development, metalinguistic awareness (including auditory segmenting), syntactic development, semantic abilities, and short- and long-term memory skills. Their analysis of the research in these areas is supplemented by discussion of instructional practices which may help to level the playing field for young children at risk for language learning problems.

Language-Learning Disabilities: Paradigms for the Nineties

Elisabeth H. Wiig

Boston University
Boston, Massachusetts

We are beginning a decade, during which many traditional paradigms in education, special education, and speech-language pathology will undergo change. Among paradigms considered promising for speech-language pathology in the schools are collaborative language intervention and strategy training for language and communication. This presentation introduces management models for developing a collaborative language intervention process, among them the Deming Management Method for Total Quality (TQ) (Deming 1986). Implementation models for language assessment and IEP planning and multicultural issues are also introduced (Damico and Nye 1990; Secord and Wiig in press). While attention to processes involved in developing and implementing collaborative language intervention is paramount, content should not be neglected. To this end, strategy training for language and communication is introduced as a viable paradigm. Macro- and micro-level process models for strategy training are featured and general issues are discussed (Ellis, Deshler, and Schumaker 1989; Swanson 1989; Wiig 1989).

Introductory Overview

The intent of this work is to introduce special educators and speech-language pathologists to new philosophies and approaches for

The Samuel Torrey and June Lyday Orton Memorial Lecture, delivered at the 41st Annual Conference of The Orton Dyslexia Society, Washington, DC., November 1, 1990.

Annals of Dyslexia, Vol. 41, 1991.

delivering services to students with language disorders and learning disabilities. Collaborative IEP planning and curriculum related language intervention are discussed as viable and more meaningful alternatives to the traditional therapies. Process models for collaborative language intervention are presented and the need to adopt a new ethic and philosophy is stressed. Because our society is multicultural, process and content models for collaborative language assessment and intervention with multicultural populations are also featured.

Traditional language intervention often focuses primarily on developing linguistic skills. While linguistic skills, related to the content (semantics), structure (morphology and syntax), and use (pragmatics) of language, are prerequisites for language maturation, learning and using strategies for communication are essential for acquiring mature communication competence (metalinguistic ability). Strategy training principles and models are therefore introduced as essential components of language intervention for the purpose of supporting the linguistic transitions expected during adolescence.

The Paradigms

It is rare to be at a point and place when times and the tide converge to make change possible. Now is such a time for special education and speech-language pathology. The nation is asking for new paradigms to improve our educational standards and products. The Federal Government is supporting research and demonstration grants that introduce new and potentially more effective paradigms for assessment and intervention of learning disabilities and language and communication disorders.

Samuel T. Orton and his associates introduced powerful and lasting paradigms for dyslexia and learning disabilities. However, as any field advances, old paradigms are modified and new paradigms are introduced. Some prove of lasting and some only of temporary value. The field of speech-language pathology and within it, language-learning disabilities, has seen many paradigm modifications, innovations, and demises in the past decades. The transformational grammar revolution (Chomsky 1965) was succeeded by the pragmatics revolution (Austin 1962; Searle 1969). Currently, the traditional, skill-based therapy paradigms are being supplanted by collaborative, strategy-based paradigms. These paradigm shifts and what is involved are the focus of this presentation.

It is a well known fact that human beings embrace status quo and resist change. Changes require paradigm shifts and these are difficult to embrace cognitively, conceptually, and affectively. The need for a paradigm shift is sometimes caused by failure and sometimes by creativity and innovation. A paradigm is defined by Kuhn (1970) as a set of beliefs and/or theories held by a scientific community. One dictionary defines a paradigm as "a set of forms all of which contain a particular element . . .; a display in fixed arrangement in such a set; an example; pattern" (Stein and Urdang 1969, p. 1045). These definitions can be broadened by considering a paradigm to be a set or fixed pattern of goals, plans, perspectives, judgments, and approaches (Wiig, Secord, and Wiig 1990).

In speech-language pathology and language-learning disabilities, we should recognize that a paradigm shift is timely and called for now, when we consider our collective service record. Leaders in speech-language pathology, among them Costello (1983), Damico (1987), Miller (1989), Nelson (1989, 1990), and Simon (1987), question the effectiveness of traditional clinical approaches to language intervention for students of school age. It appears that paradigm shifts are becoming "musts" for speech-language pathologists and special educators in the schools.

In the second half of the 80s, two promising paradigms for language intervention have emerged. They are (a) collaborative language intervention and (b) strategy training for language and communication. The following sections consider models and procedures that are already tried and tested in these areas and discusses models which need to be developed.

Collaborative Language Intervention

Management Models

The Deming Management Method. Over the last decade, the industrial world has experienced a quiet revolution, originating in Japan, spreading to Europe and now making its impact in the United States. The revolution was instigated by W. Edwards Deming and centers around the Total Quality (TQ) concept (Deming 1986; Walton 1986). TQ is now finding its way into American schools. Speech-language pathology and special education have an opportunity to be among the leaders in introducing the TQ concept and the associated collaborative intervention models (Secord 1990).

The paradigm shift required to embrace the Deming Management Method concerns the underlying principles of how organizations and people are managed and work. It advocates participatory management and embraces collaboration as a work style. It does not focus on symptoms or on surface issues. Rather, it considers the quality of our work to be the primary factor in improving the value of our work to ourselves and society and therefore in increasing the demand for our services.

Deming centers his method in 14 points for management. The nine major points, adapted, are (Deming 1986, pp. 23–24):

1. Create **constancy of purpose** towards improvement [of process] . . .
2. Adopt a **new management philosophy** [participatory management and collaboration] . . .
3. **Cease dependency on inspection** to achieve quality . . .
4. **End the practice of awarding business on price tag** [alone] . . .
5. **Improve constantly and forever** the system of production . . .
6. **Institute training** on the job . . .
7. **Institute leadership** . . .
8. **Drive out fear** . . .
9. **Break down barriers** [to collaboration] . . .

The remaining five points are closely related. They focus on aspects of implementation. The last point admonishes management to "Put everybody . . . to work to accomplish the transformation."

It should be evident that embracing and implementing Total Quality is not easy and requires a process with radical changes. The first is the requirement for a paradigm shift in perspectives, values, judgments, and approaches. The second is for collaboration and participatory management, topics to be considered next.

Collaboration. Collaboration is a philosophy, perspective, and ethic and a participatory work style that involves two or more people as equals. It must be supported by management to succeed. Furthermore, collaborative efforts, rather than individual competitive results must be rewarded by the system. Collaboration is achieved in a developmental process with well-defined stages, premises, and tenets. Phillips and McCullough (1990, p. 295) list the following as tenets and characteristics:

1. Joint responsibility for [case management and] problems.
2. Joint accountability, recognition, and reward for [case management and] problem resolution.
3. Belief that pooling talents and resources is mutually advantageous.
4. Belief that . . . problem resolution merits expenditure of time, energy, and resources.
5. Belief that the correlates of collaboration are important and desirable.

Because collaboration is a work style and ethic, success will depend, in part, on characteristics and levels of involvement by the participants (Marvin 1990; Wiig, Secord, and Wiig 1990). Consultation and collaboration readiness are important ingredients. Marvin (1990) discusses a model for levels of readiness which can be applied directly by management. The model rates the levels of readiness for consultation as *None, Social, Limited, Adequate, Informed,* and *Reciprocal.* For each level, the model describes affective, cognitive, and behavioral consultee characteristics and related consultant priorities.

Wiig, Secord, and Wiig (1990) identify knowledge, perspectives, and values that must be shared by the participants for successful collaboration. Among them are that they must:

(a) Share common goals for the collaboration.
(b) Be willing and permitted to work together.
(c) Have compatible and interactive work styles.
(d) Share enough knowledge to understand ideas and suggestions presented by other participants.
(e) Have complementary knowledge to achieve leverage.
(f) Have sufficiently different perspectives and experiences to give valid and diverse contributions.
(g) Be secure that future careers will be promoted.
(h) Find it desirable to continue collaboration.
(i) Be allowed or assigned to perform the work in collaboration as part of overall duties.

Management Decisions. Deming (1986) maintains that Total Quality can only be adopted by an organization if there is support and leadership from management in a "top-down" process. Special education and speech-language pathology are not always in positions to influence policy or educational institutions "top-down." Yet, the knowledge and perspectives for collaborative language interventions and the potential for leadership reside within these fields.

Wiig (in progress) and Wiig, Secord, and Wiig (1990) have diagrammed how a *"bottom-up"* process could be initiated to change a system towards collaboration (Figure 1). The middle section, framed for ease of identification, represents changes that must occur at the level of management. The top segment represents the knowledge and perspectives of special educators and speech-language pathologists and how these can provide input for a change process and paradigm shift. It becomes the role of special educators and SLPs to provide the insights and information needed for management to change their conceptualizations of effective service delivery models and to make it clear that collaboration is desirable and can be achieved.

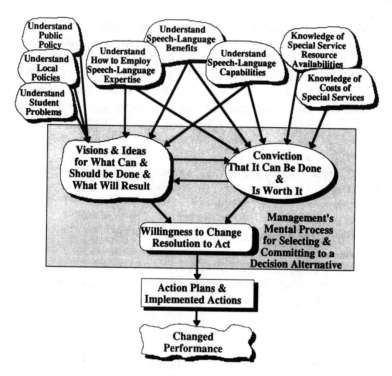

Figure 1. Conceptualization of a "bottom-up" process for developing collaborative
language intervention.
Source: Wiig, Secord, and Wiig 1990. Reprinted with permission
by authors.

Implementation Models

Problem Solving and Decision Making.   Collaboration requires problem solving at all levels and stages of development and implementation. Problem resolution is often perceived and approached as an
adversary process. The participants jostle for position. In collaboration,
competition must be abandoned for constancy of purpose to foster a
better process and product. Ishikawa proposed a multi-dimensional
problem-solving method for industry. The method relies on developing cause-effect diagrams, often called *"fishbone"* diagrams (Walton
1986, pp. 98–101).

Wiig, Secord, and Wiig (1990) provided an example of a cause-
effect diagram. It was generated in collaborative problem solving to identify and remove barriers to Total Quality SLP services (Figure 2). The
diagram shows several causes that were identified to be barriers for collaboration. These causes were first grouped into four generic categories:

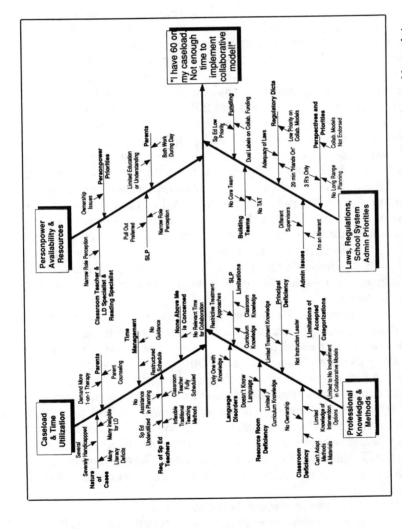

Figure 2. Illustration of a cause-effect ("fishbone") diagram for collaborative problem solving. Source: Wiig, Secord, and Wiig 1990. Reprinted with permission by authors.

9

1. *Caseload and time utilization.*
2. *Person-power availability and resources.*
3. *Professional knowledge and methods.*
4. *Laws, regulations, and school system administrative priorities.*

Within each category, such as professional knowledge and methods, impacting factors, such as funding, regulatory dictates, and role perceptions, were identified. The details of a diagrammatic representation of real and perceived barriers to delivering quality services can make it easier to identify priorities and obtain consensus for change. It can help identify what can be changed, what cannot be changed, and in sequencing the agreed-upon changes in a developmental process.

IEP Planning.   Assessment and IEP planning appear to be natural entry points for beginning collaboration in special education. Mandates, such as *Public Law 94–142*, and proposals, such as *The Regular Education Initiative*, propel us in the direction of collaboration. In spite of intentions, true cross-disciplinary collaboration rarely occurs when a child is referred for evaluation of communication status and language disorders. Generally, each discipline involved will present its data and arrive at its decisions about the case. The content, quantity, setting, and methods for language intervention are often developed with only short-term objectives, tend to be deficit driven, and are closely tied to the results of norm-referenced tests. In other words, the ensuing IEP for language intervention for a child is often clinical, rather than educational in nature.

After extensive collaborative IEP planning interactions, Secord and Wiig (in press) presented a collaborative IEP planning model. This model can be perceived to contain three major phases. The first is the data collection phase (Figure 3). During that phase, the speech-language pathologist, referring classroom teacher, LD specialist, or special educator collect observations from, among others, norm- and criterion-referenced testing, classroom observations, and teacher interviews and checklists. A diagnosis, identification of intrapersonal strengths and weaknesses, and determination of eligibility are derived from the SLP and psychoeducational test data. Teacher and other observations serve as validation and for identification of classroom difficulties and needs.

The second phase (Figure 4) encompasses *data analysis and synthesis* to arrive at intervention objectives. After all data are collected, they are compared and restructured in relation to the educational domains: listening, speaking, reading, and writing. Subsequently, classroom language adaptations, enhancement, and intervention needs are formulated and language arts curriculum objectives that are "at risk" are identified. Clinical-educational language intervention objectives are

Collaborative IEP: Data Collection

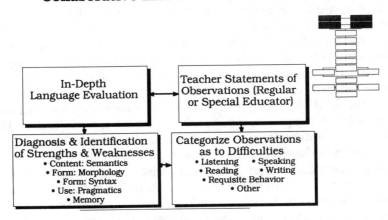

Figure 3. *The collaborative IEP planning model: Data collection.*
Source: Secord and Wiig in press. Reprinted with permission by authors.

developed next. Premises for intervention are then developed and modified until cross-disciplinary consensus has been reached. We have found the development and acceptance of premises for intervention to be critical. This process focuses the group, establishes relevant priorities, and avoids later conflicts, when short- and long-term IEP objec-

Collaborative IEP: Data Analysis and Synthesis

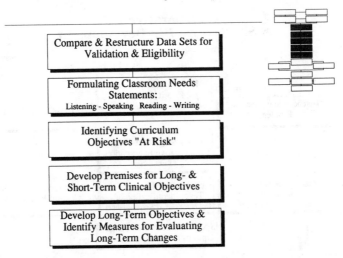

Figure 4. *The collaborative IEP planning model: Data analysis and synthesis.*
Source: Secord and Wiig in press. Reprinted with permission by authors.

tives and specific aspects of implementation are decided upon. As an example, a collaborative assessment team accepted the premise that traditional pull-out language therapy twice a week would be inadequate for the extent of the given child's language problems. As alternatives were explored, members of the group wanted to resort to pull-out therapy. By pointing to the consensus premise, all potential conflicts were curtailed.

The third phase (Figure 5) encompasses *identification and development of two or three priority areas for collaborative language intervention*. The priorities are derived from the teacher's observations, test results, statements of classroom problems, and perceived classroom language needs. Specific objectives for the cross-disciplinary collaborative language intervention efforts are then developed. The members of the collaborative team are first identified by referring to resource availability (e.g., staff, funding, materials, equipment). The roles and responsibilities of individual team members are then specified. Finally, intervention models and formats for classroom and other language interventions are specified.

The dynamic changes resulting from collaborative, rather than domain specific, IEP planning can best be illustrated by contrasting the pre- and post-collaboration IEPs for one child (Table I). The child was in Grade 1 (age 6 years, 4 months) at the time of assessment. The pre-collaboration IEP typifies SLP goals and objectives. It is deficit driven and objectives are closely tied to the norm-referenced tests used for

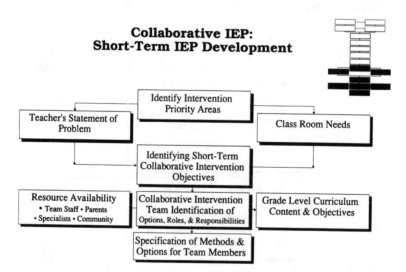

Figure 5.   The collaborative IEP planning model: Short-term IEP development.
Source: Secord and Wiig in press. Reprinted with permission by authors.

Table I
A Contrastive Overview of Pre- and Post-collaboration IEPs for a Child with a Language Disorder in Grade 1.

PRE-COLLABORATION	POST-COLLABORATION
Objective: To improve expressive language use. *Objective:* To improve understanding and use of action verbs. *Methods:* List actions of a noun. Use correct verb tense. *Objective:* To increase vocabulary. *Methods:* Group attributes; name items in a category; state likenesses and differences. *Objective:* To increase understanding and use of synonyms, antonyms, and multiple meaning words. *Methods:* State synonyms; substitute synonyms; state opposite. *Objective:* To improve auditory processing skills. *Methods:* Follow one-, two-, and three-level commands; recall and describe familiar experiences; retell familiar stories; answer questions about read stories.	*Objective:* To improve the ability to follow/carry out directions for classroom, academic, and daily living tasks. *Methods:* Develop classroom scripts and routines to support memory, organization, and inferencing. *Objective:* To improve the ability to express thoughts and needs in structurally adequate units (phrases, clauses, sentences). *Methods:* Develop linguistic rule system through interactive reading, role playing, preliteracy and integrated listening, speaking, reading, writing activities. *Objective:* To improve the ability to organize and plan classroom and daily living tasks. *Methods:* Model, break down, and analyze tasks to strengthen the awareness of scripts for action sequences and of time requirements.

assessment. In contrast, the post-collaboration IEP focuses on a few academically relevant areas and states goals and objectives for collaborative language intervention across the curriculum.

Instruction and Resource Models. Decisions about collaborative intervention options should be made within the framework of models that consider the student's needs and the available instructions and resources. Donaldson and Christiansen (1990) presented a two-phase model for collaborative decision making. The first is the entry phase, during which the student's learning problems and academic areas of need are analyzed. The second phase focuses on instruction and resource analysis. The model features a set of Yes/No questions. The answers (*Yes/No*) lead directly into decisions about instructional options.

The decision points are arranged sequentially, in a problem-solving format. The model encompasses five sets of options. They are: (1) *Behavior management;* (2) *Part-time assistance;* (3) *Instructional options* (e.g., curriculum adaptation, modification); (4) *Instructional options combined with part-time assistance;* and (5) *Full-time assistance.* The model can be applied directly to decision making for language intervention. The only requirement would be to consider the options from a language and communication perspective.

Multicultural Issues. Because we are a multicultural community, collaborative issues in serving multicultural populations must also be addressed. Damico and Nye (1990) introduce a comprehensive model for collaborative language intervention for multicultural populations. The model contains two interrelated phases. The first is the collaborative assessment program. Embedded in this phase are pre-referral, descriptive, and explanatory assessment. These assessments are followed by standardized assessments featuring task analysis, language sampling, direct observation, curriculum-based assessment, contextual analysis, and ethnographic assessment.

The second phase concerns the collaborative intervention program. The model presents three decision areas, leading to a language plan, appropriate placement, and/or an additive language-learning environment. It also presents an overview of intervention options. They are: (1) *Pragmatic/holistic paradigms;* (2) *Mediational techniques;* (3) *Curriculum modification;* (4) *Sheltered instruction;* (5) *Peer tutoring;* and (6) *Cooperative grouping.* The model holds excellent promise for quality services when implemented collaboratively.

Strategy Training

Communication as Strategic Action

Speech-language pathology is known for its frequent paradigm shifts in relation to intervention content and procedure. The field embraced transformational grammar (Chomsky 1965) whole heartedly, at the same time disregarding valid "traditional" content and procedures. In time, the field encompassed pragmatics (Austin 1962; Menyuk 1983; Searle 1969) and abandoned linguistic structure and rule learning as focii for language intervention. During the eighties, metalinguistic and strategy training paradigms for language intervention have become more and more evident (Haslett 1987; Kamhi 1987; Silliman 1987; Wiig and Secord 1985, 1989; Wiig 1982, 1985, 1989). Strategy training paradigms appear to hold promise for developing metalinguistic and metacognitive abilities essential for the transitions from concrete operational to formal operational communication and thinking with language as the tool. Fortunately, it appears that speech-language pathology has advanced to a level where it is possible to assimilate new paradigms without destroying valid traditional or prior ones in the process.

Before considering paradigms for language and communication strategy training, two underlying concepts, metalinguistic ability and strategic language use, need to be defined and differentiated. Metalinguistic ability is characterized by conscious awareness of language, ability to reflect on aspects or characteristics of language use, and ability to use language as a tool (Cazden 1972; Menyuk 1983). There is considerable overlap in the meanings of "metalinguistic ability" and "strategic language use," but there are important differences. One difference is that strategic language use presupposes metalinguistic and metacognitive abilities. The second is that strategic language use has its basis in problem solving (generating options and alternatives) and decision making (selecting among options).

Problem Solving and Decision Making

Loban (1976) identified three distinguishing features of communication in a longitudinal comparison of communicatively competent (efficient) and incompetent (inefficient) children and adolescents. The two groups differed along three continua in language production: (1) *Fluency* (rapid and consistent word finding to express semantic intents); (2) *Coherence* (planning and organizing the content of messages); and (3) *Effectiveness and control* (mastering conventional grammar, using a variety of structures, and using conditional statements to express higher level concepts). The two last features are intricately related to problem solving, decision making, and, therefore, to strategic language use.

Because mature communicators (ages 11 to 13 and up) function under a number of interactive constraints, they must problem-solve and generate communication options continuously. We can isolate some of the constraints that determine the range of options for communicating (Wiig 1990). Among them are that the speaker must:

(a) *adhere to communication principles and maxims* (quality and quantity);
(b) *respond to controlling variables* (participants, settings, media, topics, objectives);
(c) *respond to affective and conceptual listener perspectives;*
(d) *follow underlying schema and scripts* (e.g., narrative, discourse);
(e) *use linguistic and pragmatic knowledge, rules, and conventions* to formulate intentions (speech acts).

Decision making (selecting among options) for communication is also a complex affair. Selecting a communication option frequently involves *'risky' decision making* (Gilhooly 1988). This is because of the uncertainty that exists about the outcome or effectiveness of any communication approach. The decision making is complicated by the fact that *multi-attribute* and *multi-stage decisions* are often required. Several attributes of the communication context must be weighed and integrated with prior knowledge before a communication option is decided upon. Moreover, in discourse each choice leads to one of a number of options. As a result, a sequence of decisions is often required, as if the interaction were a chess game. Each of these features can be illustrated by referring to the decisions required for complaining, negotiating, and apologizing under different constraints.

Strategy Use and Expertise

There is consensus that experts in any field, including communication, use efficient, domain-specific, and/or general strategies (Dreyfus and Dreyfus 1986; Swanson 1989). The term "strategy" is often used in the context of game playing. It can be thought of as a method by which, given a decision point (node), a move is chosen which leads to an ultimate win, if a win is possible (Banerji 1987).

Within a broader context, Restle (1962) defined a strategy as a particular pattern of responses to stimuli or tasks that has been inferred over a series of trials. Either definition can be applied to language and communication. First the premise must be accepted that speaker-listener is involved in a "game." Second, we must agree that strategies are learned in a process. If these premises are accepted, a strategy can be defined as:

> A procedural routine or process that responds to underlying concepts, communication plans (schema, scripts), goals (objectives, intentions) and perspectives (affective, conceptual). The procedural routine or process (strategy) may be communication context specific or it may be context independent (Wiig 1989).

There are several views of what constitutes expertise and how it is developed. In spite of differences, all recognize that expertise is related to efficient use of domain-related strategies for solving problems and making decisions. They also agree that strategies are acquired in goal-directed processes. Beyond the similarities, Dreyfus and Dreyfus (1986) point out that experts understand situations and tasks, such as communicating, holistically and intuitively. Strategies, decisions, and actions are called up automatically and result in rapid, fluent, flexible, and coherent performance. It should be noted here, that the same characteristics were observed among competent speakers by Loban (1976). Gilhooly (1988) reminds us that in many fields expertise is achieved only after about ten years of study and practice. The similarity to the ten years normally used to achieve communication competence is startling.

Studies of normally-developing children indicate that expertise is related to strategy transformation. In the transformation, simple approaches and strategies are reworked into more efficient strategies. Several strategies may be merged into a single unit or reduced to a rule with a constant relationship and unnecessary parts are deleted (Swanson 1989). The transformations may be required before situations can be approached intuitively and holistically and strategies are used automatically.

Communication Strategy Training

Swanson (1989) summarizes recent research of students with learning disabilities by saying, "LD children experience difficulty with such self-regulating mechanisms as checking, planning, revising, and evaluating during an attempt to learn or solve problems" (p. 4). By adding the phrase "inherent in communication," the summary captures the language and communication problems observed among children and adolescents with language-learning disabilities.

Silliman (1987) suggested three, of several possible, factors related to the strategic inefficiencies observed in LLD students. They are: (1) *Insufficient content knowledge;* (2) *Inefficient processing;* and (3) *Inadequate management of available processing resources"* (p. 361). To these, Wiig (1989) added limitations in pattern recognition, reasoning approaches, problem solving, and decision making. The latter limitations were supported by Stone and Forman (1988) and Wansart (1990). Strategy training for communication seems a promising paradigm for the nineties, especially, because its efficacy has received support in controlled studies (Mandelbaum 1985; Simmonds 1990).

The advantages of strategy instruction have been captured succinctly by Swanson (1989). He states that it "focuses on what is modifiable," "allows for conscious and active rule creation," incorporates the notion that strategies may operate differently with different declarative (internal organization of prior knowledge) and procedural knowledge (knowledge about real-life performances), and "allows the child to be actively involved in the instruction" (p. 5).

While every source stresses the student's active role in strategy training, instructors also have responsibilities for structuring success (Pressley et al. 1989; Wiig 1989). First, the instructor must be able to analyze communication tasks. Second, the instructor must have knowledge of communication maxims, linguistic and pragmatic rules and conventions, controlling variables for communication, and of underlying concepts, schema (mental models), scripts (situational, cause-effect), and routines (unvarying event series). Third, the instructor must structure training within a complete model of strategy training and use. Fourth, the instructor must focus on content as well as process. In the context of communication training, linguistic skill and rule development should obviously be integrated in training.

Strategy Training Models

Strategy training for language and communication involves an active and interactive process. Wiig (1989) described the process in terms of targeted levels of competence. In the Levels of Competence Model, *Basic Training* provides structured, preferably experientially based, training to develop knowledge of (a) critical features and underlying concepts, schema, or scripts in linguistic stimuli (narrative, discourse) and (b) rules and conventions for communication in context. Deductive and inductive paradigms are also used during basic training. Among possible objectives are to decontextualize word definitions and to explicate underlying patterns, schema and scripts, often diagrammatically. In regular classroom teaching, structure, decontextualization, and explication are often missing as they may not be needed by normally developing learners.

The second level, *Extension to Pragmatic Uses*, extends the basic knowledge of features, concepts, and patterns (schema, scripts, routines) to pragmatic, every day uses. The tasks are kept fairly simple at that level. The students are allowed reference to definitions and diagrams developed in basic training. Students may be asked to problem-solve and make inferences from conversation based on established concept knowledge. They may be asked to use their knowledge of rules, schema, or scripts to analyze or produce discourse, narratives, or constraint-seeking questions. The primary learning and reasoning paradigms are deduction (exploration of prior knowledge), induction (pattern recognition and abstraction), and abduction (using facts and prior knowledge to arrive at hypothetical assertions) (Chandrasekaran 1983, 1986).

The third level, *Extension Across Media, Participants, and Contexts*, focuses on extending the established knowledge to more and more complex and/or abstract communication tasks. The objectives are generalization and independence in problem-solving and decision-making. New media (e.g., telephone, computer, written communication), participants (e.g., authority figures, strangers), and contexts (e.g., academic and curriculum, community, vocational, professional) are introduced. Students may also be asked to extend concept knowledge to figurative language use. The learning and reasoning paradigms include deduction, induction, abduction, and analogy (combines deduction and induction) (Chandrasekaran 1983, 1986).

The last level, *Self-Directed Training*, supports independent application of the acquired concepts, rules, schema, and scripts. At this level, students are given assignments to carry out and report to the group, either orally, in writing, through arts, or in computer, film, or video presentations. The objectives for training are to develop independence in planning, organizing, self-monitoring and self-evaluating, editing, revising, and automatizing strategy use. Students may be given assignments such as (1) reporting on how metaphors are used in advertising or (2) how dimensions (e.g., size, length, width, depth, volume) are described and labelled in daily life and business. Students are expected to use pattern recognition and established strategies for problem solving and decision making.

The Levels of Competence Model addresses the learning process at the macro-level. Models are also necessary for addressing problem solving and decision making for communication at the micro-level. Two strategy training models apply. The first is the *Executive Strategy* training model (Ellis, Deshler, and Schumaker 1989). The second is the Process Model for Communication Strategy Training (Wiig 1989). In a short overview, the Executive Strategy model features four steps: (1) *Focus on the problem situation;* (2) *Identify and analyze the critical features of the problem;* (3) *Generate a series of problem-solving steps;* (4) *Monitor the effectiveness of the self-generated strategy and make necessary modifications.*

Wiig's process model isolates and focuses more specially on pattern recognition, hypothesis formulation, and hypothesis testing as steps in communication strategy acquisition. It assumes that the trainer can support strategy development by (a) refocusing attention, (b) providing contrasting models to support pattern abstraction and recognition, (c) providing cues and cue reduction, and (d) rewarding divergent thinking, problem solving, and probabilistic thinking and decision making. The model itself features five steps in a process considered hierarchical, recursive, and reducable with increasing competence.

The **first step** focuses on getting the learner to actively identify features of linguistic stimuli and communication contexts that may, or may not, be significant. The **second step** focuses on getting the learner to perceive patterns in the abstracted features of linguistic stimuli and communication contexts. The **third step** requires the learner to formulate and test hypotheses about the identified features and patterns. The **fourth step** supports the learner in decision making, selecting and executing a potentially effective communication response. The **fifth step** supports the learner in self-monitoring and evaluating the efficacy of the selected response, and to repair and revise as needed. This micromodel is essentially generic and has been applied in controlled study (Mandelbaum 1985) and in field tested intervention materials (Wiig 1989).

Conclusion

This presentation emphasizes the need for a paradigm shift for providing speech-language pathology services to students of school age with language-learning disabilities. We have advocated a need for intervention practices that:

1. Respond to students' language and communication difficulties and needs in the classroom and in real life.
2. Focus on academic success and life-time adjustment.
3. Reflect long-term, holistic thinking.
4. Use highly focused short-term intervention objectives, that several professionals can implement collaboratively, across the curriculum.
5. Emphasize student strengths and use problem-solving processes to develop strategies for language and communication.
6. Are delivered in a student-centered approach that embraces Total Quality concepts.

To achieve these goals, we presented an array of process models for management, IEP planning, and intervention. The models are intended to provide a focus and give constancy in developing an effective process for service delivery. The models should not be perceived as static templates for implementation, but as dynamic modifiable plans. They should be adapted to fit individual settings and curricula. Only in that way will professionals assume ownership of the process and continue to develop and refine models to enrich the paradigms.

References

Austin, T. T. 1962. *How To Do Things With Words*. Cambridge, MA: Harvard University Press.

Banerji, R. 1987. Game playing. In S. C. Shapiro (ed.). *Encyclopedia of Artificial Intelligence*. Volume 1 (pp. 312–318). New York: John Wiley and Sons.

Cazden, C. 1972. *Child Language and Education*. New York: Holt, Rinehart, and Winston.

Chandrasekaran, B. (1983). Towards a taxonomy of problem-solving types. *AI Magazine*, 4:9–17.

Chandrasekaran, B. (1986). Generic tasks in knowledge-based reasoning: High-level building blocks for expert system design. *IEEE Expert*, Fall, 23–30.

Chomsky, N. 1965. *Aspects of the Theory of Syntax*. Cambridge, MA: MIT Press.

Costello, J. 1983. Generalization across settings: Language intervention with children. In J. Miller, D. Yoder, and R. Schiefelbusch (eds.). *Contemporary Issues in Language Intervention* (pp. 275–297). Rockville, MD: American Speech-Language-Hearing Association.

Damico, J. 1987. Addressing language concerns in schools: The SLP as a consultant. *Journal of Childhood Communication Disorders* 11:17–40.

Damico, J. S. and Nye, C. 1990. Collaborative issues in multicultural populations. *In* W. A. Secord (ed.). *Best Practices in School Speech-language Pathology: Collaboration.* San Antonio, TX: The Psychological Corporation.

Deming, W. E. 1986. *Out of the Crisis.* Boston: MIT Center for Advanced Engineering Study.

Donaldson, R. and Christiansen, J. 1990. Consultation and collaboration: A decision-making model. *Teaching Exceptional Children* 22:22–25.

Dreyfus, H. and Dreyfus, S. E. 1986. *Mind over Machine,* New York: Macmillan.

Ellis, E. S., Deshler, D. D., and Schumaker J. B. 1989. Teaching adolescents with learning disabilities to generate and use task-specific strategies. *Journal of Learning Disabilities* 22:108–119.

Gilhooly, K. J. 1988. *Thinking: Directed, undirected and creative.* New York: Academic Press.

Haslett, B. 1987. *Communication: Strategic action in context.* Hillsdale, NJ: Erlbaum.

Kamhi, A. G. 1987. Metalinguistic abilities in language-impaired children. *Topics in Language Disorders* 7:1–12.

Kuhn, T. S. (1970). *The Structure of Scientific Revolutions* (2nd ed.). Chicago: University of Chicago Press.

Loban, W. 1976. Language development: Kindergarten–grade 12. Urbana, IL: National Council of Teachers of English.

Mandelbaum, S. E. 1985. *Constraint Questions: How can they be taught to children with special needs?* Doctoral dissertation, Boston University.

Marvin, C. A. 1990. Problems in school-based, speech-language consultation and collaboration services: Defining the terms and improving the process. *In* W. A. Secord (ed.). *Best Practices in School Speech-language Pathology: Collaboration.* San Antonio, TX: The Psychological Corporation.

Menyuk, P. 1983. Language development and reading. *In* T. M. Gallagher and C. A. Prutting (eds.). *Pragmatic Assessment and Intervention Issues in Language Disorders* (pp. 151–170). San Diego: College-Hill.

Miller, L. 1989. Classroom-based language intervention. *Language, Speech, and Hearing Services in Schools* 20:153–170.

Nelson, N. 1989. Curriculum-based language assessment and intervention. *Language, Speech, and Hearing Services in Schools* 20:170–184.

Nelson, N. 1990. Only relevant practices can be best. *In* W. A. Secord (ed.). *Best Practices in School Speech-language Pathology.* San Antonio, TX: The Psychological Corporation.

Phillips, V. and McCullough, L. 1990. Consultation-based programming: Instituting the collaborative ethic in schools. *Exceptional Children* 56:291–304.

Pressley, M., Symons, S., Snyder, B. L. and Cariglia-Bull, T. 1989. Strategy instruction research comes of age. *Learning Disability Quarterly* 12:16–31.

Restle, F. 1962. The selection strategies in cue learning. *Psychological Review* 69:329–343.

Searle, J. R. 1969. *Speech Acts: An essay in the philosophy of language.* Cambridge, GB: Cambridge University Press.

Secord, W. A. (ed.). 1990. *Best Practices in School Speech-language Pathology.* San Antonio, TX: The Psychological Corporation.

Secord, W. A. and Wiig, E. H. (In press). The power of collaboration: IEP planning, *Journal of Childhood Communication Disorders.*

Silliman, E. R. 1987. Individual differences in the classroom performance of language-impaired students. *Seminars in Speech and Language* 8:357–375.

Simmonds, E. P. M. 1990. The effectiveness of two methods for teaching a constraint-seeking questioning strategy to students with learning disabilities. *Journal of Learning Disabilities* 23:229–232.

Simon, C. S. 1987. Out of the broom closet and into the classroom: The emerging SLP. *Journal of Childhood Communication Disorders* 11:41–66.

Stein, J. and Urdang, L. 1969. *The Random House Dictionary of the English Language.* New York: Random House.

Stone, C. A. and Forman, E. A. 1988. Differential patterns of approach to a complex problem-solving task among learning disabled adolescents. *The Journal of Special Education* 22:167–185.

Swanson, H. L. 1989. Strategy instruction: Overview of principles and procedures for effective use. *Learning Disability Quarterly* 12:3–15.

Walton, M. 1986. *The Deming Management Method.* New York: Perigree.

Wansart, W. L. 1990. Learning to solve a problem: A microanalysis of the solution strategies of children with learning disabilities. *Journal of Learning Disabilities* 23:164–170.

Wiig, E. H. 1982. *Let's Talk: Developing prosocial communication skills.* San Antonio, TX: The Psychological Corporation.

Wiig, E. H. 1984. Language disabilities in adolescents: A question of cognitive strategies, *Topics in Language Disorders,* 4, 51–58.

Wiig, E. H. 1985. *Words, Expressions, and Contexts: A figurative language program.* San Antonio, TX: The Psychological Corporation.

Wiig, E. H. 1989. *Steps to Language Competence: Developing metalinguistic strategies.* San Antonio, TX: The Psychological Corporation.

Wiig, E. H. 1990. Linguistic transitions and learning disabilities: A strategic learning perspective. *Learning Disabilities Quarterly* 13:128–140.

Wiig, E. H. and Secord, W. A. 1989. *Test of Language Competence-Expanded.* San Antonio, TX: The Psychological Corporation.

Wiig, E. H. and Secord, W. A. 1990. Developing a collaborative language intervention program. Working papers for seminar presentations.

Wiig, K. M. In progress. *Knowledge Management: Managing to win.* Arlington, TX: The Wiig Group.

Wiig, K. M., Secord, W. A., and Wiig, E. H. 1990. Deming goes to school: Developing total quality services in SLP. *In* W. A. Secord (ed.). *Best Practices in School Speech-language Pathology: Collaboration.* San Antonio, TX: The Psychological Corporation.

Wiig, E. H., and Secord, W. A. 1985. *Test of Language Competence.* San Antonio, TX: The Psychological Corporation.

Developmental Dyslexia Revisited and Projected

Che Kan Leong

University of Saskatchewan
Saskatoon, Saskatchewan

There are three parts to this paper. First, I review briefly the signposts from research, theory, and application in developmental dyslexia in the 1960s and the 1970s that have led us from there to here, and show the pitfalls to avoid. Second, I discuss some of the pertinent issues of the 1980s: the role of intelligence in the diagnosis of children with specific reading disabilities, the distribution of reading difficulties and disabilities, and the important place of verbal efficiency. Third, I project to the 1990s to emphasize the challenge of the computer technology as mediated learning and the challenge of "bounded rationality" and "collective rationality" in education. Throughout this survey, the paramount role of knowledgeable and caring teachers is implicit.

The Recent Past—The 1960s and the 1970s

Developmental Dyslexia Defined

I take as a convenient starting point for this overview the classic books *Reading Disability* (1962), edited by John Money, and *Developmental Dyslexia* (1964), authored by Macdonald Critchley. Money (1962, p. 9) defined the condition this way: "Dyslexia means defective reading.

Portions of this paper were given at the British Dyslexia Association Conference on Dyslexia in Bath in 1989 and The Orton Dyslexia Society Annual Conference in Washington, D.C. in 1990. The writing of the paper was assisted in part by research grant No. 410-89-0128 from the Social Sciences and Humanities Research Council of Canada

Annals of Dyslexia, Vol. 41, 1991.
ISSN 0736-9387

The reading defect may represent loss of competency following brain injury or degeneration; or it may represent a developmental failure to profit from reading instruction." The operative words for our purpose are "defective" and "developmental failure." Does defective reading mean difficulty with words or discourse above the word level? If words, does it mean decoding, and, if so, in what way? If comprehending, does it mean "functional grammar in the classroom" (Perera 1984) and/ or comprehension in general? Further, what is the role of reasoning ability in specific reading disabilities? The concepts of "defect," "deficiency," and "difference" are among those with which researchers and practitioners continue to grapple. By and large, we are dealing with inefficient processing of language and the writing system by these children (Leong 1987). The developmental aspect in Money's definition does highlight the persistence of the disabilities, if not diagnosed and treated in good time, in great intensity, and in an appropriate manner. The developmental emphasis also alerts us to the need to work with adults who continue to manifest the symptoms of "defective" reading.

It is instructive to compare the Money definition with a reasonable, neuropsychological definition offered by Steven Mattis (1978):

> Dyslexia is a diagnosis of atypical reading development as compared to other children of similar age, intelligence, instructional program, and sociocultural opportunity which, without intervention, is expected to persist and is due to a well-defined defect in any one of several specific higher cortical functions (p. 54).

The differentiation between a given observable disorder in dyslexia and in brain-damaged individuals is an important one, but one not easily made. What must be delineated are "atypical reading development," impairment in "specific higher cortical functions," and whether or not such an impairment is a deficiency which is amenable to remediation, and not just a defect as such. While the presence of a specific disorder in a critical process implies the presence of dyslexia, Mattis is careful to point out that "the absence of this specific defect does not imply the absence of the disordered reading" (Mattis 1978, p. 56).

Psychometrically, developmental dyslexia refers to a heterogeneous group of reading disabilities characterized by reading/spelling attainment significantly below the level predicted on the basis of the child's chronological age or measured intelligence (Leong 1987; Rutter 1978). Clinically, we may say that we all know a dyslexic child when we see the symptoms. Or do we?

What then are some of the things that we have learned from or some of the pitfalls to avoid? I outline below the main ones as I see them.

Modality Concept only Indirectly Relevant

There was a time in our work with dyslexics that the concept of the visual and auditory modalities was held to be of importance. Reference to visiles and audiles types of dyslexics can be found in early works (e.g., Money 1962). These modality-specific perceptual difficulties were held to differentiate ways that children learn to read. There were also training programs which purported to train "visual perception" or "auditory perception" on the grounds that so-called visual or auditory imperception would lead to reading disabilities. All the while, there was clear research evidence that the difficulties that disabled readers experience were not with the optical but the linguistic components of reading. In this regard, Orton's (1925, 1928) concept of strephosymbolia or twisted symbols was found to be too narrow. The proportion of optical reversal errors compared with consonant segment and vowel segment errors has been shown to be small with unselected second grade readers (Liberman et al. 1971), and with 8- to 10-year old developmental dyslexics (Fischer, Liberman, and Shankweiler 1977).

Eye Movements the Result of Reading

There was a time that eye movements were thought to be a "cause" rather than the result of reading difficulties and ocular training was prescribed as training for some children with specific reading disabilities. Research evidence on this issue is quite clear from the early treatise (Tinker 1958), to the more recent, elegant studies on eye movements as reflecting cognitive-monitoring processes in reading (see Rayner 1978, for review). Parenthetically, the finding by Stein and Fowler (1982a, 1982b) of visual dyslexics tending towards unstable ocular dominance in achieving fusion in binocular vision has generated some interest and has led to the reminder by Benton (1985) that visual factors in dyslexia should not be dismissed entirely.

Unwarranted Neurologizing and other Claims

There was the further claim that in working with dyslexics and even in schooling, we were teaching "right-brained children in left-brained schools." This kind of neurologizing was no doubt a misguided and unwarranted extrapolation of the studies of split-brain patients. Nobel laureate Roger Sperry (1982) rightly cautioned educators that "The left-right dichotomy in cognitive mode is an idea with which it is easy to run wild . . . The need for educational tests and policy measures to identify, accommodate, and serve the differentially specialized forms of individual intellectual potential becomes increasingly evident" (pp. 1223–1226). If it is visual-spatial ability that we would want to emphasize, there is no need to link this with hemispheric specialization. Some years ago, Macfarlane Smith (1964) wrote an informative treatise on spatial ability and its educational and social significance without any reference to hemispheric functions.

There were also dismaying and fairly large claims made which persist to the present day and which are not supported by research. As an example, there is a proposal that dyslexia results from a cerebellar-vestibular (c-v) related oculomotor dyscoordination and can be ameliorated by oculomotor training and through the use of "c-v harmonizing agents," including such anti-motion sickness drugs as methyphenidate (Ritalin), which are presumed to act on the cerebellar-vestibular system (Levinson 1980). This doubtful concept of dysmetric dyslexia (DD) because of the putative distortion of the cerebellar-vestibular function and the large claim of success needs to be evaluated with rigorous, double-blind studies (Masland and Usprich 1981).

As yet another example, the Tomatis (1978) audio-psycho-phonology training for dyslexics, practised in some school districts in Canada, is flawed. The general principle is that the voice can produce only what it hears and that many dyslexics have difficulties listening, particularly to high frequency sounds. Within this putative psychoacoustic framework, Tomatis suggests that dyslexia can occur in children whose hearing acuity is intact but whose ability to listen and to communicate is impaired. The inner ear in concert with the vestibular system is seen by Tomatis as coordinating and integrating various sensory and motor functions to achieve "central equilibrium." To maintain this balance, some "structuring dynamics" of listening and speech skills must be established. Tomatis proposes that this structuring is done through the Tomatis listening training program (LTP) which incorporates an "Electronic Ear" as the hardware of the main programming component. There are several stages in training, all emphasizing auditory stimulation and auditory vocal exercises. Suffice it to say that what evidence there is suggests only short-term gains in the achievement of the dyslexics so treated. In general, these studies are neither constructively critical of the conceptual framework, nor are they overly sophisticated in their research designs.

The one exception is the two-year study of the efficacy of the Tomatis listening training program by Kershner, Cummings, and Clarke (1986). These researchers evaluated the pretest, posttest and follow-up performance of a target group (Tomatis LTP), placebo group, and "no treatment" group of a total of 42 children aged 8 to 12 years, all with "developmental learning disabilities," from a school recognized for its remedial teaching. The pretest and posttest design was used with blind testing on a number of achievement, cognitive, neuropsychological, and psycholinguistic measures; and social-emotional and dichotic listening scores. Multivariate analyses of variance (MANOVA) with age-adjusted scores were computed. In general, the rigorous analyses show that the Tomatis listening training program did not have an effect on the children's audio-phono development tested on the key Tomatis Listening Test. There was no improved hemispheric information processing as claimed, nor were there any treatment effects on specific subtypes of learning disorders. Furthermore, any apparent gains made by the target students were found to be the "combined result of the individual care, motivation, and effective remedial instruction, and not the LTP"; and thus "time taken from school hours for such activities [LTP] is without empirical justification" (Kershner, Cummings, and Clarke 1986, p. 43).

Summary of this Section

It may be pointed out that while authors of these and other "solutions" to dyslexia and related disabilities have no doubt believed in their treatment of their patients, their basic tenets need to be substantiated and empirically verified. The onus is on the researchers to support the claims they make. To paraphrase what Darwin wrote in the *Voyage of the Beagle:* "If the misery of [dyslexics] be caused not by the laws of nature, but by our institution, great is our sin."

Lest I be misunderstood, the "unwarranted neurologizing" alluded to earlier applies only to those works on brain-behavior relationship which are not well supported by theory and not verified empirically. While the treatment of dyslexics is largely an educational enterprise, advances in unravelling the etiology come from the neurosciences. As an example, Geschwind and Galaburda (1985) hypothesized that one possible reason for the poor reading of dyslexics is their poorly formed callosal connections which lead to anomalous hemispheric specialization. In their analysis of "contemporary mainstream views" of incomplete cerebral dominance derivable from Orton (1925) in relation to reading disabilities, Gladstone and Best (1985) also emphasized the role of interhemispheric communication as a possible explanation for some types of dyslexia. Another contribution from the neurosciences to the research agenda is the putative link between left-handedness and early childhood disorders including dyslexia as attributable to the hormonal and immune environment of the individuals affected (Geschwind and Behan 1982). This possibility raises hope for intervention, and very tentative results suggest that an environment may be "controlled" biochemically so as to minimize the disabilities without negating the so-called "right-hemisphere" talents not uncommon in dyslexics (Geschwind 1983).

The Present—The 1980s to 1991

So much about the very recent past, what are some of the current issues? These issues seem worthy of attention: (a) The relationship of intelligence to achievement tests in the diagnosis of disabled readers; (b) The distribution of reading disabilities; (c) The involvement of verbal ability in reading; and (d) The covariance of phonology, morphology, and syntax in reading.

The Relationship between Intelligence and Achievement Tests

Despite the similarity of a number of items between traditional intelligence tests such as the WISC-R and the Stanford-Binet and achievement tests, the use of predicted scores from a regression between aptitude (measured intelligence) and performance (achievement) as proposed by Robert Thorndike (1963) still provides a sound psychometric means of ascertaining those children with specific learning difficulties. Elsewhere, I have made some suggestions for the improvement of aptitude-learning discrepancy based on signal detection principles (Leong 1985, 1987, 1989a).

The general idea is one of maximizing hits (those children diagnosed who are actually disabled) and minimizing misses (those children not diagnosed but actually disabled), especially false alarms, by setting up differential thresholds of cutoff scores. In the North American context, if we continue to use a well-standardized general ability test as a yardstick of learning aptitude, there are reasons for adjusting the threshold in such a way so that the hits are maximized and the misses are minimized. The degree of stringency or otherwise of the threshold depends, among other things, on the purpose of the assessment or diagnosis, on social and administrative factors.

Distribution of Specific Reading Disabilities

Whether disabled readers form a *qualitatively* different subgroup, as shown in the "hump" in the distribution of reading disabilities or whether they are part of the low reading continuum is not settled. Yule et al. (1974) found such a hump in their epidemiological study, while Rodgers (1983) using more discriminating reading tests was not able to replicate the Yule et al. findings. In his review of Vellutino's (1979) book, *Dyslexia,* Calfee (1983) stated that he actually plotted the distribution of several standardized tests on probability paper and obtained some equivocal results. He found neither evidence of a clearcut hump nor evidence of normal distribution and termed the finding a "curious puzzle" (p. 75). Further statistical evidence seems needed to make a strong claim for either the discontinuous or continuous distribution of specific reading disabilities.

There is, however, some clinical and also experimental evidence to suggest that those with specific reading disabilities are qualitatively different from those who are at the low end of the reading continuum (Leong 1987). Genetically, the males with 47, XXY chromosomes found to have language-specific difficulties with a high frequency of learning disorder (Pennington et al. 1982) may well be part of this hump. This claim of possible qualitative differences in those with specific reading disabilities and those who are "poor" readers should be compared with the finding of mainly quantitative differences between the two groups by Olson et al. (1985). Olson et al. found that the dyslexic groups lagged about two years behind the poor reading groups in word recognition, but both groups showed similar phonological coding deficits relative to "normal" readers. However, these researchers also acknowledged that there could be some unique dyslexics who deviate from the normal distribution and are difficult to detect statistically without careful behavioral, neurological, and genetic analyses.

Role of Verbal Efficiency in Reading

Mention has been made about the role of general ability in reading and its difficulties. When reading is teased out into interrelated components, general ability does not correlate very highly with these subskills. I present some evidence to support this assertion from a two-year study just completed with two cohorts of 300 grades 4, 5, and 6 children on componential analyses of reading (Leong 1988).

This developmental study was predicated on the logic of interrelated functional information processing components as an approach to understanding reading and its difficulties in preadolescent readers. The structural equation modelling involved these three latent components: (a) orthographic/phonological component; (b) morphological component; and (c) sentence and paragraph comprehension component. These components were subserved by a total of ten measurable tasks all administered on-line via the microcomputer under laboratory conditions with reaction time measures as indices of mental representation of word knowledge and sentence/paragraph comprehension. The details are given elsewhere (Leong 1988; Leong and Lock 1989). Suffice it to say that the correlations of the correct latency scores of the ten information processing tasks with the British Ability Scales (BAS) Matrix E (Elliott, Murray, and Pearson 1978) are rather low. However, the BAS correlates moderately with the Vocabulary and Reading Comprehension tests of the Canadian Tests of Basic Skills (King 1982), and there is also a moderate multiple R between BAS and the ten RT tasks and the two reading tests in a conjoint combination. Since traditional intelligence tests account for only a small proportion of the variance in different components of reading, it is likely that a considerable amount of the variation is explained by what Perfetti (1985) calls verbal efficiency.

What then constitutes this verbal efficiency? Rapid, automatic activation of word knowledge (phonological and morphological) interacting with discourse processing may be the underlying logic (Leong 1987).

Covariance of Phonology, Morphology, and Syntax

The covariance theory (van Orden 1987) states that in the development of word representation systems phonological knowledge will continue to be necessary for fluent reading but that morphemic knowledge is equally important for word processing and syntactical understanding. There are data from my two-year, two-cohort project to bear this out, at least with older readers in grades 4, 5, and 6 (Leong 1988, 1989b).

Of the different information processing tasks subserving reading, it is the Derived Morphology task which is the most predictive of reading performance as measured by an aggregate of standardized vocabulary and reading comprehension tests. The Derived Morphology task assesses the subject's knowledge of the derivation of words in sentential contexts at four levels of morphological complexity. An example of the deeper level of morphological changes is that of: *DECIDE:* Please let me know what you want: I like to have a _____. (DECISION). It should be noted that this task accounted for 32 percent, 34 percent, and 44 percent of the variance of the criterion of reading performance respectively for grades 4, 5, and 6. While there could be several explanations for this, one likely reason is that the task includes morphosyntactic representations and this involvement serves to link word meaning and paragraph comprehension as assessed by the aggregate vocabulary and reading comprehension tests scores. This interpretation can be accommodated within the covariance theory in that rule-like phonological coding is intrinsic to word identification at all levels of development and that there is also orthographic, morphemic, and syntactic aspects which contribute to reading proficiency.

Summary of this Section

While there are many issues confronting researchers and practitioners, I have chosen to highlight the continued need to examine the quantitative and qualitative differences between dyslexics and "poor" readers. In particular, reading proficiency and its difficulties are conceptualized as word knowledge interacting with discourse processing and both subserved by "world knowledge." The componential approach also offers promise of remediation.

Challenges of the 1990s

What can we say from theory, research, and practice for the immediate future? Again, there are different perspectives. I see before us for the next decade these challenges: the challenge of microcomputer technology and the challenge of education for "bounded rationality." These proposals are discussed in turn.

The Challenge of Microcomputer Technology

Without being overly euphoric about their role, we recognize that microcomputers are here to stay in our schools, in our homes, and in our work places. At the philosophical level, the potential of the computer for developing mental functioning and reorganizing higher order cognitive skills is increasingly recognized (Webb and Shavelson 1985). At the applied level, microcomputers in our schools have moved through the "tutor, tool, tutee" stages. There are now innovative computer programs to assist students in the learning of reading, writing, mathematics, and the sciences. The keynote here is *assistance* to the teacher. I will outline some approaches for work with dyslexics.

Training for Automaticity in Word Processing

One innovative computer system is the componential analysis and training of weak readers developed by Frederiksen, Warren, and Rosebery (1985a, 1985b). The general idea is to promote automaticity in accessing words so that resources can be devoted to reading comprehension. The training known as SPEED is designed to develop automatic processing of multiletter units in words, using a car race game format. An example is for the student to indicate both quickly and accurately whether or not a multisyllabic word contains the unit GEN. As the child acquires proficiency, the "game" will include larger chunks of word units. Frederiksen and his colleagues have demonstrated success with their students in a series of careful studies. The training to automaticity was found to lead to greater verbal efficiency.

"PALS" Computer System

Recently, the author of the IBM *Writing to Read* Program, John Henry Martin (1985), has extended his work upwards to train phonic subskills with a "high tech" computer environment for adult learners in a computer program known as *Principles of the Alphabet Literacy System* (PALS). Designed in a comic book format as an instructional station complete with IBM infowindow systems with personal computers, typewriters, a videodisc player, and the relevant softwares, the PALS system aims at upgrading the basic reading and spelling skills of marginally literate adults.

Training with Text-to-Speech DECtalk Computer System

For my own part, I have been undertaking some research and training studies with the sophisticated text-to-speech computer system DECtalk marketed by the Digital Corporation. The technical aspect of the conversion from unrestricted plain text to speech is documented in Allen, Hunnicutt, and Klatt (1987). The approach that I take is a concept-driven or top-down one, rather than the data-driven or bottom-up approach of PALS. The general idea is to harness the DECtalk computer system with its large vocabulary, its flexible phonemic and morphemic mechanisms, and high speech fidelity to provide both on-line and speech feedback to readers whenever they need such feedback.

There are two components to my research and training work. The research aspect seeks to study the effects of prose organization and individual differences on reading comprehension. The underlying notion is that the overt *inspection time* of segments of prose materials provides an index of reading comprehension. Further, the decomposition of the total reading time into different time segments helps to explain the variation due to different linguistic variables such as word frequency, word structure, text cohesion, and propositional units, and individual differences such as varying reading abilities (Kieras and Just 1984).

Of greater interest here is the *training aspect* of poor readers. The training uses the principle of self-paced on-line reading of appropriate text materials with *immediate* and *simultaneous* visual and speech explanation of difficult words and sentence constructions. An excerpt from an actual passage entitled "City versus Country Living" is shown below:

> Perhaps because I was born/ and brought up in the country/ I have always wanted to live/ near the heart of a great city./ Even now/ I look forward to the day/ when I can live again in Toronto./ I would like to taste again/ the diversity of the city./ I am not alone in Toronto/ even when I am alone./ . . .

The underlined difficult words (with their derivations) are explained simultaneously on-line and via DECtalk as follows: brought up [bring up]: grew up, reared; diversity [diverse]: variety, a great many activities or things. Following simultaneous on-line reading and listening to text or auding, inferential questions are asked via both the computer screen and the DECtalk speech, and the learners give open-ended answers which are immediately typed into the computer for storage and subsequent retrieval. Examples of questions and possible answers are as follows: What does the "heart" of a city mean? (The downtown area and, more importantly, the active, thriving part where there are lots of things going on.) The oral answers given by the learners obviate the need for writing on the part of the students. The transcribed versions from the computer printout can be analyzed for their levels of propositional thinking to provide another index of reading comprehension in addition to the inspection time measures on different segments of the prose materials.

Efficacy of Immediate On-Line and Computer Speech Feedback

The DECtalk computer system emphasizing the immediate bisensory feedback on-line and via computerized speech in a self-paced manner can be used with advantage for both older disabled readers and for marginally literate adults. The initial results from both the research and the training aspects are encouraging. There are, of course, conceptual, methodological, and technical problems to resolve and to refine. Some examples are the format and rate of computer and DECtalk presentation and interface, the different psycholinguistic variables used as indices of reading comprehension, and the continued fine-tuning of the computer programs. In particular, designing "usable" texts for the computer environment for efficient location and retrieval of information is one challenge facing researchers (Duffy and Waller 1985).

The Challenge of Education for "Bounded Rationality"

At the risk of being redundant, I want to reiterate the role of the computer technology as mediated learning and not as a replacement for the teacher. Computer technology as a metaphor underscores its fine-grained analysis of the step-by-step and labored learning of the novice (the disabled reader) compared with the rapid and smooth performance of the expert (the proficient reader). Furthermore, the root metaphor accents the diverse ways that learners can move forward, though some ways are shorter and easier than others. The computer metaphor should not be narrowly interpreted as dominated by boundaries and initial conditions as cognitive systems can be indeterminate and can take on continuous rather than discrete values (see, Leong 1989c, for discussion). The learner seen from this perspective is a dynamic, active information processor.

In this regard, the notion of "bounded rationality" is useful. In their review of education for reasoning within a psychological context, Shulman and Carey (1984) explained this notion as suggesting that "individuals actively make use of cognitive strategies and previous knowledge to deal with their cognitive limitations" (p. 509). While humans have the capacity to reason logically, a number of social scientists, including Nobel laureate Herbert Simon (1957), argue that rationality is

limited by certain inherent characteristics of human information processing, and that this leads to the development of mental representations of some aspects of the real world. Humans behave "rationally
with respect to this model, and such behavior is not even approximately optimal with respect to the real world" (Simon 1957, p. 199).

Cognitive Strategies

This perspective of bounded rationality positing the importance
of cognitive strategies raises a number of issues in the education of children in general and of those with learning problems in particular.
There are advances in theory and research in the promotion of thinking ability in children (see Chipman, Segal, and Glaser 1985; Nickerson, Perkins, and Smith 1985, for details). There are also training programs. These include Feuerstein's Learning Potential Assessment
Device (LPAD) and his Instrumental Enrichment (IE) as research and
remediation programs aimed at improving cognitive performance
(Feuerstein et al. 1980); and de Bono's CoRT program (de Bono 1973,
1985) designed to teach thinking in the classroom, among others.

In all these advances, one central question remains: Should training for cognitive development be domain-specific or within the context
of particular subject matters; or should this training aim at more general knowledge structure? One answer to the question of what develops in children's thinking is provided by Brown and Deloache
(1978): "That one aspect of 'what develops' is metacognition—the voluntary control an individual has over his own cognitive process"
(p. 26); and "an expanding knowledge of how to think and the ability
to monitor and coordinate the activities displayed in effective thinking" (p. 31). Metacognition is held to be important for both knowledge
and memory development, and this, of course, applies to literate activities of reading and writing. The "what develops" question must also
be studied with that of "how development occurs" or the conditions
that promote cognitive growth. In addition to the specificity or the gen-
erality question is that of engaging students *in* thinking activities and
not just teaching them *about* these activities.

Relevance to Disabled Readers

The earlier discussion of verbal efficiency and the above section on
cognitive development are relevant to our work with disabled readers.
A number of research articles in *Developmental Review* (see Crowder
1984, for representative and summary views) have rekindled debate on
the important question of whether or not the disabilities shown by disabled readers are more general than reading or written language itself.
Crowder is probably right that it is not just reading per se at which
disabled readers are poor; they are also inefficient in processing related

cognitive functions. In this regard, we are reminded of Edward Thorndike's (1917) comparison of children's reading of prose passages with the solution of mathematical problems. He wrote: "The mind is assailed, as it were, by every word in the paragraph. It must select, repress, soften, emphasize, correlate, and organize, all under the influence of the right mental set or purpose or demand" (p. 329).

In all this discussion of promoting verbal knowledge and cognitive development, we must not lose sight of learners as individuals and the pluralistic nature of learning in societies which are becoming more multicultural in nature. To some extent, it is envisioned that the microcomputer technology provides the tool for, and assists the teacher in, individualizing instruction for students with different aptitudes and cognitive abilities. In this regard, Howard Gardner (1983, 1985) eschews the uniformist or the unitary view of mind and proposes pluralistic "frames of mind" with multiple sets of capacities, which he terms *intelligences*. These capacities are relatively autonomous information processing modules triggered by specific environmental stimulation. The capacities or components are: verbal-linguistic, logical-mathematical, spatial, musical, motor-kinesthetic, inter-personal, and intra-personal "intelligences" together with "subintelligences." These interrelated intelligence domains have their biological bases and are expressed as a range of symbol systems such as linguistic, notational, pictorial, musical, kinesthetic, and affectic systems. Reading as the interpretation of symbols (linguistic system) could encompass the broad range of other symbol systems such as reading pictures and musical notations (Downing and Leong 1982).

From his pluralistic perspective of intelligences, Gardner (1988) proposes the preparation of our students for the future in greater depth with at least one area of "deep knowledge," rather than the more traditional broad approach. To maintain this breadth, he suggests alternating learning cycles of knowledge acquisition and development from breadth to depth to breadth and depth throughout the educative process. He further reiterates the importance of computer technology in matching students with suitable curricula and "optimal pedagogical approaches with those selected curricula" (Gardner 1988, p. 39).

The Learning Group

Having emphasized the role of microcomputer technology and that of the learner as an active information processor aided by the technology, I would also like to stress the social-cultural aspect impinging on our work. This is Shulman and Carey's (1984) concept of collective rationality, which is explained by them as the freedom for the learner to "transform, divide, redefine, and distribute parts of a task within a working group as needed" (p. 517). The working or learning group helps to redistribute or transform the tasks on hand and emphasizes the collective reasoning or procedures of the members to overcome the disadvantages of rational boundedness.

This notion, and indeed Feuerstein et al.'s (1980) concepts of *mediated learning experience* (MLE) and *Instrumental Enrichment* go back to Luria (1979) and mainly Vygotsky's (1934/1986) central tenet of the *zone of proximal development*. Luria explains "instrumental" as referring to "the basically mediated nature of all complex psychological functions" (p. 44). The zone of proximal development or Vygotsky's *zo-ped* is explained as:

> . . . the place at which a child's empirically rich but disorganized spontaneous concepts "meet" the systematicity and logic of adult reasoning. As a result of such a "meeting," the weaknesses of spontaneous reasoning are compensated by the strengths of scientific logic. The depth of zo-ped varies, reflecting children's relative abilities to appropriate adult structures. The final product of this child-adult cooperation is a solution, which, being internalized, becomes an integral part of the child's own reasoning. (Vygotsky 1934/1986, p. xxxv).

The learning group or the principle of collective rationality acts as a powerful means to promote learning.

Summary of this Section

In looking ahead to the 1990s, this section proposes as important the harnessing of the microcomputer technology for learning; and the promotion of cognitive strategies in learners as active information processors and as members of learning groups.

General Conclusion

I certainly cannot claim, as Sancho Panza did in reply to his master Don Quixote that "I understand no language but my own" when the two men talked about the adventures they had been through together. On the contrary, I benefit from the diverse "languages" and writings in penning this paper.

In my survey of work on developmental dyslexia in the immediate yester-years, the present times, and the coming decade, progress is clearly evident. Some 30 years ago, Macdonald Critchley (1968) discussed a number of areas worthy of further exploration in developmental dyslexia. These areas included: functional cerebral development in dyslexics; early diagnosis of "at-risk" children including the study of their speech and language development; detailed single-case studies with follow-ups; design of theory-based remedial programs and methods of instruction; understanding of cognitive strategies of these children. This listing of significant research topics was suggestive and by no means exhaustive. It can never be in a field where there is such a large number of children with special needs in a multiplicity of learning environments.

We must not cease from exploration, and at the same time let us hope that we should not "arrive where we started, and know the place for the first time," as reminded by T. S. Eliot. Without being incongruous or even macabre, this couplet from Dante's *Inferno* (xxxiv, pp. 96–97) may be an apt reminder in our way forward:

The way is long and the road is hard,
And always the sun is at mid-tierce.

We shall go forth.

References

Allen, J., Hunnicutt, M. S., and Klatt, D. 1987. *From Text to Speech: The MITalk system.* New York: Cambridge University Press.

Benton, A. 1985. Visual factors in dyslexia: An unresolved issue. In D. D. Duane and C. K. Leong (eds.). *Understanding Learning Disabilities: International and multi-disciplinary views* (pp. 87–96). New York: Plenum Publishing.

Brown, A. L. and Deloache, J. S. 1978. Skills, plans, and self-regulation. In R. S. Siegler (ed.). *Children's Thinking: What develops?* (pp. 3–25). Hillsdale, NJ: Erlbaum.

Calfee, R. 1983. [Review of Vellutino, F. R. 1979. *Dyslexia: Theory and research.* Cambridge, MA: MIT Press.] *Applied Psycholinguistics* 4:69–79.

Chipman, S. F., Segal, J. W., and Glaser, R. (eds.). 1985. *Thinking and Learning Skills* Vol. 2. Hillsdale, NJ: Erlbaum.

Critchley, M. 1964. *Developmental Dyslexia.* London: Heinemann.

Critchley, M. 1968. Topics worthy of research. In A. H. Keeney and V. T. Keeney (eds.). *Dyslexia: Diagnosis and treatment of reading disorders* (pp. 165–173). Saint Louis: C. V. Mosby.

Crowder, R. G. 1984. Is it just reading? Comments on the papers by Mann, Morrison, and Wolford and Fowler. *Developmental Review* 4:48–61.

de Bono 1973. *CoRT Thinking.* Blandford, Dorset, England: Direct Education Services Ltd.

de Bono 1985. The CoRT thinking program. In S. F. Chipman, J. W. Segal, and R. Glaser (eds.). *Thinking and Learning Skills. Vol. 1: Relating instruction to research* (pp. 363–388). Hillsdale, NJ: Erlbaum.

Downing, J. and Leong, C. K. 1982. *Psychology of Reading.* New York: Macmillan.

Duffy, T. M. and Waller, R. (eds.). 1985. *Designing Usable Texts.* New York: Academic Press.

Elliott, C. D., Murray, D. J., and Pearson, L. S. 1978. *The British Ability Scales.* Slough, UK: NFER.

Feuerstein, R., Rand, Y., Hoffman, M. B., and Miller, R. 1980. *Instrumental Enrichment:*

An *intervention program for cognitive modifiability.* Baltimore, MD: University Park Press.

Fischer, F. W., Liberman, I. Y., and Shankweiler, D. 1977. Reading Reversals and Developmental Dyslexia: A further study. *Haskins Laboratories Status Report on Speech Research, SR-51/52*, 75–89.

Frederiksen, J. R., Warren, B. M., and Rosebery, A. S. 1985a. A componential approach to training reading skills: Part 1. Perceptual units training. *Cognition and Instruction* 2:91–130.

Frederiksen, J. R., Warren, B. M., and Rosebery, A. S. 1985b. A componential approach to training reading skills: Part 2. Decoding and use of context. *Cognition and Instruction* 2:271–338.

Gardner, H. 1983. *Frames of Mind: Theory of multiple intelligences.* New York: Basic Books.

Gardner, H. 1985. *The Mind's New Science.* New York: Basic Books.

Gardner, H. 1988. Mobilizing resources for individual-centered education. *In* R. S. Nickerson, and P. P. Zodhiates (eds.). *Technology in Education: Looking toward 2020* (pp. 25–41). Hillsdale, NJ: Erlbaum.

Geschwind, N. 1983. Biological associations of left-handedness. *Annals of Dyslexia* 33:29–40.

Geschwind, N. and Behan, P. 1982. Left-handedness: Association with immune disease, migraine, and developmental learning disorder. *Proceedings of the National Academy of Sciences of USA* 79:5097–5100.

Geschwind, N. and Galaburda, A. M. 1985. Cerebral lateralization. Biological mechanisms, associations, and pathology: II. A hypothesis and a program for research. *Archives of Neurology* 42:521–552.

Gladstone, M. and Best, C. T. 1985. Developmental dyslexia: The potential role of interhemispheric collaboration in reading acquisition. *In* C. T. Best (ed.). *Hemispheric Function and Collaboration in the Child* (pp. 87–118). New York: Academic Press.

Kershner, J., Cummings, R. L., and Clarke, K. A. 1986. *Two Year Evaluation of the Tomatis Listening Training Program with Learning Disabled Children.* Toronto: The Ontario Institute for Studies in Education, University of Toronto.

Kieras, D. E. and Just, M. A. (eds.). 1984. *New Methods in Reading Comprehension Research.* Hillsdale, NJ: Erlbaum.

King, E. M. (ed.). 1982. *Canadian Tests of Basic Skills: Multilevel edition, Levels 9–12, Forms 5 & 6.* Toronto: Nelson.

Leong, C. K. 1985. Diagnosis for learning in children with special needs. *In* D. D. Duane and C. K. Leong (eds.). *Understanding Learning Disabilities: International and multidisciplinary views* (pp. 49–63). New York: Plenum Publishing.

Leong, C. K. 1987. *Children with Specific Reading Disabilities.* Lisse, The Netherlands: Swets and Zeitlinger.

Leong, C. K. 1988. A componential approach to understanding reading and its difficulties in preadolescent readers. *Annals of Dyslexia* 38:95–119.

Leong, C. K. 1989a. The locus of so-called IQ test results in reading disabilities. *Journal of Learning Disabilities* 22:507–512.

Leong, C. K. 1989b. The effects of morphological structure on reading proficiency—A developmental study. *Reading and Writing: An Interdisciplinary Journal* 1:357–379.

Leong, C. K. 1989c. A schoolman's doubtfulness: Metaphors on literacy and cognition. *In* C. K. Leong and B. S. Randhawa (eds.). *Understanding Literacy and Cognition: Theory, research, and application* (pp. 17–31). New York: Plenum Press.

Leong, C. K. and Lock, S. 1989. The use of microcomputer technology in a modular approach to reading and reading difficulties. *Reading and Writing: An Interdisciplinary Journal* 1:245–255.

Levinson, H. N. 1980. *A Solution to the Riddle Dyslexia.* New York: Springer-Verlag.

Liberman, I. Y., Shankweiler, D., Orlando, C., Harris, K. S., and Berti, F. B. 1971. Letter confusions and reversals of sequence in the beginning reader: Implications for Orton's theory of developmental dyslexia. *Cortex* 7:127–142.

Luria, A. R. 1979. *The Making of Mind: A personal account of Soviet psychology.* M. Cole and S. Cole (eds.). Cambridge, MA: MIT Press.

Martin, J. H. 1985. The writing to read system and reading difficulties: Some preliminary observations. *In* D. D. Duane and C. K. Leong (eds.). *Understanding Learning Disabilities: International and multidisciplinary views* (pp. 159–163). New York: Plenum Press.

Masland, R. and Usprich, C. 1981. [Review of Levinson, H. N. 1980. *A Solution to the Riddle Dyslexia.* New York: Springer-Verlag.] *Bulletin of the Orton Society* 31:256–261.

Mattis, S. 1978. Dyslexia syndromes: A working hypothesis that works. *In* A. L. Benton and D. Pearl (eds.). *Dyslexia: An appraisal of current knowledge* (pp. 43–58). New York: Oxford University Press.

Money, J. 1962. Dyslexia: A postconference review. *In* J. Money (ed.). *Reading Disability* (pp. 9–33). Baltimore: Johns Hopkins Press.

Nickerson, R. S., Perkins, D. N., and Smith, E. E. 1985. *The Teaching of Thinking.* Hillsdale, NJ: Erlbaum.

Olson, R. K., Kliegl, R., Davidson, B. J., and Foltz, G. 1985. Individual and developmental differences in reading disability. *In* G. E. Mackinnon and T. G. Waller (eds.). *Reading Research: Advances in theory and practice* (Vol. 4, pp. 1–64). New York: Academic Press.

Orton, S. T. 1925. "Word blindness" in school children. *Archives of Neurology and Psychiatry* 14:581–615.

Orton, S. T. 1928. Specific reading disability—Strephosymbolia. *Journal of the American Medical Association* 90:1095–1099.

Pennington, B. F., Bender, B., Puck, M., Salbenblatt, J., and Robinson, A. 1982. Learning disabilities in children with sex chromosome anomalies. *Child Development* 53: 1182–1192.

Perera, K. 1984. *Children's Writing and Reading.* London: Basil Blackwell.

Perfetti, C. A. 1985. *Reading Ability.* New York: Oxford University Press.

Rayner, K. 1978. Eye movements in reading and information processing. *Psychological Bulletin* 85:618–660.

Rodgers, B. 1983. The identification and prevalence of specific reading retardation. *British Journal of Educational Psychology* 53:369–373.

Rutter, M. 1978. Prevalence and types of dyslexia. *In* A. L. Benton and D. Pearl (eds.). *Dyslexia: An appraisal of current knowledge* (pp. 3–28). New York: Oxford University Press.

Shulman, L. S. and Carey, N. B. 1984. Psychology and the limitations of individual rationality: Implications for the study of reasoning and civility. *Review of Educational Research* 54:501–524.

Simon, H. A. 1957. *Models of Man: Social and rational: Mathematical essays.* New York: John Wiley.

Smith, I. M. 1964. *Spatial Ability: Its educational and social significance.* London: University of London Press.

Sperry, R. W. 1982. Some effects of disconnecting the cerebral hemispheres. *Science* 217: 1223–1226.

Stein, J. F. and Fowler, S. 1982a. Diagnosis of dyslexia by means of a new indicator of eye dominance. *British Journal of Ophthalmology* 66:332–336.

Stein, J. F. and Fowler, S. 1982b. Towards the psychology of visual dyslexia. *In* Y. Zotterman (ed.). *Dyslexia: Neuronal, cognitive and linguistic aspects* (pp. 49–63). Oxford: Pergamon Press.

Thorndike, E. L. 1917. Reading as reasoning: A study of mistakes in paragraph reading. *Journal of Educational Psychology* 8:323–332.

Thorndike, R. L. 1963. *The Concepts of Over- and Underachievement.* New York: Columbia University, Teachers College.

Tinker, M. A. 1958. Recent studies of eye-movements in reading. *Psychological Bulletin* 55:215–231.

Tomatis, A. 1978. *Education and Dyslexia.* France-Quebec: Les Editions.

van Orden, G. C. 1987. A rows is a rose: Spelling, sound and reading. *Memory and Cognition* 15:181–198.

Vellutino, F. R. 1979. *Dyslexia: Theory and research.* Cambridge, MA: MIT Press.

Vygotsky, L. 1986. *Thought and Language* (A. Kozulin, Trans. and ed.). Cambridge, MA: MIT Press. (Original work published 1934).

Webb, N. M. and Shavelson, R. J. (eds.). 1985. Computers, education, and educational psychologists [Special issue]. *Educational Psychologist* 20(4).

Yule, W., Rutter, M., Berger, M., and Thompson, J. 1974. Over- and under-achievement in reading: Distribution in the general population. *British Journal of Educational Psychology* 44:1–12.

The Structured Flexibility of Orton-Gillingham*

Betty B. Sheffield

Cincinnati, Ohio

This paper discusses a philosophic basis for Orton-Gillingham teaching and attempts to demonstrate how certain of the features of such multisensory teaching act to remediate language problems exhibited by many dyslexic students. The common basis of the array of programs coming from both Orton and Gillingham is addressed. Some individual strengths and minor differences between Orton and Gillingham variations are examined.

In this paper I will discuss a structure that undergirds the many successful versions of multisensory teaching, sometimes called "Orton-Gillingham." I will discuss how that structure is effective in remediating difficulties characteristic of many dyslexic students. I will also touch upon a few of the variations that give certain programs individual strength.

In fact the approach is infinitely adaptable, a philosophy not a system. Excellent reading programs developed from this philosophy have been developed world-wide (Hornsby and Shear 1976; Smelt 1976). The most complete Orton-Gillingham programs cover all aspects of our to-

---

*The author is grateful to Margaret Rawson who coined the phrase "Structured Flexibility" in her article, "The Structure of English: The language to be learned," in the *Bulletin of the Orton Society* 20:103.

Annals of Dyslexia, Vol. 41, 1991.
ISSN 0736–9387

tal written language and are built on a deep knowledge of the English language.

Many people who are unfamiliar with an Orton-Gillingham approach to the teaching of reading, writing, and spelling picture it as a monolithic and somewhat rigid system. Even a few practitioners who have been exposed to only one version of this philosophy of teaching treat it as a hidebound set of practices that must each be followed with meticulous attention or else the whole fabric of the process will shred and the student fail to learn.

The Orton-Gillingham approach is a philosophy of teaching that appears in many excellent versions. These versions succeed because they are based on a strong logical foundation of thought. They succeed as long as their teachers understand the reasons behind the teaching.

Orton-Gillingham teaching ties writing tightly into the learning process. A student is directly taught reading, handwriting, spelling, and expressive writing as part of one logical body of knowledge. He is taught language as a science. The steps of learning are built closely together. His teacher continually teaches small logical pieces of language and then connects them to what the student already knows. New learning is always linked to earlier learning.

As an aid to a flagging memory for words, the student learns to articulate sounds and words as he writes them. When he is learning a new bit of language, he hears the teacher's voice first saying a sound, a word, a sentence. Then he hears his own voice repeat. He concentrates on what his mouth is doing. He moves his own hand and then sees what he has written. His teacher gives him plenty of opportunities for practice. In this process, the student is learning strategies to integrate the visual, the auditory, and the kinesthetic channels for learning.

Orton-Gillingham programs teach what is reliable about language so that the student gains a clear idea of what he can depend on and what he must simply learn. These programs all have some kind of drill that can build mastery for a dyslexic student who has difficulties in rote memory. They all build the ability to self-teach and a joy in mastery.

Most Orton-Gillingham programs use card decks to help build mastery. The necessary phonic information for a beginning Gillingham card deck was aptly described by Wood (1976, p. 133) as, "A packet of thin paper squares containing every symbol that a child needs to learn in order to get through the primary and elementary grades, a packet only a third of an inch in depth. . . . " That "packet of thin paper squares" holds a key to literacy for many students.

Gillingham and Orton were true trailblazers back in the 1930s and 1940s. Their multisensory philosophy was designed for the teaching of a kind of structured logical mode of thinking. The structuring process threads its way through all Orton-Gillingham teaching.

Using Language for Thought

One of the strongest arguments for an Orton-Gillingham approach is that it trains logical independent thinking. It teaches children to use language as they think about language. As demonstrated by the Hanna Stanford computer study of spelling (Hanna et al. 1966), English structure is indeed logical. Dyslexic students need to learn that there are reasons for the structure of our language and discover that they can use that reasoning to build mastery.

Reading is based on a plethora of difficult abstractions. That a letter has both a name and a sound is a concept. Many dyslexic youngsters never internalize that fact. In the process of reading, sounds sequence in time and match symbols that march visually across a page. Sentences have a genuine structure. Knowledge of that structure can help both comprehension and expressive writing. Multisensory teaching shows our students that language is not a jungle. There are rules and they are comforting ones. Multisensory teaching builds in those rules, first by a constant return to basic concepts and, then, by teaching to overlearning.

Sometimes in our concentrated discussion of sounds and phonograms we forget that our underlying message does not lie in teaching children to be rote memorizers. Our greatest strength is that we teach to intelligence. We directly teach a student how to think about language and how to think independently. We teach him to play Vygotsky's category game with words (Vygotsky 1971).

Neurology and psychology teach that learning builds brain structure (Lenneberg 1970). If we train to a certain kind of thought, we are actually going to expand a student's ability for more of that type of logical thought. As Ansara (1972) fiercely advocated, we must teach our students how best to use language as an automatic tool for thinking.

Suppose we consider multisensory teaching in a kind of diagram. We first draw a central circle that represents thought and abstraction. That circle represents a youngster's computer for thought and language, his ability to play the category game with words. In a sense we are programming software for that student to make his language computer work more efficiently.

Learning Channels

Gillingham and Stillman (1956) stressed the idea of our possessing three main learning channels by which anyone learns to read or think or exist. Gillingham and Stillman believed in using the visual channel, the auditory channel, and the kinesthetic-tactile channel simultaneously to build learning.

Visual Channel

A first learning channel is the visual one. Bruner (1963) has hypothesized that a child locked into a visual mode for learning may never achieve higher levels of abstraction. Most of the remedial students I have worked with, if they have not been taught differently, will at first try desperately to process and remember visually. They will try to remember what a word looks like. They are not exceptionally good at visual memory, but a visual mode is often the only learning strategy over which they have gained any control.

Even an ordinary person does not have a strong enough visual memory to retain all of the pieces that go into a total inventory of words. It would be a remarkable person who could, by taking mental pictures, remember all words that he or she must read.

As an example, I once had a thirteen-year-old student, C.K., whose only reading strategy was to remember words as visual wholes. He had been in a school that allowed him to use what are called "bypass techniques." When he failed in reading and spelling, his school allowed him to avoid reading and spelling. He learned history and science orally. His teachers attempted to give him a great deal of affective support in a small and comforting environment, but he had to repeat two grades. When he reached a traditional Cincinnati high school, he faced desperate difficulties. The only words he could read were those that he had committed to visual memory as whole units. His spelling gave the clue to his single method for word recognition. The word "smoking" was spelled "somekin." The word "bird" was spelled "brig." The word "this" was spelled "yist." He was trying to tie words together visually with little success. He was adamant in resisting any change in strategy. For him the habit of pure visual learning was a cul de sac, an arroyo out of which he could not by himself escape. The habit of rote visual learning cut him off from building new and more successful learning strategies. He clung desperately to his rigid nonproductive set of non-learning patterns. He was an angry boy.

With the best intentions, too many teachers inadvertently lead our dyslexic students into that visual single-channel trap. They give youngsters workbooks and expect the workbooks to teach. Sometimes even the teaching of phonics is left to workbooks. A student is expected to pull from a picture a sound that he does not hear. His only recourse is reliance on visual memory. Ordinary children can often override deficiencies in books and teach themselves whatever is missing. When taught by whole words, natural readers abstract rules and categories of language. Our children learn hopelessness, passiveness, and avoidance.

Auditory Channel

The second Gillingham channel is the auditory channel of learning. I will discuss one or two facets of auditory learning that usually cause difficulty to dyslexics. The first is short-term ear memory. In describing short-term ear memory Rome and Osman (1985) use the analogy of a tape-recorder in the ear. A person with a very good ear memory can listen and play back to himself what he or she has just heard. That person can be thought of as having a long efficient memory tape.

People with good ear memories can retain thoughts long enough to process what has just been said. In lectures they can take notes on what has been said while they are listening to the next piece of information. Because they are successful in this strategy, they enjoy quantities of practice. They continue to improve proficiency. They can build skill in processing what they hear, all because of a single advantage in short-term ear memory.

On the other hand, a youngster with a poor short-term ear memory has a hard time paying attention in class. Long before kindergarten the youngster with a very short auditory "tape" has difficulty following directions. He learns early in life to turn off what he hears unless it is of extreme interest to him. It is not worthwhile to him to expend effort and agony on casual uninteresting speech. By the time he reaches third grade, his teacher complains in the teachers' lounge, "He just won't listen to me. He won't pay attention." But he knows the teacher's sentences are just too long for him to decipher. A part of his reading difficulties may hang on losing the sense of a whole sentence while he is struggling to decode the words.

An Orton-Gillingham approach builds in specific remediation for those with short-term auditory difficulties (Gillingham and Stillman 1956). When a child learns the sounds of a three-letter word and how to blend them, he is starting to build the mental ability to hold on to three pieces of language long enough to do something with them. We begin to construct this skill, small piece by small piece. As a Gillingham therapist adds decodable words, he or she starts dictating sentences. The first sentences are short. Gradually a student can manage longer and longer ones. Every word is one that the youngster has been taught and is responsible for. As retention of longer and longer sentences becomes possible, problems in short-term auditory memory lessen.

Several years ago a colleague and I ran a summer program of multisensory teaching for dyslexic youngsters. As part of our pretesting, we used the digit span from the *Wechsler Intelligence Scale for Children* (Wechsler 1949). The students had to repeat numbers in a sequence forwards and then numbers in a sequence backwards. As a matter of interest, we repeated the digit span test at the end of the summer. A majority of the youngsters who had really progressed in reading could repeat at least one more digit forward and had dropped one digit backwards. In other words, they would have gotten the same score on the WISC, but they were able to hold more material in memory, going in the direction that successful reading demands.

There is a second expectable auditory error that is characteristic of many dyslexic youngsters. Often, for example, there will be a substitution of a "t" for a "d," an "m" for a "b," or a "c" for a "g." If a child reads "became" for "began," if an adult spells "Wimbledon" as "Wimbleton," that confusion provides diagnostic information. Many dyslexic students learn to discriminate consonant sounds by how those sounds are motorically produced by their mouths. Why are "t" and "d" mutually confusable? They are produced by a similar motor touch of the tongue to the gum ridge behind the teeth. When sounds are too difficult to hear apart, our students teach themselves to sort by motor mouth movements. Sounds that are similar in motor production are often confused.

A child with severe difficulty in auditory discrimination needs a great deal of direct teaching in how two sounds may be alike and how they differ. Voicing is the key to the discrimination of similar consonant sounds. A student with a critical problem in auditory discrimination must be taught the concept of voicing so that he has some valid means for the discrimination of similar sounds. A first grader needs to know why he wrote an "m" when he should have written a "b." A 16-year-old needs to know the logic behind his mistaken spelling of the word "ladder" with two "t"s.

There are practitioners who state clearly, and I think wrongly, "Do not ever use Orton-Gillingham with a child who has severe auditory problems." These are experts who have never used an Orton-Gillingham approach. Or if they have used it, they have not done it well. Children with severe auditory problems can learn to read well with Orton-Gillingham. The tutor must teach to the student's logic and discuss with him how he produces the sounds and why those sounds are confusing.

As an example, one of my students, 45-year-old John, would write an "m" for a "b" and then moan, "Why did I make that dumb mistake?"

I would say, "But it's not a dumb mistake. It's a logical mistake. You were thinking logically to have done it. Why did you confuse those two letters?"

After a moment of thought, a look of relief would sweep across

John's face. "Oh, of course. I made them in the same place in my mouth."

To know the reason for a certain error is a great comfort to a student. That reasoning allows him to recognize his most frequent lapses and to avoid them. One by one, more pieces of English pass into his control and are no longer flagged by bewildering red marks on a handed-back page.

The vowel sounds fall into this same pattern of difficulty in discrimination. The vowel sounds cause much more trouble even than the confusable consonants. Vowel sounds by their nature are produced with no physical contact between different parts of the mouth. There is no touch that a student can feel that tells him what a vowel sound is. He has to depend on his ears and his eyes, and they are often ineffective discriminators. Sometimes what is needed is a motor gesture of some kind that will help retrieve the sound. For "short" /a/ Ansara (1971) taught the gesture of a hand held horizontally beneath a chin. Production of short /a/ causes a pronounced chin drop. A student hits his hand as he articulates the sound. Koontz (1979) uses the gesture of a hand holding an apple to key the same sound. Greene (Greene and Enfield 1986) uses the hand puppets, Miss Odd and Mr. Ed, to structure the recall of the elusive "short" sounds /o/ and /e/. If the tutor has taught the student to associate a sound with this kind of a motor cue, when the student blocks on the sound, the signal for the sound will often fire off the memory for him.

There is another severe language problem that causes dyslexic individuals a great deal of difficulty. It is a problem not of taking in information but of getting it back out again. Almost every dyslexic I've ever worked with has found it difficult to express in words all the fine ideas that he has in his mind. He may have trouble formulating sentences that say what he wishes. He may struggle to recall individual well-known names. Often the right word is a will-o-the-wisp, just out of reach of his tongue.

deHirsh, Jansky, and Langford's (1966) extensive study of first grade readiness indicates that the second best test for deciding if a kindergarten child is going to succeed in first grade is whether he can identify capital letters. Particularly in this modern day when Sesame Street bestrides Children's Television and there is such an emphasis on letters, most children who do not know the alphabet have certainly had opportunity to learn it. The same child who struggles to retrieve letter names in kindergarten looks at books in first or second grade and cannot remember the words. Sometimes he can name a word on one line. Two lines down the page repetition of the same word triggers total surprise. He has never seen that word before. He may make similar errors in oral language. A consonant becomes a "continent." He may wear "darksider" shoes. He may love band music because of the "concussion" instruments. "Jelly beans sting you on the beach." A camera might be referred to as a "picture thing." This retrieval problem is crippling for many dyslexic youngsters.

What an Orton-Gillingham approach does for this problem is to build the individual sounds for a symbol and to have the student overlearn to mastery. He can go in either direction. He can see the letter and sound it. He can hear the sound and spell it. His memory reaches a stage where it can fire off automatically without his having to deliberate. He really has to overlearn. After the dyslexic student has become a competent reader, this decoding skill is an automatic reliable lower gear to be employed when the gremlin of non-retrieval strikes.

In practical living a retrieval problem often manifests itself as sloppiness or disorganization. A dyslexic child is often the one whose mother complains, "I am never going to be able to dig through his room!" "He would go out in the middle of winter without his coat!" "He will never remember to take his homework and his pencils to school." This same youngster on the day of Halloween, waits until after breakfast when his father is about to climb in the car to drive him to school. Conscience stricken, he bleats, "Mom, I'm supposed to wear a costume of a lion today." The youngster has an organizational problem caused by a retrieval problem.

Teachers and parents can get very upset with such children because they believe the child is being deliberately careless. They may accept that the child cannot read. That is dyslexia. They may sympathize with his frightful spelling. They often do not understand that messiness and forgetfulness may be part of the same difficulty. He has to be able to remember what he must do long enough to be able to organize and as one favorite tutor friend of mine used to say, "Begin to make jello." Multisensory teaching helps to build the structure, automaticity and understanding that a student must gain in order to deal with difficulties in retrieval.

Kinesthetic-Tactile Channel

The third and most essential part of the learning triangle has been left until last. Kinesthetic-tactile is the strongest learning channel for all of us. Even in a retarded youngster, the channel which is least often adversely affected is the motor sense.

Using kinesthetic memory is helpful for any student. It is essential for a dyslexic student. He needs to feel the muscles of his throat and mouth producing a sequence of sounds. He needs to write letters and words as he sounds them. He needs opportunity to overlearn until all three channels fire off simultaneously so that retrieval can become instantaneous.

Suppose we take a time-machine back 5,000 years. If we were in a class in ancient Sumaria, the teacher would hand each of us a chunk of clay. Each of us would roll our clay into a little ball, flatten it into a saucer shape, and inscribe marks on it with a triangular stick. The symbols we would use are called cuneiform. We would be learning the symbols for lists. Ancient Mesopotamians wrote mainly lists (Chiera 1938). There would be lists of how many bottles of wine, how many loaves of bread, and how many heads of cattle were possessed. Students studying to be professional scribes learned to read symbols by writing them. Our youngsters often learn to read best by writing first.

Many years ago Lori was my student. She was severely dyslexic. She was being tutored in a group of four first graders. The children had felt letters with which to work. I found a fascinating fact about Lori. If I put the word "mat" in front of her, she could not remember the word or the individual sounds. Then I would say, "Trace it, Lori." She would put her hand up towards the letters. Instantly, that abbreviated motor action snapped in the memory of the word for her and she could read it.

It is a human tendency to teach as we ourselves have been taught. Most of us were not taught in a multisensory fashion. Consequently, our tendency is to stop having the students write so much. Teachers seldom are trained to take effective advantage of this powerful learning tool. Anyone using Orton-Gillingham must concentrate on having the students write enough.

Exemplary Programs

We have touched a little bit on the problems dyslexic youngsters have and the built-in mechanisms in an Orton-Gillingham approach for addressing these problems.

There are two main water sheds of the Orton-Gillingham approach. Each has its own strengths. Each is effective. One derives directly from Dr. Orton and one descends from the work of Anna Gillingham and Bessie Stillman.

One major difference between these two implementations of multisensory teaching lies in whether the teacher has the student sound the sounds of the phonograms as he spells, or whether the student is taught to name the letters as he spells.

Dr. Orton, as a neurologist, wanted the multisensory combination to adhere as closely to the spoken language as possible. He believed that a student spelling a word should articulate the sounds of the phonograms while writing. Those programs that derive directly from Dr. Orton's work emphasize the use of the sound when a student is writing a word. The muscles of the mouth move along with the muscles of the hand.

Gillingham and Stillman (1956) stressed teaching both the sound and the name of each letter or phonogram. However, for the multisensory part of building word retrieval they had the student name the letters as he spelled a word.

Both methods work well. What is important in both cases is that we are building memory chains that will fire automatically when a student traces a forgotten word. Having used both techniques, I suspect that the child who builds memory through sound may more quickly reach competence in reading and that perhaps the child who names letters may become a more efficient speller. The essential consideration is that there be consistency in using one system or the other with a particular child or in a particular school.

Another apparent difference between the Orton and Gillingham streams is that the adherents of Gillingham seem to place a heavier emphasis on the routine use of key words to trigger sound memory. Those who follow Dr. Orton are more inclined to use key words only when an individual student needs them.

Another difference lies in the teaching of the schwa sound. The decoding of words in the original Gillingham Red Manual (1956) was based on older dictionaries that did not include the schwa sound. Consequently Gillingham taught to clear stressed vowel sounds. Some Gillingham programs today follow that model. In the Gillingham Green Manual (1960), later edited by Sally Childs, pronunciation was shifted to conform to updated diacritical markings which included schwa. McClelland (1989) reported that Gillingham was never comfortable with the use of schwa. Many Gillingham therapists do not teach it. In contrast, the Orton programs radiating out from Rochester and Bloomington, Minnesota directly teach the use of schwa (Greene and Enfield 1986; Rome and Osman 1985). The concept of schwa is an integral part of their successful teaching of accent.

Another extremely minor but intriguing difference between the Red and Green Manuals is the pronunciation of final suffix "-y" in a word such as happy. Kinder to Midwestern ears, the Red Manual and Rome and Osman have final "-y" rhyme with /ee/ as in "feet." The newer Green Manual considers that "-y" rhymes with the /i/ in the word "hit." According to Childs (1970), the logic behind this change was to make all the sounds for the letter "y" be the same as those for the letter "i."

Those Gillingham programs designed for one-to-one tutoring put strong emphasis on cursive writing. They do an efficient and thorough job of teaching writing. There are excellent reasons for using cursive. Among these reasons is the fact that the use of cursive philosophically puts a word together as a single unit. The Rochester Orton group puts a less heavy emphasis on the type of writing. They are more likely to check if an older student has consistent writing with which he is comfortable and go with it, even if the letters are made somewhat idiosyncraticly.

Programs of Direct Orton Derivation

The work of Peter Gow (1991) in upper state New York and that of Marian Monroe (1932) in Iowa and Chicago represent two of the earliest testing and teaching implementations of Dr. Orton's theories. Founded in 1926, the Gow School is the oldest College Preparatory School that was specifically designed for the teaching of bright dyslexic high school students. Its "Reconstructive Language" program evolved from the early association between Peter Gow and Dr. Orton.

Monroe's research into testing and remediation for the clinic of the Institute for Juvenile Research in Chicago represented a replication and elaboration of a similar study at the University of Iowa in 1928 (Monroe 1932). The clinical insights and teaching techniques in her book *Children Who Cannot Read* are still as fresh as tomorrow. Her *Iota Reading Tests* remains in use today in several parts of the country. As she mentions in her book: "Dr. Samuel T. Orton first called my attention to the unusual facility which poor readers sometimes have in mirror-reading and mirror-writing, to their reversal errors and problems suggested by such observations."

Three nuclear programs that evolved directly from Dr. Orton are June Orton's work in North Carolina (Orton 1976), that of Rome and Osman in Rochester, Minnesota (Rome and Osman 1985), and Spalding's *Writing Road to Reading* (Spalding 1962). In Winston-Salem those who studied with June Orton speak of using Orton-Orton. The published teaching material available is her *Guide to Teaching Phonics* (Orton 1976), a small book with a strong effective sequence for presentation of phonic elements. It articulates well with *The Language Tool Kit* by Rome and Osman.

Paula Dozier Rome studied directly with Dr. Orton and with her uncle, Paul Dozier. Her work and that of her partner Jean Osman continues at the Reading Center in Rochester, Minnesota. Their *The Language Tool Kit* contains a set of cards that are chock full of language information. Part of the program's strength lies in what it can teach a tutor about basic language. There is a slim excellent manual that goes with it. Some of their materials on higher-level prefixes and suffixes and roots will soon be published. These materials demonstrate how we build meaning through pieces, morphemes of words. Another strength that they have for me personally is their technique for drilling. They show cards and ask for sounds. They say sounds and the child repeats, hears his own voice, and writes the letter. In the third part of the drill the cards have been sorted out into three piles with possible beginning consonants first, vowel sounds in the middle, and possible ending consonants at the end. This stack of nonsense words is ideal for teaching the concept of blending, particularly to teenagers or adults. Since older students may have many real words on total inventory, they may not be truly building the concept of blending when reading lists of real words.

The Writing Road to Reading was developed by Romalda Spalding after her initial contact with Dr. Orton (Spalding 1962). For a time Spalding was consultant and teacher trainer for a remedial program at the Lincoln Schools near Boston. At that time, remedial students in the Lincoln Schools were evaluated by the Massachusetts General Language Clinic. Designed for an entire classroom, her program is based on a progressive direct teaching of language structure using phonogram cards for drill. Literature-based trade books are used rather than basal readers. There is much useful material for teaching manuscript writing. From personal experience, however, I find that this excellent program goes too fast for many dyslexic students.

A second Orton program for use in the general classroom is *Project Read* which is designed to be used with the bottom reading group across an entire school system. *Project Read* has a complete progression which integrates reading and writing and includes decoding, vocabulary, sentence structure, paragraph structure, and comprehension. Greene and Enfield's work stresses that dyslexic students need both structure and the creative aspects of our language. Creativity without form leads dyslexics to chaos, but form without creativity becomes "boring, boring, boring" (Greene 1982).

Programs of Direct Gillingham Derivation

Many programs have derived from Gillingham and Stillman's original work. Jane McClelland on the West Coast was trained directly by Anna Gillingham. The Shedd Program, (Shedd and Shedd 1967) with its modifications that are widely used in the Southern United States, was derived from a course clinical psychologist Charles Shedd took with Gillingham therapist, Rita Buchan (Shedd 1973).

Three major Gillingham programs are readily available, the teacher-training program at Massachusetts General Hospital, *Slingerland*, and *Alphabetic Phonics*.

Dr. Edwin Cole, like Dr. Samuel Orton, was certified both as a neurologist and a psychiatrist. In 1934 he participated in Orton's "second full-scale language research project" at the New York Neurological

Institute. The Institute staff included Paul Dozier and Anna Gillingham. Dr. Cole went on to initiate, as part of the Language Unit of the Massachusetts General Hospital, a language training program for teachers that required 300 hours of supervised teaching. That training program is still in full operation. In 1967 Dr. Cole helped found the Carroll School specifically for dyslexic children (Orton 1968).

The Slingerland Program (Slingerland 1971) is a complete strong classroom program developed by Slingerland during her close association with Gillingham. Slingerland is in wide use in the Western United States, from California to Washington State and across to Hawaii. Designed to be taught to an entire classroom, the program, like Spalding's, uses trade books or basal readers. A specific set of reading books is not required. *The Slingerland Program* is an excellent program for any public school. Beth Slingerland studied directly with Anna Gillingham. She adapted Gillingham techniques for youngsters in a public school. The program is to be used with any kind of basal reader. A phonic progression is directly taught. Those sight words that the youngsters need to learn are directly taught. As with *Project Read*, many dyslexic students in Slingerland classes never need special expensive outside help.

Alphabetic Phonics was initiated by Gillingham therapist Sally Childs and developed at Scottish Rite Hospital in Dallas by Aylett Cox under the aegis of Dr. Lucius Waites. There is training and a wealth of published material available for both *Slingerland* (1971) and *Alphabetic Phonics* (Cox 1984). *The Slingerland Program* contains excellent materials for the teaching of manuscript writing and *Alphabetic Phonics* is a strong source for a structure for teaching cursive writing.

Angling for Words was also developed in Dallas and designed for college preparatory students, fourth grade and older (Bowan 1972).

Original Gillingham manuals are in print. The Red Manual is older, but is still preferred by many therapists. The manuals are difficult to use without training. The Green Manual is the basis for the therapist training program for language therapists at Massachusetts General Hospital. Designed for fourth grade and above, the manuals are gold mines of materials, concepts, and lists and lists of words.

Conclusion

All Orton-Gillingham programs can be effective. They depend on the skill, knowledge, and dedication of their teaching professionals. They may be the only remedial programs that are valid for many struggling children and discouraged adults. Their individual successes have been written in the history of many salvaged lives.

References

Ansara, A. 1972. Language therapy to salvage the college potential of dyslexic adolescents. *Bulletin of the Orton Society* 22:123–139.

Ansara, A. 1971. Presentation at Marian College, Indianapolis.

Bowan, C.C. 1972. *Angling for Words*. Novato, CA: Academic Therapy Publications.

Bruner, J. 1963. *The Process of Education*. New York: Random House.

Chiera, E. 1938. *They Wrote on Clay*. Chicago: University of Chicago Press.

Childs, S. 1970, November. Presentation at the annual meeting of the Orton Society, Washington, D.C.

Cox, A. 1984. *Alphabetic Phonics: Structures and techniques*. Cambridge, MA: Educators Publishing Service.

deHirsch, K., Jansky, J., and Langford, W. 1966. *Predicting Reading Failure*. New York, Harper and Row.

Gillingham, A. and Stillman, B.W. 1956. *Remedial Training*. Cambridge, MA: Educators Publishing Service.

Gillingham, A. and Stillman, B.W. 1960. *Remedial Training*. Cambridge, MA: Educators Publishing Service.

Gow Addresses Need for Teacher Training. 1991. *Gow Magazine*, 2,1:p. 5.

Greene, V. 1982. Teaching Comprehension. Presentation for the Ohio Valley Branch of the Orton Society, Cincinnati.

Greene, V. and Enfield, M.I. 1986. *Phonology Guide*. Bloomington, MN: Language Circle Press.

Hanna, P.R., Hanna, J.S., Hodges, R.E., and Rudorf, E.H. 1966. *Phoneme-Grapheme Correspondences as Cues to Spelling Improvement*. Washington: U.S. Government Printing Office.

Koontz, A. 1979, August. *Specific Language Difficulties*. Course taught at the University of Cincinnati.

Hornsby, B. and Shear, F. 1976. *Alpha to Omega* (2nd ed.). London: Heinemann Educational Books Ltd.

Lenneberg, E.H. 1970. The neurobiology of language. *Bulletin of the Orton Society* 20:7–13.

McClelland, J. 1989. Personal conversation. Dallas.

Monroe, M. 1932. *Children Who Cannot Read*. Chicago: University of Chicago Press.

Orton, J.L. 1968. Presentation of the Samuel T. Orton Award to Edwin M. Cole, M.D. *Bulletin of the Orton Society;* 18:vii–x.

Orton, J.L. 1976. *A Guide to Teaching Phonics*. Cambridge, MA: Educators Publishing Service.

Rome, P.D. and Osman J.S. 1985. *Language Tool Kit*. Cambridge, MA: Educators Publishing Service.

Shedd, C.L. and Shedd. M. 1967. *Alphabetic-Phonetic Structural Linguistic Approach to Literacy*. Lafayette, LO: Authors.

Shedd, C.L. 1973. Personal conversation. Lafayette, Louisiana.

Slingerland, B. 1971. *A Multi-Sensory Approach to Language Arts for Specific Language Disability Children*. Cambridge, MA: Educators Publishing Service.

Smelt, E.D. 1976. *Speak, Spell and Read English*. Victoria, Australia: Longman Australia Pty Limited.

Spalding, R. 1962. *The Writing Road to Reading*. New York: William Morrow.

Vygotsky, L.S. 1971. *Thought and Language* (E. Haufmann and G. Vakar, Trans.). Cambridge, MA: M.I.T. Press.

Wechsler, D. 1949. *Wechsler Intelligence Scale for Children*. New York: the Psychological Corporation.

Wood, M.H. 1976. Dyslexic in the regular classroom. *Bulletin of the Orton Society* 26:124–140.

Early Language Intervention: A Deterrent to Reading Disability

Diane J. Sawyer

Middle Tennessee State University
Murfreesboro, Tennessee

Katharine Butler

Syracuse University
Syracuse, New York

Reading is a language art! In acquiring competence in reading we build on pro-ficiencies already available in the primary (spoken) language system. Language is made up of three primary components that impact on reading—phonology, or the sound structure of language including syllables and phonemes; syntax, or the rules governing the sequential ordering of words in phrases and sen-tences; and semantics, or the meaning system that is attached to words and phrases as a consequence of experiences in a variety of contexts. All three de-pend upon adequate short- and long-term memory capacities and functioning for their growth and refinement. Additionally, the bridging of speech to print, or the task of establishing sound/symbol correspondences in beginning reading draws not only upon phonological competencies and memory, it is also depen-dent upon the discovery that words are made up of smaller and isolable parts. This knowledge is often referred to as auditory segmenting which is one aspect of metalinguistic awareness.

This paper will discuss these five language roots of reading. The authors will report on research that demonstrates that children, upon school entrance,

Annals of Dyslexia, Vol. 41, 1991.
Copyright © 1991 by The Orton Dyslexia Society
ISSN 0736–9387

do not all possess equal levels of competencies in these five critical language areas. Since success in beginning reading is dependent upon the adequate development and functioning of each of the five language areas noted above, early school experiences should be directed toward language development, as well as reading instruction, if we are to reduce the incidence of reading difficulties in our schools. Finally, we will offer suggestions for enhancing language competencies that will support and promote the acquisition of reading.

Phonological Development and Reading

Phonology refers to the sound structure of the language—the speech sounds (syllables and phonemes) we produce and the rules governing the combining of sounds in a given language. In written English, as in other alphabetic languages, speech sounds are coded by means of letters. Learning to read involves, in part, learning to establish the sound/symbol correspondences between speech units and letters. Vellutino (1977), in his review of a range of research studies considering the performance of poor readers on various kinds of language processing tasks, concluded that deficits in either the phonological or syntactic or semantic processing of language, or any combination thereof, probably account for the severe difficulties many children experience in acquiring reading. This verbal deficit hypothesis has gained considerable support over the past ten years from a wide variety of research reports. Such a deficit may result from either of two conditions: 1) inadequate experiences with language that result in limited access to language for communication or problem solving; or 2) neurological processing difficulties that result in delayed or disordered language. A brief discussion of how each of these conditions affects the development of phonology and, ultimately, reading acquisition follows.

Experiences with Language

While humans are born with a biological predisposition to acquire language (Lenneberg 1967), infant involvement in a language rich environment appears essential to promote acquisition. Early studies of the emergence of language have documented delays in reaching developmental milestones in vocal and verbal behavior among children raised in institutions where contact with adults primarily involves attention to physical needs (eg., Brodbeck and Irwin 1946; Provence and Lipton 1926). Similarly, first-born children show better language development at given ages than do subsequent born, and single babies are similarly better off than are twins or triplets (McCarthy 1954). Talk must be directed toward an infant to stimulate babbling and vocal play. Such adult stimulation appears to be critical for language development throughout childhood. Recent studies suggest that differences in language stimulation in the home may have long-term effects on childrens' language acquisition and school achievement.

Badian (1988), in a study of 116 children followed from kindergarten through grade eight, found that among the main characteristics distinguishing poor readers from good readers were birth position, speech delay, and socioeconomic status. When compared to the total group of good readers, the poor readers were 3.3 times less likely to be first born, 3.4 times more likely to have a speech delay, and 3.6 times more likely to belong to the lowest two SES groups (of a five-category classification based on fathers' occupations). Broman, Bien, and Shaughnessy (1985) report similar findings for a longitudinal study involving 35,000 children followed from gestation through age seven. Of 169 variables considered as possible contributors to poor intellectual and academic attainment, eight environmental factors were found to be most highly related to low achievement at age seven. Overall, the low achievers had a higher birth order and came from larger families. When the poorest readers (lowest 10 percent of the distribution of scores among low achievers) were compared to matched controls, the best discriminators of low achievement were maternal IQ, maternal education, housing density, and indices of cognitive and motor development. The researchers conclude that the power of sociocultural factors in this study to discriminate low achievers lends indirect support to the verbal deficit hypothesis. They argue that since those aspects of the family environment associated with low achievement are also the ones associated with opportunities for verbal-conceptual learning, the lower SES, larger family size, and higher birth order of low achievers could all have contributed to the restriction of these opportunities (p. 116).

Neurological Processing Difficulties

Growth in mastery over language is tied to brain growth and advances in the organization of the brain. Lenneberg (1967, 1968) demonstrated that the appearance of increasingly complex speech and language behaviors, in infancy and early childhood, paralleled milestones in motor development. He related the two behaviors to the growth of connecting tissue linking brain cells. As these dendrite connections increase in number and complexity, infants are increasingly able to perform more complex perceptual, motor and lingustic feats.

Eimas et al. (1971) noted that infants as early as one month of age can distinguish between broad categories of speech sounds (ie. voiced/voiceless consonants). Over the next seven months, maturation of the central nervous system and listening experiences in their linguistic environments, lead children to distinguish increasingly finer phonetic features of language (Eimas 1979). But some children are handicapped in their abilities to take in auditory information. Beyond the obvious problems associated with hearing loss are those that involve difficulties processing the speech signal (abstracting, or organizing information). It appears that such children acquire language more slowly and generally experience difficulties in learning to read as well (deHirsch 1961; Menyuk 1976).

Children with hearing loss, whether permanent or intermittent loss over a long time, do not benefit from normal language stimulation sufficiently to maintain the normal time line for language acquisition. Reading performance among the deaf and hearing-impaired is usually significantly retarded. However, many children with normal hearing, still evidence lags in linguistic development and accompanying reading retardation. Satz, Friel, and Rudegeair (1976) suggest that extreme difficulties in acquiring reading may be explained as a consequence of a lag in the maturation of the brain, leading to delay in acquiring early sensori-perceptual skills, such as auditory discrimination and phonological development, and later conceptual-linguistic skills, such as syntax and semantics, that are critical to the acquisition of reading.

Children with auditory processing difficulties seem not to be able to respond efficiently to normal levels of language stimulation and thus are also unable to maintain the normal acquisition time-line. Similarly, some children may have difficulty establishing efficient connections between cognition and motor performance to allow them effectively to articulate the features of language they have grasped intellectually. Tallal (1987), in a longitudinal study involving subtypes of language-impaired children, noted that neuropsychological deficits, rather than deficits in linguistic knowledge per se, distinguish among subgroups of language-impaired children.

It seems reasonable to ask if the consequences of anomalies in neuropsychological processes can be observed in the language development of presumably normal children and whether such anomalies might be related to later reading achievement. Stark (1988) studied the phonological development among 45 first-born infants, ages two weeks to 18 months, who were apparently normal according to birth histories and pediatric reports. She examined 30 of these children again when they were in second grade. Stark concluded that subsequent difficulties in reading could be predicted on the basis of an early identified lag in phonological development. She suggested that a significant lag in development of speech motor skills should be considered as predictive of reading difficulty. Broman, Bien, and Shaughnessy, in the study of low achievers cited earlier, noted that low-achieving boys tended to have a history of early speech production problems and intelligibility problems, suggestive of a maturational lag among boys in acquiring language. Low-achieving girls in this study tended to have histories of more serious developmental language difficulties, including expressive language problems and lower verbal IQs.

It appears that anomalies of the central nervous system, whether related to rates of maturation or to analyzing and expressing linguistic information, lead to difficulties in acquiring phonology and other aspects of language and in acquiring reading. Kamhi and Catts (1986), in a study comparing the performance of language-impaired, reading-impaired and normal children on tasks requiring the encoding and retrieval of phonological information, found that the language-impaired were significantly worse than the reading-impaired on only three measures (all requiring word and sentence repetition). Their findings suggest that the two groups are really quite similar with respect to phonological processing difficulties and should, perhaps, be considered as sub-groups of the learning-disabled population who differ primarily on the basis of the severity of their phonological processing abilities.

Auditory Segmenting and Reading

Auditory segmenting involves the ability to focus attention consciously on sub-units of a spoken word (syllables, letter clusters such as blends, and single sounds or phonemes). This is considered an essential skill in learning to read an alphabetic language because letters code speech units. If one is to learn the letter/sound correspondences of a language, one must be consciously able to isolate those units from the stream of speech. However, spoken language is delivered in a continuous stream of sound. There are no physical breaks between words unless the speaker pauses. Children must learn to create psychological separations where physical separations do not exist. The same holds for recognizing syllables and phonemes as separate units. For example, Liberman et al. (1967) have demonstrated that a consonant cannot be voiced without an accompanying vowel. Children must learn to ignore that reality and behave as if /be/ were a single sound instead of the combination of sounds that "buh" is in reality. In learning to read, children must disengage themselves from the message and focus attention, instead, on the form or how the message is constructed.

Children learn to isolate the words, syllables, and phonemes of the speech stream, or to segment speech auditorially, between the ages of three and seven years. Downing (1970) noted that most five-year-olds lack a clear understanding of the referent for the term "word" as used by their teachers. Rosner and Simon (1971) found that some children had not acquired phoneme segmentation by sixth grade, and

Dougherty (1981) found that many developmentally-disabled adults, aged 21–60, had not mastered the range of segmenting tasks.

Numerous studies have found that the ability to segment phonemes at the time that reading instruction is begun is predictive of subsequent levels of reading achievement. (eg., Bradley and Bryant 1978; Fox and Routh 1980; Liberman 1973; Lundberg, Olofsson, and Wall 1980; Sawyer et al. 1985). Further, Durkin's (1966) study of children who learned to read before school suggests that among more than half of the early readers, phonemic awareness (evident in their interest in learning to print and spell) was apparent before they showed an interest in learning to read. She states that ". . . for some early readers, ability to read seemed almost like a by-product of ability to print and spell." (p. 137).

Recently, researchers have demonstrated that segmenting skills can be taught and that such instruction does result in higher levels of reading achievement (Bradley and Bryant 1983, 1988 personal communication regarding a follow-up investigation of performance among children in the 1983 study when they reached eighth grade; Lundberg 1988; Sawyer 1988). Further, Sawyer (1988) found that when beginning reading insruction approaches were matched to individual levels of segmenting ability at school entrance, and this was coupled with ongoing instruction in language segmentation, reading achievement for all students was enhanced. Within this program, the achievement differences usually observed between the poor and average segmenters were blurred—standardized test scores were practically and statistically similar. Attainment of explicit awareness of language segments, particularly of phonemic units, appears to contribute significantly to success in reading acquisition, but beginning reading instruction need not be postponed until phonemic segmenting is acquired. Children can learn much about the reading process and can develop confidence in themselves as readers, while acquiring segmenting skills if the instructional program provides them with reading tasks that build upon the level of segmenting abilities (word and/or syllable) that they do possess.

Syntactic Development and Reading

Syntax refers to the sequential ordering of words for the expression of meaning. For example, "The boy chased the dog," means something quite different from "The dog chased the boy." The shift in meaning is solely the result of an exchange in the order of two words. Learning to read requires sensitivity to meaning that is coded by means of the syntax of a language. Competent use of syntax in spoken language provides the foundation for effective use of syntactic cues to comprehension of written text.

Smith (1971) makes the point that efficient reading involves going from meaning to print; constructing the meaning coded in text as a consequence of expectations for what ought to be coded there. Such a process is heavily dependent upon prior knowledge of the permissible ways that words may be strung together in the language and how meaning is affected by that stringing together.

Children continue to develop syntactic competence throughout the elementary school years. During the course of this development we may expect that all children will have difficulty comprehending some of the syntactic structures they meet in text despite the fact that their oral language syntax appears quite sophisticated. Ruddell (1965) found that fourth graders had difficulty comprehending passages made up of some of the same structures they were using in spoken language. When reading passages contained syntactic structures that were used with a high degree of frequency in their spoken language, fourth graders' comprehension was significantly better than when passages were constructed using structures that appeared only infrequently in their oral expression. Apparently, the infrequently occurring structures were just beginning to be "tried out" but were not fully understood. Boys experienced greater difficulty comprehending the low frequency structures than did girls. Again, a slower growth rate for language among boys is suggested.

Numerous studies have shown that language-impaired children lag behind their normal age mates in their acquisition of syntax (see review by Leonard 1982). While they may use many of the same structures as their age mates, they use them with considerably less frequency. As suggested in the Ruddell study cited above, infrequently used structures are just beginning to be understood, and understanding may be greatly assisted by the circumstances, the context, in which the form is used. Written text is highly decontextualized. There are no gestures or facial expressions or vocal expression cues to aid comprehension. If children are lagging behind their classmates in the comprehension of oral syntax, they will surely have greater than usual difficulties comprehending their textbooks and standardized test passages.

Some language-impaired children show syntactic abilities that are not only less mature than their age mates, but different from that of normal, younger children at similar levels of language development (again see Leonard's 1982 review). Such children may well be those whose language deficits are rooted in neurological process deficits.

Menyuk (1978) suggests that difficulties in recognizing that words in each grammatical category (nouns, verbs, etc.) are somehow different from those in other categories could interfere with a child's ability to acquire a range of grammatical structures. Such children would use only a small number of different grammatical forms and would become confused when faced with the problem of having to work out the meaning of more complex structures such as those met in print. Vogel (1975) examined the relationship between syntactic ability in oral language and reading comprehension among normal and dyslexic children. She found that oral syntactic competence accounted for approximately 50 percent of the variance in reading comprehension at second grade. She notes that this is remarkable since second graders still devote a great deal of their attention to the process of decoding and so one would expect decoding competence to account for a very large portion of the variance.

Kean (1984), in a study of adults who had been dyslexic children, found that their adult syntactic abilities were significantly deviant from normal. They had difficulties both in judging the grammatical correctness of sentences and in interpreting the meaning of sentences. Their problems were related to recognition and use of grammatical constraints governing the interpretation of, as well as dependency relations associated with, different classes of noun phrases, including regular nouns, pronouns, and anaphors (backward referencing as with pronouns and auxiliary verbs). Kean's work lends support to Menyuk's conjecture regarding the nature and possible origin of syntactic difficulties. It appears that these problems may persist into adulthood and may well be the consequence of deficits in neurological processing, since deficits stemming from maturation or from experience in the linguistic community would not be expected to persist into adulthood.

Semantic Abilities and Reading

Semantics has been identified as the psycholinguistic system that patterns the content of an utterance, intent, and meanings of words and sentences (ASHA 1982). Thus this language root relates to how children come to understand the content of their language. However, content is affected by the way words are strung together into sentences. In fact, so close is the relationship between the sequential ordering of words and the meaning of those words that Menyuk (1988) suggests the development of each is intertwined with the other and perhaps should be described as the development of "semantax." However, it may be helpful to think about syntax as being the *form* which language takes (including phonological and morpholigical constraints) while semantics deal with *content* of language. While syntax reveals the sentence structure, semantic analysis conveys the underlying meaning, or semantic structure.

Kuczaj (1982) noted that individuals create the meaning of words, since in order to be "able to interpret, integrate, conceptualize, and organize information in the world in order to 'know' things about the world . . .one must also interpret, integrate, conceptualize, and organize information from the world (including memory of such information) in order to decide what a word means." (p. 101). He adds that words and their meanings may lack a constant relationship, and, in fact, that is usually the case. Indeed, it is frequently necessary to respond to one of the multiple meanings of a single word, and awareness of multiple meanings is a common objective in developing childrens' vocabularies.

Identifying what a word means is a complex matter. Within semantic memory is the lexicon, or the speaker's mental dictionary. This provides information about words and their meanings and pronunciations as well as associational contexts. As a consequence, a word's meaning is activated *within* the context in which it is read. In other words, the context available helps the child sort out which of several meanings is appropriate, when and if he has sufficient world knowledge.

Helpful to this process are schemas. Schemas are organized chunks of knowledge in long-term memory. Schemas relate to word meanings, concepts, and daily events and actions. They assist reading comprehension and recall of texts because they provide the child with an opportunity to organize incoming information in relation to prior knowledge. Thus, when a teacher asks a child to "Tell me what this word in our book means," an interactive sequence of mental events is required, from comprehending the teacher's instruction to accessing the lexicon in semantic memory and providing the correct response accurately and quickly. Such verbal processing requirements may be easily accomplished by good readers, but poor readers' failures are most likely due to deficiencies or malfunctions in one or more aspects of such processing (Vellutino and Scanlon 1982).

Good readers combine information heard or read with their own "world knowledge" in semantic memory to create a new entity inside-the-head that represents the meaning of the text or discourse (Sternberg and Powell 1983). Obviously, children who have imperfect or insufficient knowledge of the world and difficulty in lexical access or retrieval may display semantic processing problems (Butler 1986a). Such difficulties may be encountered in story reading or story telling, i.e. narrative discourse. Below is an example of such a failure. A six-year-old kindergartner is asked to respond to a teacher's oral story:

Teacher: Okay, Burt, now listen to this story and then say it back to me . . . tell me the *whole* story: "One day, a little boy went to school. He went up the steps of the school and opened the door. The boy went into his classroom and started playing with his friends. The teacher said, 'Time to come to circle.' The boy put away his toys and sat down on the rug."

Burt: A teacher . . . a boy played with a teacher's toys . . . time for us to come to circle . . . and it's the end.
          (Butler 1986b, p. 23.)

Retelling requires the linking of background knowledge and schemas stored in long term memory to the newly presented story sequence. This linking supports the accuracy of recall. The pauses in Burt's response reflect the period of time wherein Burt presumably searched for the to-be-remembered information in long-term memory. Burt's lack of success at this task suggests the potential for difficulties when reading is formally introduced. A language evaluation by both the teacher and the speech-language pathologist might reveal disabilities in speaking and listening as well as in reading readiness. If so, early language intervention holds promise (Nye, Foster, and Seaman 1987).

Normal readers, even young readers, can typically access words, retrieve meanings, and apply schemata without undue effort. In fact, it is this ability to deal with multiple tasks efficiently and without undue effort or attention that assists good readers, since their efforts are devoted to comprehension of the text rather than direct attention to retrieval strategies (Perfetti 1986). Obviously, then, comprehension of text is dependent upon recall from short- and long-term memory.

Short- and Long-Term Memory Development

The ability to remember, i.e. to code, store, and retrieve information from memory is crucial to the acquisition of speaking, listening, reading, and writing. While various definitions of "short-" and "long-" term memory exist, suffice it to say that the general concept of short-term memory is that of being of relatively brief duration, reflecting as little as one or two minutes, including digits, word lists of limited length, brief reading passages, and so forth as measures of retention in short-term (working) memory. Conversely, long-term (permanent) memory is considered to reflect the accumulation of increasingly complex knowledge about events as well as linguistic stimuli. Knowledge stored in long-term memory that derives from children's experiences or events is referred to as episodic memory, and is made up of auto-biographical, temporally-dated events.

Asking a preschool child to tell about birthday parties may bring a response such as "I get presents. Ice cream and cake." A fourth grader, however, will go far beyond the recall of an episode. Typically a ten-year-old will state: "You know, it's to celebrate, kind of. Have kids over; play games; have a birthday cake with candles and stuff. Sometimes you get a big present—like a ten-speed or somethin'. It's more like Christmas, only usually not as good." Evident here is the ability of the fourth-grader to abstract similarities between events, to reflect on memories generated from repeated episodes and to assign lexical items such as "celebrate" to such occasions, a stage of semantic development that is unavailable to a younger child. The fourth grader can go beyond autobiographical data and produce a script about birthdays in general.

Very young children's memory is thought in some ways to be all episodic and only later to develop a semantic component (Ornstein 1978). Semantic memory, as noted earlier, reflects the organized knowledge one possesses about words and other verbal symbols, their meaning and referents, about relations among them, and about rules for manipulating these symbols, concepts, and relationships.

In order to recall information from long-term memory, retrieval strategies are necessary (Klatzky 1984). Some information is retrieved automatically, e.g. one's name, address, and telephone number, while other information may require controlled search, e.g. retrieving the name of the fourth President of the United States, or providing the precise definition of "zeitgeist." Young children, and children with limited language skills, may have considerable difficulty retrieving from long-term memory the acceptable definitions or descriptions of words or objects. For example, a language disordered first-grader may respond to a question such as "Tell me about a bicycle," with "Ride it." Or, a four-year-old in nursery school, if shown a picture of an object, such as a stove, might reflect momentarily and abandoning the long-term memory search, state: "I have to go potty. It's a cookin'."

Such oral language difficulties, noted in the preschool, may well be predictive of later reading problems. In fact, a fifteen year follow-up study on children with reported language processing problems at entrance to kindergarten found there was a highly significant relationship between language and attentional deficits at four or five, and reading disabilities at third grade ($P < .001$), at eighth grade ($P < .01$) and at twelfth grade ($P < .05$) (Butler 1988). This finding is consonant with other studies of the interaction between reading and early language problems.

As we have shown, the search for meaning requires a search of long-term memory, and therefore brings into play not only appropriate reading strategies, but appropriate memory retrieval strategies as well. Such strategies include automatic and controlled search of long-term memory. When information is located quickly requiring little attention or effort, the retrieval strategy is said to be automatic, whereas if one must expend effort and conscious attention to seek among alternatives, it is referred to as controlled (Klatzky 1984).

Automaticity is of importance for fluent reading, as all teachers have observed. Children who "know their words" very well are able to access them quickly and to activate appropriate schemas rapidly as well. Perfetti and Curtis (1986) conclude that "the hall mark of skilled reading, indeed, is the rapid and effortless activation of a word concept from a letter string" (p. 33). Note that Perfetti is focusing upon a word *concept*, not the rote sounding out of a word. But automaticity is not all; its value lies in freeing the child to engage fully in other comprehension processes and to monitor his understanding. "Knowing" whether or not one comprehends is an important part of the listening and reading process, knowing, for example, when there are problems in recall or there are inconsistencies in the spoken or written text itself. While automaticity implies rapid lexical retrieval, comprehension implies a number of higher-order cognitive strategies that permit the speaker/ reader to assess both memory processing and output actively.

Space constraints do not permit a lengthy discussion of short-term and long-term memory attributes. Certainly, the interrelationship between short and long memory is complex. If short-term encoding is inefficient (as it may be in poor speakers and readers), long-term memory may suffer (Worden 1983). If short-term memory strategies for encoding are poor, the information stored (and retrieved) from long-term memory may be incomplete. Beyond the initial stages of reading, higher order strategies are helpful in placing information in long-term memory. The work of Palincsar and Brown (1984) in teaching middle school children to monitor their listening comprehension through reciprocal teaching (including summarizing, questioning, clarifying, and predicting) has been successful in teaching comprehension strategies in the classroom and providing a structured context in which learning may take place.

Implications for Instruction

Most children will continue to acquire new linguistic forms and to develop control over their comprehension and use of language throughout the elementary school years. Language development can be fostered through the models of language processing and language use that are made available to children. In this section we will discuss classroom practices specifically intended to promote growth in language and in reading.

Enhancing Phonological Abilities

Difficulties in the reception or production of speech sounds must be addressed by specialists in audiology and speech pathology. However, two practices that will particularly support these children, and are also beneficial in encouraging the communication efforts of all children, involve wait-time and responses to requests to repeat what has been stated. Children with production problems may be reluctant to verbalize and may also require more time to organize and produce a statement. Teachers must consciously monitor their behavior to ensure that every child has ample time to organize for and initiate a response. Typically, teachers assume that if a response is not initiated within one or two seconds the child cannot respond and another child is called on. Wait-time of at least five seconds is recommended for normal children; phonologically-impaired children may require more wait-time.

Children with receptive problems, whether due to a hearing loss or to a perceptual processing difficulty, will have significant difficulties grasping a message in a noisy setting or when speech is rapid (Tallal 1987). Yet background noise is pervasive in a classroom, and rapid speech is often used in reprimands as well as in attempts to hurry children along. Some of us normally speak more rapidly than others. A pattern of asking for directions to be repeated may signal the need for teachers to assess the levels of background noise in their classroom or their own rates of speech as possible factors interfering with students' reception of language in the classroom.

Among apparently normal children who come to school with lags in phonological development (many boys as well as children from low language stimulation homes), numerous opportunities for language stimulation should be provided. Such stimulation should include reading regularly (daily) from a variety of books and one-to-one conversations that involve children in talk about objects, events, or situations of special interest to each.

In general, encouraging phonological development in the classroom requires a conscious effort to engage children in interesting listening and speaking situations that stimulate them to focus attention on the productions of others and to extend and refine their own productions. Interestingly, the very children who need this stimulation the most, are likely to receive the smallest amounts. Quay and Jarrett (1986) found that teachers of lower SES children had fewer verbal communications with them than with other adults in the classroom setting. Teachers of middle SES children initiated higher rates of positive exchanges with their students. Further, teachers of middle SES children had a higher rate of negative exchanges with boys, but among teachers of lower SES children these rates were not different for boys and girls. If we are to have a positive impact on language development in the schools, teachers must become as concerned with developing a rich and positive listening/speaking atmosphere in the classroom as they have previously been with demonstrating (teaching) decoding skills and math processes.

Promoting Auditory Segmenting Abilities

Specific attention to spoken language as an entity that may be considered apart from the meaning it conveys can be fostered through various game-like activities, structured auditory analysis exercises, and reading related tasks.

Clapping out the words of an often repeated sentence in a fairy tale (eg., "Someone's been eating my porridge.") or a line from a nursery rhyme or poem or song helps to build word awareness. Marching to nursery rhyme/songs (eg., Ba Ba Black Sheep) that have one word per beat is also effective in promoting word awareness. Syllable awareness can be encouraged by clapping the parts (syllables) children hear in each other's names (eg., Keith, Don - ald, Car - o - lyn) and listening for changes in the length of words as affixes are added (eg., run/running; happy/happiness; tie/untie) or deleted. (For a more complete description of informal activities to promote word, syllable and phonemic awareness see Sawyer et al. 1985.)

Auditory segmenting skills are a critical component of phonological processing skills as they relate to reading acquisition. Attention should be given to developing these skills in the classroom. As little as five minutes per day of segmenting activities can have a significant effect upon reading acquisition (Sawyer 1988).

Promoting Syntactic Development

Reading to children and promoting the habit of regular reading may be the easiest, most enjoyable and effective means for promoting syntactic development. In a ground breaking study Chomsky (1972) found that the amount of exposure to childrens' books (reading and listening) was related to the stage of syntactic development achieved among children ages six to ten. She demonstrated that normal children achieve earlier comprehension of later developing or more complex syntactic structures as a consequence of frequent reading (or listening to books read) experiences in the home. Exposure to more syntacticly complex books was associated with higher levels of linguistic attainment. Interestingly, Chomsky noted less exposure to books and exposure to less syntacticly complex books in lower SES homes.

Alverman (1983) compared a sample of six- to ten-year-old disabled readers to the children in Chomsky's study. She examined the order of emergence of the syntactic structures tested by Chomsky, comprehension of those structures, and the relationship between linguistic development and reading exposure as well as reading achievement. Alverman found that 60 percent of the disabled readers passed through the same sequence of stages as Chomsky's subjects but at a slower rate. While Chomsky's subjects all mastered the easiest construction (stage 1) by age 7–1, Alverman's disabled readers did not master this construction until age 9–4. Further, among Chomsky's subjects only 36 percent were at stage 2 or below while 80 percent of the disabled readers in Alverman's study were at those stages. Alverman concluded that disabled readers have less well developed listening comprehension for certain language structures than their normal age mates. When Alverman considered reading exposure as it related to language development, she also found that the relative syntactic complexity of the books read or listened to correlated significantly with the stages in language development attained. Alverman interpreted the data to imply that parents and teachers should consider reading material to disabled readers that is well above their reading level. Since reading achievement in this study was highly correlated with the stage of syntactic complexity attained and since linguistically more complex materials were read or listened to by those with higher levels of linguistic attainment, it seems reasonable to assume that linguistic development and reading achievement both may be fostered by planned exposure to linguistically more complex books than disabled readers are capable of reading themselves. Alverman suggests that reading to disabled readers may build listening comprehension for more complex syntactic structures which, in turn, will be available to serve reading comprehension. For some, perhaps, reading achievement can be even more effectively served through the ears (listening comprehension) than through the eyes (word attack).

Talking should go hand-in-hand with listening. Heath (1982) found that among families who did read to children, those whose families discussed the real world relevance of stories were better readers by third grade than those whose parents only read to them even though they were about equal at school entrance. By third grade children are expected to think and reason about what they read. Children who have had the advantage of early models for going beyond enjoyment of books, to consider actions and motives and relevance to real life, are better able to cope with the independent pursuit of these issues when reading begins to be a primary vehicle for learning. Teachers must provide these models for children whose homes do not.

Teachers can also involve themselves directly in developing children's syntactic structures. Responding to children's communication with models of expanded forms or with questions to help extend, shape, and control language to fit their purposes will help children to acquire more complex structures. Encourage peer responses to serve the same end—clearer statements of meaning from the speaker, better comprehension on the part of the listener. Efforts to achieve greater clarity and specificity in spoken language will be accompanied by increased ability to comprehend written texts.

Promoting Semantic/Lexical Abilities

As noted in the previous section, reading to children may promote syntactic development. The same is true, of course, for developing semantic relationships, lexical storage, and vocabulary acquisition. It was earlier suggested that Palinscar and Brown's (1984) recent work has helped children extend, shape, and control language through use of direct instruction and teacher modeling. This four-step process helps children put into their own words their monitoring strategies and to use the verbal resources of the other students in the reading group and the teacher to support this effort. For example, in studying a text, or in responding to a read-aloud story, children stop and summarize periodically, using the language of the text or the story. They then attempt to formulate questions that rephrase the main idea of what they have heard. Third, they attempt to clarify what it is they might not have understood, whether it is an inconsistency in the text or a misunderstanding of the language they have heard or read. Finally, they are asked to infer by predicting what it is the author will go on to say. The teacher first models the approach and then gives the children many opportunities to practice. Interwoven throughout is the exploration of meaning as a part of classroom discourse and instruction.

Lexical processing is typically referred to in the schools as vocabulary instruction. It is, as can be seen from preceding information, a task to be undertaken within the context of what is known about semantic processing. To be considered is just "how" vocabulary instruction relates to how children encode, store, and retrieve information, those three essential and sequential processes (Murdoch 1982). Particularly for children in the early stages of reading, many of the words used in the classroom may be unknown or perhaps partially known. Children may be able to *recognize* certain words' meaning in a given context, but not be able to *recall* such meanings unassisted. Recognition implies partial "knowing" but not mastery.

There are innumerable suggestions that might be provided to assist teachers in promoting semantic and lexical abilities. Four broad areas are briefly discussed below.

Direct Instruction.   Nagy and Herman (1987 p. 33) suggest that teachers:

1. Provide exposures to instructed words;
2. Provide students with words in meaningful contexts;
3. Provide varied and rich information about words;
4. Provide links between old and new information, i.e., help the student use his prior knowledge and experience to gain word meaning;
5. Have students become active, rather than passive, in the word-learning process;
6. Have students attend to affixes, context clues and awareness of words and their meanings.

Curtis (1987) suggests that teachers focus on words that appear most frequently in print, and that since high-frequency words have multiple meanings, direct instruction should focus on the several *meanings* of a word that students will need to know (p. 49).

Semantic Organizers and Realias. So called "semantic organizers" may be helpful to younger as well as older children (Pehrsson and Robinson 1985). In the very early school years (kindergarten-first grade) children use realia organizers, which help them relate an activity

> . . . represented by a picture such as eating dinner, playing ball, cleaning house, . . . with real objects (such as specific tools) that could be used within the context of that topic. The emphasis is on activity right from the introduction of basic readiness activities . . . A child constructs a realia organizer by using a large picture, pieces of rope and real objects to demonstrate relationships involving a topic and related activities . . . Teachers provide pictures and cut five pieces of rope about two feet long and a sixth of a foot long, then demonstrates the activity. The core is a large picture of a group of people eating at a dinner table. Holding a plate, the teacher asks the children if it belongs with the picture. If all agree, the plate is placed on the table near the large picture. Next a two-foot piece of rope is used to connect the picture and the plate. The teacher shows other items such as a cup, glass, and knife and, when children agree that these are related, connects them individually to the picture with a two-foot piece of rope for each (inclusive categories) (pp. 38–39).

Pehrsson and Robinson go on to describe that children are then presented with something that does not belong to the category, and a one-foot piece of rope is placed at right angles across a connecting rope to represent "no," or a minus sign. Children then follow the teacher's lead, with each child conducting his/her own experiment.

Such realias lead to pencil-and-paper organizers and the teaching of verbs, nouns, concepts, and episodic events. The organizers can become quite sophisticated. Pehrsson and Denner (In press) have constructed instruction related to older children's needs in deciphering curriculum content. Almost all organizers rely on children's use of visual or graphic approaches to organizing needed information, with the generation of the information being sought by the teacher from the children as they explore new information and the meaning of words inherent in that situation.

Semantic Feature Analysis.   Semantic feature analysis is considered useful for extending and clarifying word meanings (Johnson and Pearson 1984) and has been used successfully with such disabled populations as the hard-of-hearing and deaf and the learning disabled. A matrix is provided which contains a set of related words on one axis and a set of attributes on the other. This matrix is then discussed in detail by the group of students and decisions are made about whether or not each attribute (feature) can be found with each object. For example, if the related words were *igloo, castle, tent,* and *log cabin,* each could be judged on various attributes: Is it made of wood? Stone? Ice? Is it expensive? Is it found in large cities? Can you make a fire in it? A minus signifies it is not an appropriate attribute, while a plus indicates that it is highly likely it will be found in that structure.

Semantic Networking.   Semantic networking, when used as an instructional strategy, is another visual way of making the relationships among words evident. A group activity sometimes useful to students is to select a common word, such as *rain,* and place it on the center of a chalk board, followed by asking students to indicate what comes first to their minds. The teacher then records those associations, and may receive such responses as "wind," "umbrella," "clouds," "puddles," "raincoat," "sleet," "snow," or other responses which do not appear primarily linked to the network associated with rain. Each response is given respectful attention and discussion and the "closeness" to the initially drawn word within a group semantic network is defined by drawing lines between the items. Frequently, discussion will reveal how such words as *fog* or *cat's feet* have come to be idiosyncratically associated in a student's semantic map.

Vocabulary in Context.

As Samuels (1987) suggests, to determine if the vocabulary of a text is a probable source of difficulty, simply ask the student to give the meanings of difficult words. He states: "A simple, useful but frequently ignored technique for helping students comprehend the texts used in school is to introduce new and difficult vocabulary in the same context as found in the text" (p. 318). It would appear that, simple, or sophisticated, direct attention to vocabulary and its acquisition help.

Promoting Short-Term Memory Skills.

Worden (1983) reported that studies that deal with motivation and rewards, rehearsal training, rehearsal plus reinforcement training, the teaching of cumulative rehearsal strategies, as well as temporal chunking, have been found to be of assistance to children with learning and reading problems. Thus for poor readers, teachers may wish to explore such memory strategy training. As Waters and Andreassen (1985) note, there is sufficient literature on memory development and early use of strategies by children to permit teachers to arrange learning conditions that will enhance memory processing by provision of materials that lead to chunking and clustering of information, by direct instruction in how to organize information, how to rehearse effectively, and so forth.

For example, with young children, the use of prosody (rhythm) can assist in storing information. Most of us remember learning the alphabet through the rhythm of the Alphabet Song, and so well ingrained is that rhythm that even adults can confidently recall both the letters of the alphabet and the prosodic elements which tied this seemingly disparate group of symbols to the spoken word. Rhyming is also a widely recognized method of not only teaching similarities and differences, but for providing a "hook" on which to hang information.

Rehearsal strategies are helpful in storing information in short-term memory, and while not typically used by younger children, rehearsal which is active (i.e., the child attends in some particular way to the stimuli), has been shown to be superior to rote rehearsal. Thus having children whisper the words or the names of pictures to be remembered during "study times," or having them name *all* of the words or pictures before being asked to recall the information has been shown to result in increased retention (Hagen and Stanovich 1977). Even among first-grade children, those who engage in spontaneous rehearsal did much better in learning specific tasks than those who were non-rehearsers, and those who engaged in active rehearsal did better than those who engaged in rote rehearsal (Waters and Andreassen 1985). For example, memorizing the products of various states (Idaho: potatoes; Florida: orange; Wisconsin: cheese) may be done through simply repeating the information over and over. However, rehearsing it actively, perhaps by pasting pictures of the products on a colorful map of the United States, would provide an additional context for this task.

Interestingly, children who engage in rehearsal also benefit from increased wait time (up to ten seconds between stimuli). There is evidence that good and poor processors alike benefit from sufficient time to retrieve information from short- and long-term memory. While poor processors may need such time to accomplish the task if they fail to use efficient memory strategies, good processors use that time to provide elaborated answers, having had sufficient time to recall further details and additional associations and schemas. The key is to process the *meaning* of the material, i.e., semantic processing. While children may learn on their own how to organize incoming information, they tend to learn it later in the elementary school years, yet children as young as first grade can benefit from structured conditions which, when provided by the teacher, offer them an opportunity to take advantage of semantic category instruction.

Finally, instruction in vocabulary learning is essentially an associative task, and much of what is done in the classroom provides multiple cues to the children (Pressley, Forres-Pressley, and Miller 1985, p. 31). Teachers can help children by making explicit the required associations and by not taking for granted that children may have sufficient prior knowledge or schemas to make instant "connections" between old and new information.

The key word method is a mnemonic (memory) device which involves

> . . . construction of interactive visual images. The learner generates an image of the definition referent interacting with a key word, which is simply a familiar concrete word that resembles a salient part of the unfamiliar vocabulary word. For example, the English word *carlin* means old woman. Using the key word *car*, a learner might generate an image of an old woman driving a car. When presented *carlin* later, ready retrieval of car occurs because of its acoustic similarity to *carlin*, which leads to recall of the linking image containing the old woman. (Pressley, Levin, and McDaniel 1987).

This vocabulary remembering strategy is reported to be quite successful. In essence, it is real-world associative learning, according to Pressley, Levin, and McDaniel, who note that vocabulary remembering is an associative task wherein the student must form connections between new, unfamiliar words and their definitions (p. 119). These authors are less positive regarding inferring word meanings from internal context (i.e. the inspection of word parts) indicating that it has not been fully studied. They raise the intriguing issue of possibly combining mnemonic and semantic strategy approaches (p. 122).

Promoting Long-Term Memory Skills

Strategies that affect short-term memory skills may also result in some long-term memory enhancement. For example, Pressley et al.

(1982) neatly summarized memory strategy instruction with children and noted that "mnemonic strategies are courses of actions or plans, which are deliberately undertaken by memorizers in order to enhance remembering." (p. 127). While space does not permit an extensive discussion of memory strategies, research specific to reading suggests that self control training, including reciprocal teaching strategies, where teachers model how to summarize information that has been read, how to ask questions and to seek clarification of the passage, and how to predict outcomes can be helpful for children as young as six (Pressley et al. 1985). In addition, mnemonic strategies such as the key word method for learning new vocabulary, as noted earlier is recommended by the research literature (Pressley, Levin, and McDaniel 1987). It should be stressed that teaching strategies to learners should be done only after careful analyses of what the learner is doing spontaneously, what the learner does under instruction and what the task requirements may be. It is important to note that not all children require instruction in strategy usage. However, poor readers may be able to develop complex information processing strategies through direct instruction.

Kamhi and Catts (1986) note that reading- and language-impaired children may approach reading/listening strategies in a passive, nonstrategic manner. They suggest that teachers and speech-language pathologists should work together to facilitate oral and written comprehension by training children to be more active in their communicative strategies, including training to recognize breakdowns in comprehension and to request clarification when instructions, assignments, and conversation are misunderstood. Such classroom collaboration should be initiated early so that children who reveal serious language/literacy problems may have appropriate instruction and intervention.

Summary

Each of the components of language discussed has provided a brief glimpse of the interaction among them. There is consensus that a child first learns language, oral language, which serves as a base for using language to learn—learning to read and learning to write. While there is some thought that learning to read and write also contributes to the acquisition of spoken language, and this interactive view may be upheld, it is our thesis that reading competence builds on proficiencies available to the child from his/her preschool experiences, whatever they may have been. Certainly, we now know that all children do not come to formal education with the same proficiencies in place. However, careful instruction that builds on knowledge of how the language roots of reading and writing affect achievement can yield more effective language users as well as more competent readers and writers.

References

Alverman, D. 1983. Reading achievement and linguistic stages: A comparison of disabled readers and Chomsky's 6-to 10-year-olds. *Journal of Research Developments in Education* 16:26–31.

American Speech-Language-Hearing Association. 1982. Definition: Communication disorders and variations. *ASHA* 24 (11):949–950.

Badian, N. A. 1988. The prediction of good and poor reading before kindergarten entry: A nine-year follow-up. *Journal of Learning Disabilities* 21 (3):98–103.

Bradley, L. and Bryant, P. E. 1978. Difficulties in auditory organization as a possible cause of reading backwardness. *Nature* 271 (5647):746–747.

Bradley, L. and Bryant, P. E. 1983. Categorizing sounds and learning to read—a causal connection. *Nature* 301:419–421.

Brodbeck, A. J. and Irwin, O. C. 1946. The speech behavior of infants without families. *Child Development* 17:145.

Broman, S., Bien, E., and Shaughnessy, P. 1985. *Low Achieving Children: The first seven years.* Hillsdale, N.J.: Lawrence Erlbaum Associates, Publishers.

Butler, K. G. 1986a Semantic factors in language development and disorders. *Topics in Language Disorders* 6 (4):pp. iv–v.

Butler, K. G. 1986b *Language Disorders in Children.* Austin, Tx: Pro.Ed.

Butler, K. G. 1988. Preschool language processing performance and later reading achievement. *In* R. L. and M. W. Mashland (eds.). *Preschool Prevention of Reading Failure* (pp. 19–51). Parkton, MD: York Press.

Catts, H. W. and Kamhi, A. G. 1986. Intervention for reading disabilities. *Journal of Childhood Communicative Disorders* 11 (1):67–79.

Chomsky, C. 1972. Stages in language development and reading exposure. *Harvard Educational Review* 42 (1):1–33.

Curtis, M. E. 1987. Vocabulary testing and vocabulary instruction. *In* M. G. McKeown and M. E. Curtis (eds.). *The Nature of Vocabulary Acquisition.* Hillsdale, NJ: Lawrence Erlbaum Associates.

deHirsch, K. 1961. Studies in tachyphemia: Diagnosis of developmental language disorders. *Logos* 4:3–9.

Dougherty, C. 1981. Segmenting ability as a predictor of adult mentally handicapped learner's reading performance. Unpublished manuscript. Syracuse University, Syracuse, N.Y.

Downing, J. 1970. Children's concepts of language in learning to read. *Educational Research* (12):106–112.

Durkin, D. 1966. *Children Who Read Early.* New York: The Teachers College Press.

Eimas, P. D. 1979. The processing of speech: some implications for language development. *In* Ludlow, Doran-Quine. *The Neurological Basis of Language Disorders in Children Methods and Directions for Research.* No. 79–440. (National Institutes of Health, Bethesda, Md.)

Eimas, P. D., Fiqueland, E. R., Jufczyk, P., Vigorito, J. 1971. Speech perception in infants. *Science* (171):303–306.

Fox, B. J. and Routh, D. K. 1980. Phonetic analysis and severe reading disability in children. *Journal of Psycholinguistic Research* 9:115–119.

Hagen, J. W. and Stanovich, K. G. 1977. Memory: Strategies of Acquisition. *In* R. V. Kail and G. H. Hagen (eds.). *Perspectives on the Development of Memory and Cognition.* Hillsdale, NJ: Lawrence Erlbaum Associates.

Heath, S. B. 1982. Protean shapes in literacy events: Ever shifting oral and literate traditions. *In* D. Tannen (ed.). *Spoken and Written Language.* Norwood, N.J.: Ablex, 1982.

Johnson, D. D. and Pearson, P. D. 1984. *Teaching Reading Vocabulary.* New York: Holt, Rinehart and Winston.

Kamhi, A. G. and Catts, H. W. 1986. Toward an understanding of developmental language and reading disorders. *Journal of Speech and Hearing Disorders* 51:337–47.

Kean, M. L. 1984. The question of linguistic anomaly in developmental dyslexia. *Annals of Dyslexia* 34:137–54.

Klatzky, R. L. 1984. *Memory and Awareness: An information processing perspective.* New York: W.H. Freeman.

Kuczaj, S. A. 1982. Acquisition of word meaning in the context of the development of the semantic system. *In* C. J. Brainerd and M. Pressley (eds.). *Verbal Processes in Children: Progress in cognitive development research* (pp. 95–124). New York: Springer Verlag.

Lenneberg, E. 1967. *Biological Foundations of Language.* New York: Wiley.

Lenneberg, E. 1968. The affect of age on the outcome of central nervous system disease in children. *In* Isaacson, (ed.). *The Neuropsychology of Development.* New York: Wiley.

Leonard, L. 1982. The nature of specific language impairment in children. *In* S. Rosenberg (ed.). *Handbook of Applied Psycholinguistics.* Hillsdale, N.J.: Lawrence Erlbaum Associates Publishers.

Liberman, I. Y. 1973. Segmentation of the spoken word and reading acquisition. *Bulletin of the Orton Dyslexia Society* 23:65–77.

Liberman, A. M., Cooper, F. S., Shankweiler, D. and Studdert-Kennedy. 1967. Perception of the speech code. *Psychological Review* 74:431–461.

Lundberg, I. 1988. Preschool prevention of reading failure: Does training in phonological awareness work? *In* R. Masland and M. Masland (eds.). *Preschool Prevention of Reading Failure.* Parkton, Md.: York Press.

Lundberg, I., Olofsson, A. and Wall, S. 1980. Reading and spelling skills in the first school years, predicted from phonemic awareness skills in kindergarten. *Scandinavian Journal of Psychology* 21:159–173.

McCarthy, D. 1954. Language development in children. *In* L. Carmichael (ed.). *Manual of Child Psychology.* New York: Wiley.

Menyuk, P. 1976. Relations between acquisition of phonology and reading. *In* J. Guthrie, (ed.). *Aspects of Reading Acquisition.* Baltimore, Md.: Johns Hopkins University Press.

Menyuk, P. 1978. Linguistic problems in children with developmental dysphasia. *In* M. Wyfe (ed.). *Developmental Dysphasia.* London: Academic Press.

Menyuk, P. 1988. *Language Development: Knowledge and use.* Glenview, IL: Scott, Foresman/ Little Brown.

Murdoch, B. B. 1982. Recognition memory. *In* C. R. Puff (ed.). *Handbook of Research Methods in Human Memory and Cognition* (pp. 1–27). New York: Academic Press.

Nagy, W. E. and Herman, P. A. 1987. Breadth and depth of vocabulary knowledge: Implications for acquisition and instruction. *In* M. E. McKeown and M. E. Curtis (eds.). *The Nature of Vocabulary Acquisition* (pp. 19–36). Hillsdale, NJ: Lawrence Erlbaum.

Nye, C., Foster, S. H., and Seaman, D. 1987. Effectiveness of language intervention with the language/learning disabled. *Journal of Speech and Hearing Disorders* 52:348–357.

Ornstein, P. A. 1978. *Memory Development in Children.* Hillsdale, NJ: Erlbaum.

Palincsar, A. S. and Brown, A. L. 1984. Reciprocal teaching of comprehension-fostering and comprehension-monitoring activities. *Cognition and Instruction* 1 (2):117–175.

Pehrsson, R. S. and Robinson, H. A. 1985. *The Semantic Organizer Approach to Writing and Reading Instruction*. Rockville, MD: Aspen Publishers.

Pehrsson, R. S. and Denner, P. In press. *Study Strategies: The semantic organizer approach*. Rockville, MD: Aspen Publications.

Perfetti, C. 1986. Cognitive and linguistic component of reading ability. *In* B. Forman and A. Siegel (eds.). *Acquisition of Reading Skills* (pp. 1–41). Hillsdale, NJ: Erlbaum.

Perfetti, C. A. and Curtis, M. E. 1986. Reading. *In* R. F. Dillon and R. J. Sternberg (eds.). *Cognition and Instruction* (pp. 13–59). Orlando, FL: Academic Press.

Pressley, M., Heisel, G. E., McCormick, C. B. and Nakamura, G. V. 1982. Memory strategy instruction with children. *In* C. J. Brainerd and M. Pressley (eds.). *Verbal Processes in Children: Progress in cognitive development research* (pp. 125–160). New York: Springer-Verlag.

Pressley, D. L., Forres-Pressley, D. E. and Miller, G. 1985. Children's use of cognitive strategies, how to teach strategies and what to do if they can't be taught. *In* M. Pressley and C. J. Brainerd (eds.). *Cognitive Learning and Memory in Children: Progress in cognitive development research* (pp. 1–47). New York: Springer-Verlag.

Pressley, M., Levin, J. R., and McDaniel, M. A. 1987. Remember versus inferring what a word means: Mnemonic and contextual approaches. *In* M. G. McKeown and M. E. Curtis (eds.). *The Nature of Vocabulary Acquisition* (pp. 107–128). Hillsdale, NJ: Lawrence Erlbaum.

Provence, S. and Lipton, R. 1926. *Infants in Institutions* New York: International Universities Press.

Quay, L. and Jarrett, O. 1986. Teachers' interactions with middle and lower SES preschool boys and girls. *Journal of Educational Psychology* 78:495–498.

Rosner, J. and Simon, D. 1971. The auditory analysis test: An initial report. *Journal of Hearing Disabilities* 4:384–392.

Ruddell, R. 1965. The effect of oral and written patterns of language structure on reading comprehension. *Reading Teacher* 270–275.

Samuels, S. J. 1987. Factors that influence listening and reading comprehension. *In* R. Horowitz and S. J. Samuels (eds.). *Comprehending Oral and Written Language* (pp. 295–328). San Diego, CA: Academic Press.

Satz, P., Friel, J. and Rudegeair, F. 1976. Some predictive antecedents of specific reading disability: A two-, three-, and four-year follow-up. *In* J. Guthrie, (ed.). *Aspects of Reading Acquisition*. Baltimore, Md.: Johns Hopkins University Press.

Sawyer, D. J. 1988. Studies of the effects of teaching auditory segmenting skills within the program. *In* R. Masland and M. Masland (eds.). *Preschool Prevention of Reading Failure*. (pp. 121–142). Parkton, Md.: York Press.

Sawyer, D. J., Dougherty, C., Shelly, M., and Spraanenburg, L. 1985. Auditory segmenting performance and reading acquisition. *In* C. Simon (ed.). *Communication Skills and Classroom Success: Assessment of language-learning disabled students*. San Diego: College-Hill Press.

Smith, F. 1971. *Understanding Reading*. New York: Holt, Rinehart and Winston, Inc.

Stark, R. 1988. Are prelinguistic abilities predictive of learning disability? A follow-up study. *In* R. Masland and M. Masland (eds.). *Preschool Prevention of Reading Failure*. Parkton, Md.: York Press.

Steinberg, R. J. and Powell, J. S. 1983. Comprehending verbal communication. *American Psychologist* 48:878–893.

Tallal, P. 1987. Interagency Committee on Learning Disabilities Report to the U.S. Congress: Developmental Language Disorders.

Vellutino, F. R. 1977. Alternative conceptualizations of diplexia: Evidence in support of a verbal deficit hypothesis. *Harvard Educational Review* 47 (3):334–354.

Vellutino, F. R. and Scanlon, D. M. 1982. Verbal processing in poor and normal readers. *In* C. J. Brainerd and M. Pressley (eds.). *Verbal Processes in Children's Progress in Cognitive Development Research* (pp. 189–264). New York: Springer-Verlag.

Vogel, S. 1975. *Syntactic Abilities in Normal and Dyslexic Children.* Baltimore, Md.: University Park Press.

Waters, H. S. and Andreassen, C. 1985. Children's use of memory strategies under instruction. *In* M. Pressley and J. R. Levin (eds.). *Cognitive Strategy Research: Psychological foundations* (pp. 1–24). New York: Springer-Verlag.

Worden, P. E. 1983. Memory strategy instruction with the learning disabled. *In* M. Pressley and J. R. Levin (eds.). *Cognitive Strategy Research: Psychological foundations* (pp. 129–154). New York: Springer-Verlag.

Part II
Issues and Programs

As educators and the public become more aware of the incidence of dyslexia and the effects it has on all segments of the population, researchers and curriculum developers turn their attention to aspects previously given little attention. Such issues as the nonacademic, social implications of dyslexia, the impact of dyslexia on post-secondary instruction, and the role of early educational practices are among those receiving much needed investigation.

Perhaps the most publicized of these issues relates to the widespread adoption in schools of the reading-language program referred to as "whole language." In recent years the merits of this program compared to and contrasted with the merits of multisensory programs have been widely debated. The Orton Dyslexia Society's recent publication, *All Language and the Creation of Literacy,* and Marilyn Adams' landmark study, *Beginning to Read: Thinking and Learning about Print,* and the 1989–90 *Phi Delta Kappan* Chall-Carbo papers, attest to the importance of this issue.

In "Teachers' Opinions of the Whole Language Approach to Reading Instruction," Patrick Groff concludes that primary-grade teachers remain dubious about the claims of whole language proponents. While this study reflects opinions expressed by one group of teachers, it suggests that teacher views have yet to be sought and analyzed and that the top-down adoption of curriculum remains the practice of preference in most schools.

Not surprisingly, many dyslexic and language-disabled students encounter serious difficulty when they undertake foreign language studies. In "Use of an Orton-Gillingham Approach to Teaching a Foreign Language to Dyslexic/Learning-Disabled Students: Explicit Teaching of Phonology in a Second Language," Richard Sparks and his colleagues examine this issue from the other end— investigating students who have such difficulty and determining what oral and written language weaknesses they share. They find that whether previously diagnosed as dyslexic or not, these students are deficient in handling the phonological and semantic codes in their first language and that, when provided with a multisensory structured approach to foreign language, they are more successful than when immersed in the "natural" approach frequently used in foreign language instruction.

Susan R. Butler, in "Reading Program—Remedial, Integrated, and Innovative," describes a remedial reading program designed to overcome the pattern of poor reading which, despite years of remedial instruction, compounds itself over time for the majority of children. She reports on the success of an integrated remedial program which reflects research findings in the areas of behavior and psycholinguistic and cognitive learning theories and which focuses on phonological processing strategies.

One of the most persistent and difficult presenting problems in low-achieving students is behavioral. While occurring at all ages, it often manifests itself during adolescence. In "Nonverbal Learning Disabilities and Remedial Interventions," Jean M. Foss describes students who not only fail to achieve but who lack social skills and generally have poor peer relations. Foss then details intervention strategies for such students which combine academic responsibility with the gradual improvement of feelings of personal worth and effectiveness.

Teachers' Opinions of the Whole Language Approach to Reading Instruction

Patrick Groff

San Diego State University
San Diego, California

This article reports the findings of a study of the opinions of first- and first/second-grade teachers of certain comments made about the whole language approach to reading instruction by leading advocates of this procedure. The investigation revealed that these teachers rejected as "false" more of these comments about the whole language approach than they accepted as "true." The findings of this study, apparently the first of their kind that have been reported, suggest that less progress has been made in persuading teachers that the whole language approach to reading instruction is the preferred teaching procedure than some leaders of the whole language movement previously have claimed.

It is clear that the "whole language" (WL) approach to the teaching of reading has gained in popularity of late with leaders of reading instruction. The increasingly favorable recognition among education professors to the WL approach is noticeable in the growing number of articles they publish in its praise in well-known educational journals. For instance, *Language Arts,* an official organ of the National Council of Teachers of English, at present devotes a large majority of its pages to a positive treatment of the WL approach to the development of reading and other aspects of literacy.

Support for the whole language approach also is found today among prominent English language educators at the state level. For example, the *English-Language Arts Framework,* published by the Cali-

Annals of Dyslexia, Vol. 41, 1991.
ISSN 0736–9387

fornia State Department of Education, was developed by 20 "leading English-language arts educators" from that state, of whom four were teachers, as a guideline for recent reading textbook adoption procedures (Quinby 1987, p. vii).

"Children learn to read by reading," this document announces (p. 40). "The more difficult task of learning individual words" can best be left "until after students have experienced the delight of understanding meaning in sentences," (p. 40). These precepts of the whole language approach have been adopted by the "strong whole language movement in the United States," (Goodman 1986, p. 62) notes. Such "whole language views are represented in official documents and innovative practices all across Canada" as well, he observes (p. 62). The growing acceptance for WL-based reading schemes also is found in New Zealand, England, and Australia, Goodman et al. (1988) believe. "Never have I witnessed anything like the rapid spread of the whole-language movement," Pearson (1989, p. 231) agrees.

The Present Study

The extent to which today's rank-and-file elementary school teachers endorse these and other precepts of the whole language approach to reading instruction has yet to be determined. So far, there appears to have been no systematic attempts to ascertain the degree of acceptance among teachers of young children of the tenets of the WL approach elucidated by the most renowned and prolific advocate-writers of this instructional procedure. The present study is an attempt to investigate this question.

It has been observed that "the definition of whole language seems to vary considerably" among the proponents of this approach (Just and Carpenter 1987, p. 531). Considering the volume of their writing on this issue, and the extent to which their writings are favorably cited or subscribed to by other advocates of the WL approach, it nonetheless appears fair to conclude that the views of Frank Smith, Kenneth Goodman, Judith Newman, and Constance Weaver represent as near to a consensus about this topic as one can find. When asked, who are the authors of "classic studies" in reading, professors who teach university reading courses named Smith and Goodman most often (Froese 1982). Books on the WL approach to reading instruction in the elementary school have also been written by Anderson (1984), Ferreiro and Teberosky (1982), Goodman and Burke (1980), Harste, Woodward, and Burke (1984), Holdaway (1979), and Hittleman and Hittleman (1983).

The Questionnaire of the Study

The present study asked primary-grade teachers their opinions about certain aspects of the whole language approach to reading instruction. For this purpose 15 different conclusions about reading instruction were abstracted from the writings of prominent advocates of the WL approach. Primary-grade teachers were sent a questionnaire containing these 15 statements and asked to respond to each as either "true," "false," or "undecided" (if teachers were unsure in any way about a statement). It was decided that the purposes of the study did not require more than three categories of response, True, False, and Undecided. These three categories were presented to respondents as equivalents to the (1) strongly agree—agree, (2) undecided, and (3) disagree—strongly disagree categories of the Likert scale. The distinction made in the Likert scale between strongly agree—agree, for example, was not needed to achieve the purposes of the study, it was concluded.

The 15 statements presented in the questionnaire, and the sources in the published literature about the whole language approach to reading instruction from which they were extracted, are as follows:

1. *The intensive and systematic teaching of phonics hinders reading comprehension.* WL advocates would agree. Smith (1978, p. 141) argues that the application of phonics information results in "so much delay that short-term memory will be overloaded," and as a consequence, children "will lose the sense of what they are reading." Weaver (1988, pp. 76–77) agrees that learning much phonics information "seems highly unnecessary."

2. *Children need to recognize individual words before they can read with comprehension.* WL proponents disagree. Weaver (1988, p. 29) believes that there is a mutual antagonism between "meaning centered" and "word centered" reading. It is true, Newman (1985a, p. 57) says, with their "emphasis on word identification" reading programs "make learning to read difficult." This is because "meaning identification does not require the identification of individual words," Smith (1986b, p. 166) avers. "A reader therefore, can only recognize . . . the constituent words when the meaning of an entire statement is known" (Hittleman and Hittleman 1983, p. 353).

3. *English is spelled too unpredictably for phonics too work well.* True, say WL supporters. English is spelled so unpredictably, Smith (1985, p. 53) contends, that there is "no way of predicting when a particular [speech sound-letter] correspondence ap-

plies." Weaver (1980, p. 86) agrees that "only a few of the frequently taught [phonics] rules are consistent enough or relate to enough words to make them worth teaching."

4. *Children learn to read best the same way they learned to speak.* Promoters of the WL approach concur. Newman (1985a, p. 60) observes that "there is evidence which indicates literacy can develop in the same 'natural' way as spoken language." *"We do not directly teach children how to talk,"* Weaver (1988, p. 178) stresses. "Neither can we directly teach 'rules' for reading" (p. 222). Beginning readers thus must "develop writing and reading strategies by and for themselves," she insists (p. 222). Goodman (1986, p. 26) notes that "teaching kids about language will not facilitate their use of language." He applies this principle to reading as well.

5. *Children should not be taught to recognize words by "sight" as "wholes."* Proponents of WL find this false. "We recognize words in the same way that we recognize all the other familiar objects in our visual world—trees and animals, cars and houses, cutlery, crockery, furniture and faces—on sight," Smith (1985, p. 57) explains. "It is easier for a reader to remember the unique appearance and pronunciation of a whole word like *photograph*, for example, than to remember the unique pronunciations of meaningless syllables and spelling units," Smith (1978, p. 146) submits. Before children reach the "grapho/phonemic stage" of word recognition, Weaver (1988, p. 206) attests, they can "recognize" some words, can "pick out individual words," and can read a story "by heart" (p. 209). Beginning readers should learn 200 "whole words," Holdaway (1979, p. 98) advises.

6. *Children at age 6 do not need oral language development before being taught to read.* Those who favor the WL approach affirm this idea. "Many children of two and three years of age have learned to read," Smith (1986b, p. 189) opines. "A child does not need to be very mature to learn to read," he holds (1983, p. 113). This is because "there is nothing unique about reading, either visually or as far as language is concerned" (Smith 1986b, p. 188). Goodman (1986, p. 34) maintains that "whole language firmly rejects" the belief that "there are substantial numbers of learners who have difficulty learning to read or write for any physical or intellectual reason." Thus if a child displays hardship in learning to read, the teacher should "change the material rather than to try to change the child" (Smith 1986b, p. 183).

7. *Children should guess at written words, using sentence context cues.*

Those who espouse WL approve. The strategy children should use most in reading, after trying to skip over unrecognizable words, is "making use of the context to eliminate unlikely alternatives for what the unfamiliar word might be," counsels Smith (1986b, p. 145). "The most effective and efficient readers are those who use a maximum of nonvisual information (content) and a minimum of phonics," Weaver (1980, p. 90) tells teachers. To this effect, Smith (1973, p. 79) calculates that "one word in five can be completely eliminated from most English text with scarcely any effect on its overall comprehensibility."

8. *Learning names of the alphabet is important in beginning reading.* WL exponents do not subscribe to this. "Literacy is not achieved by learning the so-called basics or mechanics of reading and writing, such as names of the alphabet," Smith cautions (1984, p. 143). Learning the alphabet is a by-product of reading," he insists (1986b, p. 184). It does not "facilitate learning to read." Therefore, the fact that written words are made up of letters is "irrelevant" (Smith 1985, p. 57).

9. *The length and complexity of words and sentences is of little consequence in beginning reading instruction.* Advocates of WL second this proposal. It is wrong for teachers to believe that short words are easier for children to learn to read than are long words, Smith (1986a, p. 93) imparts. He claims that children can read more three-syllable words than monosyllabic ones. Newman (1985a, p. 59) adds that research "raises serious doubts about using word frequency as a basis for preparing reading material for young readers." It is not possible to put restrictions on the type of syntax used in this material and "at the same time create a natural text," Goodman, et al. declare (1988, p. 88).

10. *There are otherwise normal children who cannot learn phonics and must be taught by a purely "visual" approach.* WL theorists accept this view. Weaver (1988, p. 103) hypothesizes that "children who seem unable to learn phonics are quite able to comprehend what they read." This is because "it may be difficult if not impossible for some children to hear and identify the separate sounds in words" (p. 103). These conclusions appear to be based on Carbo's (1987, p. 432) contention that some children who have normal speaking and listening abilities "cannot hear any difference among vowel sounds." These children "will not profit from instruction in phonics, regardless of when it is provided," Carbo (p. 434) encourages teachers to assume.

11. *Children can teach themselves to read. Formal instruction is unnecessary.* Smith (1983, p. 113) judges that "there is abundant evidence that children have learned to read without the benefit of formal instruction." He attests that "many children have learned to read, often spontaneously, as young as three years of age" (Smith 1986b, p. 185). Children "can develop and use an intuitive knowledge of letter-sound correspondences," Weaver (1980, p. 86) reports, "even though they may never have had phonics instruction." Newman (1985a, p. 60) agrees that "children are able to learn to read without deliberate instruction from adults." She stresses that she is "not advocating we teach our students about the language cue systems in any formal way" (Newman 1985b, p. 104). These beliefs seem based on the idea that learning to read is not the direct result of teaching (Goodman et al. 1988, p. 125).

12. *Children should learn a hierarchy of reading skills of ever-increasing difficulty.* WL proponents object to this proposal. Reading programs should not involve "careful intervention by the teacher using a carefully sequenced instructional program," Newman advises (1985a, p. 60). Goodman also deduces that "there is no hierarchy of sub-skills" that should be taught (1986, p. 39). "Reading has no one sequence of skills," Anderson echoes (1984, p. 186). "There is no empirical evidence that justifies the use of one hierarchy of skills," Hittleman and Hittleman point out (1983, p. 140). Goodman et al. also contend that "the evidence from science—recent theory and research—" is that reading is best developed without "this tight control" (1988, p. 125).

13. *Intensive phonics teaching makes learning to recognize words hard for children.* Those who uphold WL defend this view. A reliance on phonics information by children "makes the task of reading inordinately difficult, if not impossible," Weaver protests (1980, p. 86). From her perspective, children's "sounding out a word is cumbersome, time-consuming, and unnecessary" (p. 86). Worse yet, warns Smith, children practicing this activity "are likely to develop into disabled readers" (1985, p. 54). It is clear, he thinks, that one main way to make learning to read difficult is to "ensure that phonics skills are learned and used" (1979, p. 138). According to Goodman, this is because "matching letters with sounds . . . is a flat-earth view of the world," one that "rejects modern science about reading" (1986, p. 37).

14. *Workbooks and worksheets should be used in reading instruction.* WL advocates disagree. These materials should not be used in

reading instruction Goodman et al. remonstrate because "the workbooks focus on skills; use shorter, less complete texts; and reduce reading instruction focus to parts [words] rather than the whole" (1988, p. 83). Also deploring the fact that workbooks "focus at the outset on skills for identifying words" is Weaver (1988, p. 43). She reminds teachers that "meaning does *not* take care of itself once words are identified" (p. 43).

15. *The basal reader system is the optimum system for teaching reading.* WL defenders take an opposite position. "No published instructional program has ever provided the generalizations and concepts that people must develop to learn to read," says Goodman (1984, p. 109). Basal readers also are undesirable, Goodman et al. argue, because they "do not easily permit modification [by the teacher] in any but superficial ways" (1988, p. 124). Moreover, "there appear to be misconceptions, inconsistencies, misdirection, and misapplication" in the basal reader system, Goodman et al. charge (1988, p. 125). Worst of all, they feel, basal readers "control language; they control learners; they control teachers" (p. 125).

Respondents to the Questionnaire

The fifteen-statement questionnaire used in the study was submitted to 253 first-grade teachers and to 64 first-second combination-grade teachers. These 317 teachers taught in 104 different elementary schools in San Diego, California.

These 317 teachers consisted of all those in San Diego schools who conducted "regular" or "normal" classes in grades one or one-two combination. Not included in the study were teachers at these grade levels whose classrooms were designed to teach children who spoke a foreign language, who were mentally retarded, academically gifted, or emotionally handicapped. The teachers in the study therefore could be said to have conducted "regular" or "normal" classes.

In sum, the questionnaire was sent to the entire group of "regular" first-grade and first-second combination-grade teachers in a large-city school district. Of the 317 teachers so contacted, 275 or 86.7 percent returned the questionnaire.

Findings of the Study

The findings of the study are presented in Table I. Shown here are the percents of "true," "false," or "undecided" responses from the teach-

Table I
Teachers' Responses to Statements Related to WL Instruction

Statement	% of Teachers Responding		
	True	False	Undecided
1. The intensive and systematic teaching of phonics hinders reading comprehension.	9	74	17
2. Children need to recognize individual words before they can read with comprehension.	67	25	8
3. English is spelled too unpredictably for phonics to work well.	11	72	17
4. Children learn to read best the same way they learned to speak.	36	26	38
5. Children should not be taught to recognize words by sight as wholes.	8	77	15
6. Children at age 6 do not need oral language development before being taught to read.	1	95	4
7. Children should guess at written words, using sentence context cues.	78	12	10
8. Learning the names of the alphabet is important in beginning reading.	68	22	10
9. The length and complexity of words and sentences is of little consequence in beginning reading.	6	84	10
10. There are otherwise normal children who cannot learn phonics and must be taught by a purely visual approach.	61	17	22
11. Children can teach themselves to read. Formal instruction is unnecessary.	4	80	16
12. Children should learn a hierarchy of reading skills of ever-increasing difficulty.	78	8	14
13. Intensive phonics teaching makes learning to recognize words hard for children.	3	91	6
14. Workbooks and worksheets should be used in reading instruction.	64	12	24
15. The basal reader system is the optimum system for teaching reading.	18	41	41

ers in the study to 15 statements related to the whole language approach to reading instruction. As can be seen in Table I, the items of the questionnaire were posed as both negative and positive statements about the whole language approach. The questionnaire presents a random order of true versus false statements about the tenets of this approach.

The findings of the study must be qualified, of course, in that they represent the opinions of first- and second-grade teachers in one major U.S. city, San Diego, California. There are indications, however, that the opinions of these teachers might be considered fairly close to those of teachers in general. For one thing, they teach a wide representation of the ethnic group of the nation. San Diego's schools enroll 41 percent white students, 23 percent Latino, 16 percent black, 18 percent Asian, and 2 percent unidentified.

In addition, San Diego is not a provincial or isolated demographic area. In fact, there is relatively high migration into this city and lesser out-migration. The San Diego Association of Governments data show that 31 percent of this city's population had migrated into it during 1975–1980 from other states. The population of San Diego at present therefore seems more representative of people from all parts of the nation than does the population of some large cities in the Midwest, East, and South. The in-migration character of the San Diego population is exemplified by the fact that, according to San Diego city schools personnel data, 44 percent of its teachers received their training in education outside of California.

Discussion

The findings of the study present both good and unfavorable news about the extent to which the opinions of leading proponents of the WL approach about this instructional scheme are accepted by primary-grade teachers. These advocates of WL doubtless will be encouraged by the findings that 77 percent of teachers in the study believe that children should be taught to recognize whole words by "sight," and that 78 percent opine that children should guess at words when reading. That only 18 percent of these teachers accept the basal reader system as the optimum one for teaching reading could also be considered a favorable sign by the enthusiasts of the WL approach. That 61 percent of teachers in the study think that there are children who cannot learn phonics information also suggests the WL point of view has gained notable acceptance. Proponents of the WL approach also would be heartened to learn that 74 percent of these teachers either feel that children learn to read best the same way they learned to speak, or at least are undecided about this issue.

An analysis of the findings could not explain, however, why 36 percent of the teachers accept the idea that children should learn to read the same way they acquire speaking ability, but that only 4 percent agree that children can teach themselves to read without formal instruction. Apparently the supposition that children learn to read naturally, i.e., the same way they learned to speak, is too attractive for teachers to resist. Upon second thought, however, teachers seem significantly less willing to concede the logical consequence of this assumption: a totally informal program of reading instruction in which the teacher has only indirect influences.

These endorsements or partial agreements by teachers of the views of leaders of the WL movement stand in contrast with the greater number of generally negative opinions these teachers have of the WL tenets they were asked to appraise. To this effect, about two out of three of the teachers reject the WL premises that children do not need to recognize words in order to read with comprehension, that workbooks are unnecessary, and that learning names of the alphabet is unimportant. About three out of four of the teachers rebuff the proposition that English is spelled too unpredictably for phonics to work well, that the intensive teaching of phonics impedes reading comprehension, and that children should not be taught a hierarchy of reading skills.

Even larger percents of the teachers repudiated the precepts that children can teach themselves to read (80 percent), that the length and complexity of words and sentences is of little concern (84 percent), that intensive phonics teaching makes learning to recognize words hard (91 percent), and that children do not need oral language development before being taught to read (95 percent).

Implications of the Findings

The teachers in the present study responded to 15 opinions about the whole language approach to reading instruction taken from the writings of leading advocates of this approach. These teachers tended to reject more of these opinions as false than they accepted as true. It appears significant that these teachers' schools are in a state whose Department of Education strongly advocates WL language precepts that teachers tend to disavow.

If the WL approach to the teaching of reading is to prevail over its competitors in this educational process, it thus appears that its proponents have a substantial task remaining to convince first- and second-grade teachers to accept some of its maxims. The resistance by teachers to certain aspects of the WL approach may be greater than has been predicted by its instigators.

The findings of the study therefore suggest that less progress has been made in persuading educational professionals at the grass roots level of school systems that the WL approach is the preferred instructional procedure than some leaders of the WL movement have claimed. The findings of the study thus call into question the supposition that "It is not the psycholinguistic gurus but the teachers who have created the whole-language movement" (Goodman 1989, p. 70). The findings might also suggest that teachers are not trained sufficiently in methods of reading instruction courses about the whole language approach.

The study thus implies that to teachers some of the aspects of the whole language approach are at best controversial matters. It is clear that teachers who disapprove of, or are unsure about certain axioms of the WL approach can find reading experts who share their misgivings (e.g., Adams 1990; Anderson et al. 1985; Carnine, Silbert, and Kameenui 1991; Chall 1983, 1989; Feitelson 1988; Groff 1987; Liberman and Liberman 1990; Perfetti 1985).

Knowledge of the discrepancies that appear to exist between the support given to the WL movement by leaders of this plan and by some classroom teachers may give some additional insights into the "great debate" over reading instruction that currently ensues (Chall 1989). Teachers' opinions about this debate seem rarely solicited. If a workable resolution to this dispute is to be realized, however, it is important to take into consideration the attitudes and perceptions of teachers about it.

In this regard, now that there is evidence that teachers, as well as reading experts, are split as to whether the entire WL approach to reading instruction should be adopted, teachers who favor or disagree with selected WL tenets could be asked to explain the basis of their acceptance of or adversion to these principal ideas. This procedure would present a means for teachers to talk back to reading experts on both sides of the reading debate. This kind of dialogue, noticeably absent at present, might act to constrict or modify the extreme nature of the polemics sometimes now used in the "great debate," and thereby help smooth the road toward a consensus view as to how reading should be taught.

This open discussion between advocates of the whole language approach and those who endorse the direct, systematic, and intensive teaching of a hierarchy of discrete reading skills need not result in the conclusion that every student should be taught to read by a single, "official" methodology. Nonetheless, if the number of conflicting contentions about reading instruction that currently are held by various reading experts could be reduced significantly, it is likely that more effective reading instruction for students in general (i.e., those taught by the teachers in the present study) could be instigated.

References

Adams, M. J. 1990. *Beginning to Read: Thinking and learning about print*. Cambridge, MA: MIT.

Anderson, G. S. 1984. *A Whole Language Approach to Reading*. Lanham, MD: University Press of America.

Anderson, R. C., Hiebert, E. H., Scott, J. A., and Wilkinson, I. A. G. 1985. *Becoming a Nation of Readers*. Washington, DC: U.S. Department of Education.

Carbo, M. 1987. Reading styles research: "What works" isn't always phonics. *Phi Delta Kappan* 68:431–435.

Carnine, D., Silbert, J. and Kameenui, E. 1990. *Direct Reading Instruction*. Columbus, OH: Merrill.

Chall, J. S. 1983. *Learning to Read: The great debate*. New York, NY: McGraw-Hill.

Chall, J. S. 1989. Learning to read: The great debate. 20 years later—a response to "Debunking the great phonics myth." *Phi Delta Kappan* 70:521–538.

Feitelson, D. 1988. *Facts and Fads in Beginning Reading*. Norwood, NJ: Ablex.

Ferreiro, E. and Teberosky, A. 1982. *Literacy Before Schooling*. Exeter, NH: Heinemann.

Froese, V. 1982. Classics in reading: A survey. *Reading Teacher* 36:303–306.

Goodman, K. 1986. *What's Whole in Whole Language?* Exeter, NH: Heinemann.

Goodman, K., Shannon, P., Freeman, Y., and Murphy, S. 1988. *Report Card on Basal Readers*. Katonah, NY: Richard C. Owen.

Goodman, K. S. 1989. Whole language is whole: A response to Heymsfeld *Educational Leadership* 46 (6):69–70.

Goodman, Y. 1984. The development of initial literacy. *In* H. Goelman, A.A. Oberg, and F. Smith (eds.). *Awakening to Literacy* (pp. 102–109). Exeter, NH: Heinemann.

Goodman, Y. and Burke, C. L. 1980. *Reading Strategies: Focus on comprehension*. Katonah, NY: Richard C. Owen.

Groff, P. 1987. *Preventing Reading Failure*. Portland, OR: National Book.

Harste, J. C., Woodward, V. A., and Burke, C. L. 1984. *Language Stories and Literacy Lessons*. Exeter, NH: Heinemann.

Hittleman, D. R. and Hittleman, C. R. 1983. *Developmental Reading, K–8: Teaching from a psycholinguistic perspective*. Boston, MA: Houghton Mifflin.

Holdaway, D. 1979. *The Foundations of Literacy*. Exeter, NH: Heinemann.

Just, M. A. and Carpenter, P. 1987. *The Psychology of Reading and Language Comprehension*. Boston, MA: Allyn and Bacon.

Liberman, I. Y. and Liberman, A. M. 1990. Whole language vs. code emphasis: Underlying assumptions and their implications for reading instruction. *Annals of Dyslexia* 40:51–76.

Newman, J. M. 1985a. Using children's books to teach reading. *In* J.M. Newman (ed.). *Whole Language: Theory in use* (pp. 55–64). Exeter, NH: Heinemann.

Newman, J. M. 1985b. What about reading? *In* J.M. Newman (ed.). *Whole Language: Theory in use* (pp. 99–110). Exeter, NH: Heinemann.

Pearson, P. D. 1989. Reading the whole-language movement. *Elementary School Journal* 90:231–241.

Perfetti, C. A. 1985. *Reading Ability*. New York, NY: Oxford.

Quinby, L., (ed.). 1987. *English-Language Arts Framework for California Public Schools*. Sacramento, CA: California State Department of Education.

Smith, F. 1973. *Psychology and Reading*. New York, NY: Holt, Rinehart and Winston.

Smith, F. 1978. *Understanding Reading*. New York, NY: Holt, Rinehart and Winston.

Smith, F. 1979. *Reading without Nonsense*. New York, NY: Teachers College, Columbia University.

Smith, F. 1983. *Essays into Literacy*. Exeter, NH: Heinemann.

Smith, F. 1984. The creative achievement of literacy. *In* H. Goelman, A. A. Oberg, and
    F. Smith (eds.) *Awakening to Literacy* (pp. 102–109). Exeter, NH: Heinemann.
Smith, F. 1985. *Reading.* New York, NY: Cambridge University.
Smith, F. 1986a. *Insult to Intelligence.* New York, NY: Arbor House.
Smith, F. 1986b. *Understanding Reading.* Hillsdale, NJ: Lawrence Erlbaum.
Weaver, C. 1980. *Psycholinguistics and Reading.* Cambridge, MA: Winthrop.
Weaver, C. 1988. *Reading Process and Practice.* Exeter, NH: Heinemann.

Use of an Orton-Gillingham Approach to Teach a Foreign Language to Dyslexic/Learning-Disabled Students: Explicit Teaching of Phonology in a Second Language

Richard L. Sparks

College of Mt. St. Joseph
Cincinnati, Ohio

Leonore Ganschow

Miami University
Oxford, Ohio

Silvia Kenneweg

Hathaway Brown School
Shaker Heights, Ohio

Karen Miller

St. Paul's School for Girls
Brooklandville, Maryland

Annals of Dyslexia, Vol. 41, 1991.
Copyright © 1991 by The Orton Dyslexia Society
ISSN 0736–9387

Recent research findings suggest that students who have difficulty learning a second language have weaknesses in oral and written native-language skills which affect their performance in the foreign-language classroom. These weaknesses involve understanding the phonological, syntactic, and semantic codes of language. Evidence suggests that dyslexic/learning-disabled and other "at risk" students who struggle in the second language classroom exhibit particular difficulty with the phonological and syntactic codes of the language. The Orton-Gillingham method, a multisensory, structured language approach which adheres to the direct and explicit teaching of phonology, is presented as an alternative to the "natural" communication approaches recently developed by foreign-language educators to teach a second language. A method for adapting this approach for teaching Spanish is described.

It is well recognized among professionals who work with college-bound or college-enrolled students with dyslexia/learning disabilities that the study of a foreign language poses inordinate difficulties for most of them (Fisher 1986; Ganschow and Sparks 1987; Javorsky, Sparks, and Ganschow in press; Levine 1987; Pompian 1986; Sparks, Javorsky, and Ganschow 1990). Recent findings suggest that relative weaknesses in their native language may affect the ability of these students to perform successfully in foreign language classrooms, especially when they are exposed to a second language for the first time in high school or college (Ganschow and Sparks 1986, 1987; Sparks and Ganschow 1981; Sparks, Ganschow and Javorsky in press; Sparks, Ganschow, and Pohlman 1989; Sparks, Javorsky, and Ganschow 1990). Furthermore, there is evidence to indicate that these young men and women have latent difficulties with the phonological and syntactic aspects of their native language which have gone unnoticed or have been compensated for over their years of schooling (Dinklage 1971; Levine 1987). However, when confronted with a new symbol system—with new sounds, letter combinations, and syntactic structures—the students' basic difficulties with the "linguistic codes" of the language re-emerge and they are "thrown back" into a situation similar to that which they encountered when learning to read and write their native language.

One of the missions of The Orton Dyslexia Society is to encourage the training of teachers in a methodology that has been shown over the years to be successful for students with reading, writing, and spelling difficulties in their native language. This methodology, a "multisensory, structured language" approach, is being used in a few schools across the country to teach beginning Spanish to students with dyslexia/learning disabilities (Kenneweg 1988; Miller 1990). In general, however, students with dyslexia/learning disabilities have not been exposed to this teaching approach because it simply is not known in foreign language circles, and special educators have devoted their time to

focusing on teaching native language skills. These students tradi-
tionally have had few options: (1) to struggle with the foreign language
on their own in regular classroom environments; (2) to apply for
waiver/substitution of the foreign language requirement in school settings where this option is available; or (3) to change their academic or
career goals to avoid foreign language study entirely.

Despite the widespread use of multisensory, structured language
techniques and the positive reports from practitioners that these techniques work, there has been little empirical data to validate their effectiveness (Clark 1988). Recently, however, some evidence has been generated which supports the use of these techniques when teaching
students to read, spell, and write their native language (Brightman
1986; Enfield 1976, 1988; Frankiewicz 1984; Guyer and Sabatino 1989;
Hutcheson, Selig, and Young 1990; Vickery, Reynolds, and Cochran
1987; White 1986). Given the support that multisensory instruction has
received and the positive experiences cited by the few teachers who
have expertise in both foreign language instruction and structured
language training (Kenneweg 1988; Miller 1990), it would seem to be a
viable approach to beginning foreign language instruction for dyslexic/
learning-disabled students.

In this paper, we lay the groundwork for the importance of focusing on language-based variables when teaching a foreign language. We
begin with a brief review of the literature, in which we examine explanations for foreign language learning differences. Evidence is presented to support our view that "foreign" language learning problems
involve difficulties with the phonological syntactic and semantic codes
of the language, which we refer to as the "Linguistic Coding Deficit
Hypothesis." We also describe some of our research findings which
suggest that students with histories of foreign language learning problems have particular difficulties with the sound/symbol (phonological)
and syntactic "codes" of language. A description of the approach in a
foreign language classroom is provided by two teachers (Kenneweg
and Miller) who have training in both foreign language instruction and
the Orton-Gillingham method and have been practicing this approach
when teaching Spanish in classrooms for dyslexic/learning-disabled
students for a number of years. Last, we present implications of Orton-
Gillingham instruction for foreign language education.

Review of the Foreign Language Literature

Over the years, foreign language professionals have expressed
concern about students' failure to learn a second language. Studies
have focused on the role of intelligence as well as affective variables.

Recently, the influence of individual learning strategies and learning styles has been hypothesized to be a factor in foreign language failure. Aptitude for learning a foreign language also has been a widely researched area. A summary of the foreign language literature includes research related to foreign language learning and IQ, affect, learning styles and strategies, and aptitude.

Intelligence, Affective, and Learning Strategy/Style

Intellectual, affective, and learning strategy/style explanations for foreign language learning differences have received considerable attention in the foreign language research literature. Intelligence has not been shown to be a critical variable in foreign language learning; in fact, measures of general intelligence have been shown to be relatively independent of language aptitude (Carroll 1985; Gardner 1985; Gardner and Lambert 1965, 1972; Genessee 1976). Wesche, Edwards, and Wells (1982), for example, found that foreign language aptitude tests measured abilities distinctly different from mental abilities on IQ tests.

Affective variables, such as attitude/motivation (Gardner and Lambert 1972; Gardner 1985), anxiety (Horwitz, Horwitz, and Cope 1986; Horwitz 1990), and social distance from the second language group (Schumann 1976) have been proposed as reasons for success or failure to learn a second language. Research findings on anxiety have been equivocal, however, and not all types of anxiety are felt to be detrimental to second language learning (Horwitz 1990; Scovel 1978). While theories of attitude and motivation have been widely disseminated throughout the foreign language teaching profession, such models have also been viewed as empirically unsound because of methodological and measurement problems associated with the self-report instruments that are used to form the basis of the theories (Oller 1979, 1981; Oller and Perkins 1978a, b). Au (1988) has criticized Gardner's Socio-Educational theory on several points including the model's inability to generate concrete empirical evidence that attitudes and motivation are the *cause* of foreign language failure. Sparks and Ganschow (1991) have suggested that high levels of anxiety, low motivation, and poor attitudes are the by-products of foreign language learning problems, and that these affective differences occur *as a result of* overt or subtle native language learning difficulties.

Recently, emphasis in the foreign language literature has shifted to finding alternative methodologies for specific types of students (Horwitz 1990) and has focused on the role of learning strategies and learning styles (Oxford 1989, 1990). Specific aspects of learning style which have been hypothesized to affect second language learning are brain hemisphericity, sensory modality preferences, tolerance for ambiguity, field dependence-independence, and Myers-Briggs dimensions (e.g., extraversion-introversion, sensing-intuition, thinking-feeling, and judging-perceiving). Learning strategies are thought to be related to sex and age of the learner, career orientation, and affective and personality factors. Oxford writes, however, that neither style nor strategy contributions to second language learning have been rigorously investigated, and that many learning style instruments have not been shown to be empirically reliable or valid. Corbett and Smith (1984) also have emphasized that further refinement of learning style instruments is necessary before they are used in a foreign language classroom. In subjects other than foreign language, dimensions of learning style such as the use of sensory modality testing and modality teaching have not been shown to be effective (Arter and Jenkins 1977; Kampwirth and Bates 1980; Kavale and Forness 1987, 1990; Larrivee 1981; Stahl 1988; Tarver and Dawson 1978). Likewise, the modality model in reading and learning disabilities has generated little empirical support (Adams 1990; Glass 1988).

Foreign Language Aptitude

Research on aptitude for learning a foreign language began with the work of Carroll (1958, 1962, 1973, 1981, 1985). In conjunction with Stanley Sapon (Carroll and Sapon 1959), he developed a test of foreign language aptitude, the Modern Language Aptitude Test (MLAT). By using measurements of cognitive abilities and "work sample" methods, Carroll was able to distinguish four variables that made independent but significant contributions to the prediction of success in learning a foreign language: (1) phonetic coding ability—the ability to learn, recognize, and remember correspondences between particular sounds of a language and their printed symbols; (2) grammatical sensitivity—the ability to recognize the grammatical functions of words and other components of sentences as well as apply grammatical rules; (3) inductive language learning ability—the ability to infer linguistic rules, forms, and patterns from new linguistic content; and (4) rote learning ability—the capacity quickly to learn a large number of phonetic and grammatical associations. The four variables form the basis of the MLAT; Carroll speculated that each contributed a distinct piece of information about foreign language aptitude (although he did not hypothesize which might be the most important variable). Thus, the total score on the MLAT was seen as predictive of a learner's probable success in learning a foreign language in a traditional classroom format.

In a later article though, Carroll (1968) suggested that ". . . the language tester would do well to sample different areas—phonological, syntactic, and lexical—in order to obtain a satisfactory profile of an individual's competence in his native language . . ." (p. 52) because differences might exist in a person's oral vs. written or expressive vs. receptive language skills. He indicated, for example, that ". . . cases are reported in which a learner cannot discriminate two foreign language phonemes spoken by others and yet is able to produce them in a distinctive fashion; the reverse case is even more frequent" (p. 53). Carroll speculated that an individual might exhibit greater competence in one part of language (syntax) and a lesser degree of skill in another (phonology), and later acknowledged that first and second language learning have "common properties . . . both require the capacity to remember and reproduce sounds and to apply grammatical rules" (1973, p. 6).

Pimsleur and his colleagues (1962, 1964, 1966, 1968) also conducted research on foreign language aptitude. A portion of their work focused on "underachievers," a group comprised of individuals who had significantly less success in foreign language courses than in other subjects. Through his work, Pimsleur also developed a test of foreign language aptitude, the Language Aptitude Battery (LAB) (1966). This test consisted of three parts: (1) verbal intelligence—the familiarity with words in the individual's native language and the ability to manipulate verbal material; (2) motivation—for which he designed an interest test; and (3) auditory ability—measured by sound discrimination and sound-symbol association tasks.

It was this third component, in particular, that appeared to interest Pimsleur, who indicated that auditory ability ". . . has not been recognized nor accorded its true importance . . ." (1968: p. 102). In his research studies it was found to be the variable which accounted for deficiencies in second language learning not explainable by lower intelligence or a lack of motivation. Like Carroll, he (1966) cited cases in which underachieving students did as well as high achievers on tests of vocabulary and verbal reasoning but performed more poorly on the tests of "auditory ability." He made reference to the "many fascinating research problems" presented by this factor in relation to second language learning. Pimsleur also wondered if this ability could be affected by training or if it were really a "physiological phenomenon," and he questioned if "auditory ability" might play a part in learning to read and write one's native language. He called for a "serious research attack" on this ". . . special factor beyond intelligence and industriousness which accounts for how well an individual succeeds in a [foreign] language course" (1964, p. 135).

While the research literature suggests that foreign language aptitude tests can be important predictors of second language learning potential, they do not appear to have been widely used by the foreign language teaching profession. Data on the predictive validity of aptitude tests such as the MLAT and LAB indicate that validity coefficients on the average were .51, but varied widely depending on many factors. In studies where language aptitude tests were combined with other variables (intelligence, motivation, attitude), aptitude tests have accounted for as large, or a larger proportion of the variance as the other variables (Edwards, Wesche, and Smyth 1976; Gardner 1985; Gardner and Lambert 1972; Pimsleur, Sundland, and McIntyre 1964).

Linguistic Coding Deficit Hypothesis

The possibility of similarities between first and second language learning has been suggested in the foreign language literature (Carroll 1973; Oller 1981). Recently, the connection between native and foreign language learning has been described by two of the authors and a colleague in the context of a "Linguistic Coding Deficit Hypothesis" (Sparks, Ganschow, and Pohlman 1989). This hypothesis, derived from research by Vellutino and Scanlon (1986) on children with reading disabilities, speculates that foreign language learners have a deficiency in one or more of the linguistic codes of the language system—phonological, syntactic, and semantic. Our research group has conducted five studies to date related to this hypothesis; they are reported here.

In our first pilot study (Sparks, Ganschow, and Pohlman 1989) we found deficits in the native phonological and syntactic, but not semantic, language skills of 22 college students who had petitioned and received a waiver from their university's foreign language requirement after course failure. The difficulties with sounds and grammar seemed to have an immediate impact on these learners, most of whom failed in the first or second semester of the foreign language.

In a study of successful foreign language learners and unsuccessful learners who had petitioned and received a waiver from the foreign language requirement in college (Ganschow et al. in press), significant differences between the two groups were found on tests of phonology, word identification, spelling, and grammar (i.e., phonology and syntax), but not reading comprehension or vocabulary (i.e., semantics). There were no differences in intelligence on the WAIS-R between the groups, but significant differences were found on both the Short and Long forms of the MLAT, as well as all MLAT subtests. This finding was similar to a study by Gajar (1987) with students with learning disabilities at Penn State.

Another recent study by the authors and colleagues (Sparks et al. 1991a, b) focused on the native and foreign language aptitude skills of "low" risk, "high" risk, and school-identified learning-disabled high school students enrolled in first-year foreign language classes. "Low" and "high" risk students were identified by means of an author-developed (Ganschow and Sparks in press) self-reported screening instrument, first quarter grades in the foreign language course, and teacher recommendation. Significant differences were found between the "low" and "high" risk groups and "low" risk and LD groups on all phonological, syntactic, and semantic measures of both native and foreign language aptitude (word identification, phonology, spelling, grammar, vocabulary, reading comprehension, all MLAT subtests). Significant differences were found between the "high" risk group and students with LD on all measures of syntax and semantics; no significant differences were found on phonological and rote memory tasks. In interpreting these results, the authors speculated that the "high" risk learners had not been identified as "at risk" *before* enrolling in the foreign language course because their native language syntactic and semantic skills (as evidenced by this group's scores which were in the average range on word identification, reading, reading comprehension, written language and grammar tasks) were relatively intact. However, the "high" risk group and students with LD were characterized by similar performance on phonological tasks in reading and foreign language aptitude as well as rote memory difficulties on the MLAT. This finding suggested that both non-LD at risk learners and students with LD share similar deficits in phonological coding.

We examined students with and without learning disabilities with respect to their self-reported attitudes toward foreign-language learning (Javorsky, Sparks, and Ganschow in press). Results indicated that college students with LD perceived themselves as less capable and possessing fewer skills to manage the oral and written language requirements of the foreign language course. No differences between the two groups' motivation to learn a foreign language were found, but the students with LD felt more anxious when asked to study or perform the second language. Here, we speculated that the higher level of anxiety perceived by students with LD was related to their relative weakness in oral and written language.

In a recently completed study (Ganschow and Sparks in press), the Linguistic Coding Deficit Hypothesis was investigated further through the use of a self-reported screening instrument designed to screen college students who were likely to be "at risk" for having difficulty in traditional college classroom settings. The instrument (Sparks and Ganschow in preparation) contained questions which might reveal overt or subtle oral and/or written language difficulties similar to those experienced by students with LD. The instrument was administered to three groups of students (N = 637) as well as to a population of students who had petitioned for substitution of the foreign language requirement. Results indicated that a number of language-related questions were important discriminators of "high" and "no" risk students: ease of learning to read, spell, and learn phonics; ease of studying English; understanding what was read; grades in reading and spelling; and ease of note-taking. Based on limited measures, the instrument showed a high degree of validity and reliability, though it did not appear to be a very good predictor of foreign language course grades. Nevertheless, over 80 percent of the students who had petitioned for substitution of the foreign language requirement scored in the "high" risk category on the instrument. The authors speculated that the instrument could be a useful screening device in college-level foreign language classrooms.

The results of these studies have led the authors to hypothesize that the foreign language learning problems of learning-disabled and "high" risk students result primarily from deficiencies in phonology and associated short-term (rote) memory deficits. There is a group of students with foreign language learning problems that is distinguished not by phonological problems, but by semantic (and sometimes syntactic) deficits. Thus far, however, this group has been found to be numerically much smaller than the group with phonological difficulties. Like the "phonological-core variable-difference model" developed by Stanovich (1988, 1990) to explain the deficient processing mechanism of students with dyslexia/learning disabilities, the Linguistic Coding Deficit Hypothesis speculates that a similar processing deficit is responsible for the problems experienced by students in learning a second language.

Connections between the Foreign Language and LD Literature

Before moving into a description of the Orton-Gillingham approach as it applies to the teaching of a foreign language, we attempt here to synthesize for the reader the manner in which the evidence from three perspectives—that of foreign language educators, special educators, and reading researchers—converges to clarify the links between native and foreign language learning.

John Carroll's research focused on language variables that appeared to make a difference in the acquisition of a foreign language. He hypothesized that an individual might have varying abilities in the phonological, syntactic, and semantic components of language, and also that one's expressive/receptive and oral/written language skills might be discrepant. His research findings and speculations about language learning are consistent with the notion that the academic problems evidenced by students with LD are language-based (Catts 1986, 1989; Catts and Kamhi 1986, 1987; Liberman 1982; Vellutino 1979, 1987; Wallach and Butler 1984; Wiig and Semel 1980). Carroll's hypotheses are further supported by research which has found that students with LD exhibit oral communication deficits which cause a variety of oral language processing and production deficits (Johnson and Myklebust 1967; Magee and Newcomer 1978; Newcomer and Magee 1977; Vogel

1974; Wiig and Semel 1973, 1976, 1980; Wiig, Semel, and Crouse 1973). Increasing evidence has shown that these oral communication deficits do not disappear, but instead persist into adulthood (Blalock 1982; Johnson 1980; Morris and Leuenberger 1990; Vogel and Adelman 1990; Wiig and Semel 1975; Wiig and Fleischmann 1980). Oral language deficits also may play a causal role in later written language disabilities (Butler 1988; Liberman 1982; Liberman and Shankweiler 1979; Perfetti 1985; Vellutino 1979).

Pimsleur's "auditory ability" factor, in particular, provided evidence which resembles the deficits in phonological ability exhibited by reading- and learning-disabled students recently described in the literature (Blachman 1989; Bradley and Bryant 1983; Liberman 1987; Liberman and Shankweiler 1985; Lundberg 1987; Stanovich 1986; Wagner and Torgesen 1987). While Pimsleur cited a "paucity of information" about foreign language underachievement, scarcity of evidence is not the problem in the learning and reading disabilities literature, where "converging evidence" has accumulated which indicts differences in students' phonological skills as the source of variance in reading ability (see review by Stanovich 1986). Additional studies have suggested some commonality of processing between reading and listening (Sinatra 1990), and others have indicated that children and adults with reading disabilities have deficits in listening comprehension (Berger 1978; Chall 1983; Curtis 1980; Daneman and Carpenter 1980; Jackson and McClelland 1979; Jenkins and Pany 1981; Kotsonis and Patterson 1980; Stanovich, Cunningham, and Feeman 1984). Furthermore, reading-disabled children show limited awareness and sensitivity to the speech-sound structure of language as well as poor verbal short-term memory and word-finding and naming problems (Bradley and Bryant 1983; Brady, Shankweiler, and Mann 1983; Catts 1986, 1989; Mann and Liberman 1984; Mann, Shankweiler, and Smith 1984; Wolf, Bally, and Morris 1986). A recent study by Crain (1989) supported the view that the spoken language comprehension failures of poor readers arise from limitations in phonological processing, and also involve working memory.

It seems evident from the foreign language aptitude research that poor "auditory ability" or "phonetic coding" might cause difficulties in learning a foreign language, just as deficits in phonological ability cause problems in learning to read and write one's native language. Research also suggests that if a student has significant difficulties with reading, concomitant deficits may also exist in oral communication, particularly listening comprehension. These findings appear to indicate that such a student would have problems in both the oral and written language activities of a traditional foreign language classroom. With this background in mind, we now turn to describing how a methodology that is used to teach phonology in one's native language might be applied successfully to the teaching of a foreign language.

Orton-Gillingham Methodology and Foreign Language Learning

Recent approaches developed by the foreign language teaching profession have focused on methodologies that espouse "natural" approaches to language learning, and recommend that students learn a second language in much the same way they learn their first; i.e., listening precedes speaking which precedes reading and writing. The authors have examined this view and speculate that this principle may cause difficulties for students with language and learning disabilities (Ganschow and Sparks in press; Javorsky, Sparks, and Ganschow in press; Sparks and Ganschow 1991). Because these students have difficulties not only with written language, but also oral language, such "natural" approaches have the potential to create the same problems as the primarily reading and writing approaches formerly used by foreign language teachers. Instead, we propose that a multisensory, structured language approach be used because a methodology which adheres to the direct and explicit teaching of the phonology of the second language and at the same time enables the students to "see," "hear," and "do" (write) the language simultaneously might be the key that enhances a student's ability to unlock or crack the code of a foreign language (Javorsky, Sparks, and Ganschow in press; Kenneweg 1988; Myer et al. 1989; Sparks and Ganschow 1991).

One such strategy is the Orton-Gillingham approach (Gillingham and Stillman 1960; Orton 1966). The similarity of this approach to the authors' instructional recommendation is evident, as the method espouses the direct and explicit teaching of phonology in a highly structured, step-by-step fashion (Williams 1987). The approach also recommends that only a small amount of material be presented at one time with thorough mastery of that material through multisensory presentation practice. Numerous remedial programs that teach reading, spelling, and writing have been developed that adhere to the fundamental principles of the method (Cox 1985; Greene and Enfield 1985a, b; Slingerland 1971; Traub and Bloom 1975).

A foreign language class that is taught using the Orton-Gillingham method is distinguished by its use of a multisensory approach so that the student's auditory, visual, and kinesthetic (motor) pathways are engaged simultaneously. The motor pathway at the high school level may be engaged via writing on the board or on paper. Letters (graphemes) that represent sounds (phonemes) are presented to the students and immediately synthesized into words. By introducing the graphemes and their corresponding foreign language phonemes through multiple modalities, students are not restricted to one form of input (i.e., auditory as in a "natural" communication approach), and can "see" sounds and words by writing them, a request often made by students having difficulty in a foreign language classroom (Ganschow and Sparks 1986). Thus, the students are simultaneously listening, speaking, reading, and writing the second language. While such an approach may seem "unnatural" to those for whom both the first and a second language were easily learned, it may be necessary for students who have histories of oral language (listening and speaking) difficulties which, as previously mentioned, seem to affect the acquisition of written language (reading and writing skills).

It is important to point out that the multisensory approach recommended here is not similar to the process strategy model which evaluates modality preferences (visual, auditory, tactile-kinesthetic) to determine particular "learning styles" that are used in programs emphasizing "visual" or "auditory" materials. Instead, a multisensory approach would suggest that all modalities influence the learning process. By using such an approach, it is hypothesized only that students would have access to more than one form of input. It is critical to recognize, though, that the input is directed toward making sense out of language, in this case the phonology of the foreign language. Students who lack "phonemic awareness," or Pimsleur's "auditory ability," have not been able to grasp intuitively that spoken words are composed of sound segments, and they generally have difficulties with listening comprehension as well. A multisensory approach uses auditory, visual, and tactile-kinesthetic input simultaneously not to train a visual (e.g., visual discrimination, visual-motor), tactile-kinesthetic (e.g., fine or gross motor skills), or auditory (auditory memory or blending) process, but to provide additional forms of input which are always directed to learning the structure of the language.

Because the student who is learning a second language must learn more than phonology, the Orton-Gillingham method, when applied to foreign language learning, must go beyond the teaching of sounds and pronunciation of words. It must also address all of the fundamental components of language learning: phonology, grammar, and semantics; expressive and receptive language; and oral and written language. Certain rules must be observed in order to make the course consistent from an Orton-Gillingham standpoint and to keep its integrity as a foreign language class. These rules are:

1. The course must be taught entirely in Spanish; the use of English should be reserved for clarifying difficult grammar points.

2. It must be a structured class with well-defined daily activities.
3. There must be frequent review.
4. It must emphasize consistently simultaneous writing and pronunciation so that the students can "see," "hear," and "do" the language.

Because students with language and learning disabilities have difficulty with both phonology *and* syntax, any full-class approach to second language learning must attempt to teach these language concepts *directly.* Thus, an Orton-Gillingham class would include daily teaching of sounds and grammar in a multisensory fashion. It is essential that the foreign language teacher be aware of the need for explicit instruction, as the teaching of the sounds (which leads to words) and syntactic rules paves the way for communication (i.e., listening and speaking) in the second language.

Teaching the Phonology and Syntax of Spanish

The phonetic structure of Spanish is regular and may seem easy to teach to students with dyslexia/learning disabilities; however, it should be remembered that the students are still learning the phonology of a new language system. Thus, a daily lesson plan should be followed which includes these recommended class activities:

1. Blackboard Drills (10–15 minutes)—phonology and grammar.
2. Oral Sound Drills (2–3 minutes)—review of sounds just learned at the blackboard.
3. Grammatical Concepts (10 minutes)—introduction and review of grammar.
4. Vocabulary Teaching (10 minutes)—introduction of new vocabulary words which use new and previously-learned sounds.
5. Reading/Communicative Activities (10 minutes)—practicing "real" communication in the second language.

Blackboard drills. The teaching of phonology is done daily at the blackboard. The teaching should be done in the following manner: (1) the teacher pronounces a sound and the students repeat it; (2) the teacher writes the letter and pronounces the sound simultaneously and the students imitate; (3) the teacher writes simple Spanish words on the board that contain the new sound while pronouncing each word aloud, and the students imitate; (4) the teacher dictates these same words to the students as they simultaneously pronounce and write the words. Only one sound is taught each day, and the teacher should make provisions for frequent review of previously learned sounds. Flash cards with each phoneme may also be used for review (consonants written in black ink, vowels in red ink). Additional cards are added as each new sound is learned.

The order of presentation of the Spanish sounds should be: (1) all vowels; (2) consonants that are the same in both English and Spanish; (3) consonants that are different in English and Spanish; and (4) special blends of sounds (i.e., diphthongs and consonant blends) such as consonant -*u*- vowel, which makes the *u* sound like "w." Once the vowels have been learned, the blackboard drills should combine consonants with the vowels (*ma, me, mi, mo, mu*). The teacher can then begin to dictate easier multisyllabic words as more consonants are introduced (*lata, lana, tela, lelo, elena*, etc.). A few sounds can be learned before a larger review takes place, although daily repetition is important. The review of previously learned sounds can include new words. As the year progresses, the time spent on the blackboard drill of sounds may decrease as the students' automaticity in using the phonology of the new language increases. Instead, phonetic phrases and sentences can be used.

Oral sound drills. This part of the lesson follows the blackboard drills and takes place while the students are seated at their desks. The purpose is to review orally and visually the sounds just learned at the blackboard or to review a sound that was taught previously. The teacher displays a card with a specific grapheme. One student should say the phoneme (sound), then attempt to recall words with that sound. In a small class, each student might pronounce a consonant in combination with the five vowels; in a larger class, each student might pronounce only one syllable. All of the students should prepare sound (flash) cards to review as part of their homework routine (consonants in black, vowels in red).

Grammatical concepts. This activity is done at the blackboard and follows the oral sound drills with the purpose of reinforcing the syntax of Spanish. Because students with dyslexia/learning disabilities struggle to learn the syntax of their own language, it is important that the teacher develop explicit methods for inducing the grammatical rules of an unfamiliar language (i.e., rules should be arrived at, not given). These exercises should review one previously taught grammatical concept and reinforce the concept taught the day before. The teacher might review time, weather, days of the week, dates, adjectives, or verbs. For example, when reviewing possessive adjectives the teacher would:

1. Bring students to the board and say aloud a subject pronoun and an object (*ella, medias*), which the students would simultaneously repeat and write.

2. Ask a student to give the correct possessive adjective and the object (*sus medias*).
3. Ask the students at the board to write and repeat simultaneously.

As the syntax increases in complexity, the teacher can begin asking questions involving possessive adjectives (*?De que color son tus zapatos?*). One student answers the question orally (*Mis zapatos son negros*). When the answer has been accepted and/or corrected, the class simultaneously says and writes the sentence.

When teaching grammatical concepts in the second language, the teacher might also have the students "act out" the language as much as possible so that they are "doing" its structure. For example, when teaching the concept of the negative, the teacher might have a student write *Sara es cubana* on the board. Three students come to the front of the room. Each is assigned a part of the sentence (*sujeto, verbo,* and *adjetivo*), and pronounces his/her part aloud (*Sara, es, cubana*). A fourth student holding a square of construction paper with the word "no" written on it enters the sentence aided by the teacher while the sentence written on the board is also changed by a designated student. Each student again pronounces his/her part in the sentence. Using this simple exercise, syntax becomes very real and concrete for students with language learning difficulties.

Vocabulary teaching.   Vocabulary is taught with the help of visuals. Students with dyslexia/learning disabilities frequently ask to "see" a picture of the word they are pronouncing and writing, particularly in the early stages of second language learning. Often, this is made easier by textbook companies which provide transparencies to accompany vocabulary words. The number of words taught daily may vary according to the length and difficulty of the words. For example, there may be 18 words to learn in a lesson. The teacher may divide the list, teaching nine words one day and nine words the next. A list of new vocabulary words may not be introduced until one to two days later when a new lesson begins. When feasible, new vocabulary words should be limited to those which include only those phonemes (sounds) that the students have learned. Once the vowels are mastered, however, the students can learn a variety of new words at one time. Because the vowels are introduced first, many new words can often be introduced within the first one to two weeks of the course.

The methodology used to teach vocabulary words is similar to the teaching of sounds at the blackboard:

1. The teacher pronounces the new word and the students repeat it.

2. The teacher simultaneously pronounces and writes the words on the blackboard.
3. The students imitate by pronouncing and writing at the blackboard.
4. The teacher might also divide the word into syllables to illustrate the sounds and syllables more concretely.

Students are encouraged to make vocabulary cards for the new words (consonants in black, vowels in red) so that the words can be reviewed as often as necessary.

Communicative activities. For most dyslexic/learning-disabled students enrolled in foreign language courses that employ "natural" communication approaches, listening and speaking of the second language is the point at which instruction begins. The students, in effect, are required to use their three language systems—phonological, syntactic, and semantic—to listen to and speak the foreign language before, or in conjunction with, reading and writing. Like many students who have not mastered reading and writing in their native language, dyslexic/learning-disabled students in a foreign language usually have not received *explicit* instruction in the phonology or syntax of the new language. Instead, they are expected to "intuit" the phonology and grammar of the second language independently. The *direct* teaching methods of the Orton-Gillingham approach allow the student the opportunity to learn the phonological and syntactic system of the new language *at the same time* that she/he is asked to use the semantic system for communication. Thus, a structured language approach enhances and allows "real" communication to take place. Far from preventing "creativity" or "spontaneity," a structured approach to second language learning allows students to develop proficiency when using the new language for communicative purposes.

Communicative activities can also be done using a multisensory approach. One such activity, for example, could involve a previously taught grammatical concept presented in the following manner:

1. Each student is asked to prepare four index cards that each contain one pronoun: *lo, la, los, las.*
2. Then, each student is instructed to write several sentences on a sheet of paper. Each sentence is to contain a subject, verb, and direct object (noun).
3. Next, students are separated into pairs. One student (#1) reads a sentence to his/her partner (#2).
4. Student #2 selects the card with the correct direct object pronoun and repeats aloud the sentence with the direct object pro-

noun in its proper place. (If time allows, Student #1 may also write the response given by his/her partner next to the original sentence.)

Other communicative activities in the classroom might include listening to the teacher's (or another student's) question and giving a verbal response, allowing students to question each other, answering written questions in writing, reading a question and responding verbally, and listening to tapes of dialogue (while reading along with the tape) and then answering written or oral questions. Success in communicative activities such as this is the result of not only an efficient semantic coding system but also well-developed phonological and syntactic systems which enable the student to make automatic, spontaneous responses in the second language.

Implications for Foreign Language Education

The five parts of a Spanish lesson which use Orton-Gillingham methodology represent a highly structured daily lesson plan. The approach presented in this paper, most likely, sounds familiar to many LD and reading specialists who are aware of the problems of dyslexic/learning-disabled students. We have found, though, that foreign language educators generally are not aware of methodologies that emphasize explicit instruction in the phonology of the second language. LD and reading specialists should not be surprised by this state of affairs in the foreign language teaching profession, however, as the debate in their own field continues to rage as to whether direct instruction in phonology is important in learning to read and spell one's native language, or whether "natural" approaches such as "whole language" are more beneficial to students with language learning problems.

Language instructors' reluctance in acknowledging the importance of explicit teaching of phonology and grammar, perhaps, is a "natural" consequence of their being "good" language learners. Teachers of second languages, in particular, are likely to have highly developed native language skills. Consistent with the speculation of the Linguistic Coding Deficit Hypothesis, their phonological, syntactic, and semantic coding systems probably function so well that acquisition of both the first and second language did, indeed, seem to occur "naturally" (although perhaps not without effort). "Good" language learners automatically access the linguistic codes and apparently have a high degree of "metalinguistic awareness" (Adams 1990; Kavanagh and Mattingly 1972).

Because such learners have been able to learn the codes rapidly and automatically (perhaps without any, or a minimum of direct instruction), they may not have a *conscious* awareness of the manner in which they have mastered the language so easily. As teachers, then, they may not be sympathetic to, or conscious of, the needs of some learners for *direct* instruction in phonology (and grammar). Our recent research in second language learning lends support to this argument. It remains for foreign language and special educators who are knowledgeable about the unique language-based difficulties of students with dyslexia/learning disabilities to meet the challenge of implementing effective teaching methodologies.

References

Adams, M. 1990, *Beginning to Read: Thinking and learning about print*. Cambridge, MA: MIT Press.

Arter, J. and Jenkins, J. 1977. Examining the benefits and prevalence of modality instruction. *Journal of Special Education* 11:282–298.

Au, S. 1988. A critical appraisal of Gardner's social-psychological theory of second-language (L2) learning. *Language Learning* 38:75–100.

Berger, N. 1978. Why Johnny can't read? Perhaps because he's not a good listener. *Journal of Learning Disabilities* 11:633–638.

Blachman, B. A. 1989. Phonological awareness and word recognition. *In* A. Kamhi and H. Catts (eds.). *Reading Disorders: A developmental language perspective*. San Diego: College-Hill Press.

Blalock, J. 1982. Persistent auditory language deficits in adults with learning disability. *Journal of Learning Disabilities* 15:604–609.

Bradley, L. and Bryant, P. 1983. Categorizing sounds and learning to read—A causal connection. *Nature* 310:419–421.

Brady, S., Shankweiler, D., and Mann, V. 1983. Speech perception and memory coding in relation to reading ability. *Journal of Experimental Child Psychology* 35:345–367.

Brightman, M. 1986. An Evaluation of the Impact of the Alphabetic Phonics Program in the Kinkaid School from 1983 through 1985, Report No. 2. Houston: Neuhaus Foundation.

Butler, K. 1988. Preschool language processing performance and later reading achievement. *In* R. Masland and M. Masland (eds.). *Preschool Prevention of Reading Failure*. Parkton, MD: York Press.

Carroll, J. 1958. A factor analysis of two foreign language aptitude batteries. *The Journal of General Psychology* 59:3–19.

Carroll, J. 1962. The prediction of success in intensive foreign language training. *In* R. Glaser (ed.). *Training and Research in Education*.

Carroll, J. 1968. The psychology of language testing. *In* A. Davies (ed.). *Language Testing Symposium: A linguistic approach*. London: Oxford University Press. Pittsburgh: University of Pittsburgh Press.

Carroll, J. 1973. Implications of aptitude test research and psycholinguistic theory for foreign language teaching. *International Journal of Psycholinguistics* 2:5–14.

Carroll, J. 1981. Twenty-five years of research on foreign language aptitude. *In* K. C. Diller (ed.). *Individual Differences and Universals in Language Learning Aptitude*. Rowley, MA: Newbury House.

Carroll, J. 1985. Second language abilities. In R. Sternberg (ed.). *Human Abilities: An information processing approach.* New York: W. H. Freeman & Co.

Carroll, J. and Sapon, S. 1959. *Modern Language Aptitude Test.* New York: Psychological Corporation.

Catts, H. 1986. Speech production/phonological deficits in reading disorderd children. *Journal of Learning Disabilities* 19:504–508.

Catts, H. 1989. Defining dyslexia as a developmental language disorder. *Annals of Dyslexia* 39:50–66.

Catts, H. and Kamhi, A. 1986. The linguistic basis of reading disorders: Implications for the speech-language pathologist. *Language, Speech, and Hearing Services in the Schools* 17:329–341.

Catts, H. and Kamhi, A. 1987. The relationship between reading and language disorders: Implications for the speech-language pathologist. *Seminars in Speech and Language* 8:377–392.

Chall, J. 1983. *Stages of Reading Development.* New York: McGraw-Hill.

Clark, D. 1988. *Dyslexia: Theory and practice of remedial instruction.* Parkton, MD: York Press.

Corbett, S. and Smith, W. 1984. Identifying student learning styles: Proceed with caution! *Modern Language Journal* 68:212–221.

Cox, A. 1985. Alphabetic phonics: An organization and expansion of Orton-Gillingham. *Annals of Dyslexia* 35:187–198.

Crain, S. 1989. Why poor readers misunderstand spoken sentences. In D. Shankweiler and I. Liberman (eds.). *Phonology and Reading Disability: Solving the reading puzzle.* Ann Arbor, MI: University of Michigan Press.

Curtis, M. 1980. Development of components of reading skill. *Journal of Educational Psychology* 72:656–659.

Daneman, M. and Carpenter, P. 1980. Individual differences in working memory and reading. *Journal of Verbal Learning and Verbal Behavior* 19:450–466.

Dinklage, K. 1971. Inability to learn a foreign language. In G. Blaine and C. McArthur (eds.). *Emotional Problems of the Student.* New York: Appleton-Century-Crofts.

Edwards, H., Wesche, M., and Smyth, F. 1976. Psychological Predictors of Success in Second Language Training. Report of the Independent Study on the Language Training Programs of the Public Service of Canada. Ottawa: Government of Canada.

Enfield, M. 1976. An alternate classroom approach to meeting special learning needs of children with reading problems. Ph.D. diss., University of Minnesota, Minneapolis.

Enfield, M. L. 1988. The quest for literacy. *Annals of Dyslexia* 38:8–21.

Fisher, E. 1986. Learning disability specialist looks at foreign language instruction. *Hilltop Spectrum* 4(1):1–3.

Frankiewicz, R. 1984. An Evaluation of the Impact of the Alphabetic Phonics Program in Cypress Fairbanks Independent School District from 1981 through 1984. Houston: Neuhaus Foundation.

Gajar, A. 1987. Foreign language learning disabilities: The identification of predictive and diagnostic variables. *Journal of Learning Disabilities* 20:327–330.

Ganschow, L. and Sparks, R. 1986. Learning disabilities and foreign language difficulties: Deficit in listening skills? *Journal of Reading, Writing, and Learning Disabilities International* 2:305–319.

Ganschow, L. and Sparks, R. 1987. The foreign language requirement. *Learning Disabilities Focus* 2:116–123.

Ganschow, L. and Sparks, R. In press. A screening instrument for the identification of foreign language learning problems: Evidence for a relationship between native and second language learning problems. *Foreign Language Annals.*

Ganschow, L. and Sparks, R. In press. "Foreign" language learning disabilities: Issues, research, and teaching implications. *In* B. Vogel (ed.). *Success for College Students with Learning Disabilities.* New York: Springer-Verlag.

Ganschow, L., Sparks, R., Javorsky, J., Pohlman, J., Bishop-Marbury, A. In press. Identifying native language difficulties among foreign language learners in college: A "foreign" language learning disability? *Journal of Learning Disabilities.*

Gardner, R. 1985. *Social Psychology and Second Language Learning: The role of attitudes and motivation.* London: Edward Arnold.

Gardner, R. and Lambert, W. 1965. Language aptitude, intelligence, and second language achievement. *Journal of Educational Psychology* 56:191–199.

Gardner, R. and Lambert, W. 1972. *Attitude and Motivation in Second Language Learning.* Rowley, MA: Newbury House.

Genessee, F. 1976. The role of intelligence in second language learning. *Language Learning* 26:267–280.

Gillingham, A. and Stillman, B. 1960. *Remedial Training for Children with Specific Disability in Reading, Writing, and Penmanship.* Cambridge, MA: Educators Publishing Service.

Glass, G. 1988. Controversial practices. *In* K. Kavale, S. Forness, and M. Bender (eds.). *Handbook of Learning Disabilities: Methods and interventions,* Vol. II. Boston, MA: College-Hill Press.

Greene, V. and Enfield, M. 1985a. *Project Read Reading Guide: Phase I.* Bloomington, MN: Bloomington Public Schools.

Greene, V. and Enfield, M. 1985b. *Project Read Reading Guide: Phase II.* Bloomington, MN: Bloomington Public Schools.

Guyer, B. and Sabatino, D. 1989. The effectiveness of a multisensory alphabetic phonetic approach with college students who are learning disabled. *Journal of Learning Disabilities* 22:430–434.

Horwitz, E. 1990. Attending to the affective domain in the foreign language classroom. *In* S. Magnan (ed.). *Shifting the Instructional Focus to the Learner.* Middlebury, VT: Northeast Conference on the Teaching of Foreign Languages.

Horwitz, E., Horwitz, M., and Cope J. 1986. Foreign language classroom anxiety. *Modern Language Journal* 70:125–132.

Hutcheson, L., Selig, H., and Young, N. 1990. A success story: A large urban district offers a working model for implementing multisensory teaching into the resource and regular classroom. *Annals of Dyslexia* 40:79–96.

Jackson, M. and McClelland, J. 1979. Processing determinants of reading speed. *Journal of Experimental Psychology* 108:151–181.

Javorsky, J., Sparks, R., and Ganschow, L. In press. Perceptions of college students with and without learning disabilities about foreign language courses. *Learning Disabilities: Research and Practices.*

Jenkins, J. and Pany, D. 1981. Instructional variables in reading comprehension. *In* J. T. Guthrie (ed.). *Comprehension and Teaching.* Newark, DE: International Reading Association.

Johnson, D. 1980. Persistent auditory disorders in young dyslexic adults. *Bulletin of the Orton Society* 30:268–276.

Johnson, D. and Myklebust, H. 1967. *Learning Disabilities: Educational principles and practices.* New York: Grune and Stratton.

Kampwirth, T. and Bates, M. 1980. Modality preference and teaching method: A review of the research. *Academic Therapy* 15(5):597–605.

Kavale, K. and Forness, S. 1987. Substance over style: Assessing the efficacy of modality testing and teaching. *Exceptional Children* 54:228–239.

Kavale, K. and Forness, S. 1990. Substance over style: A rejoinder to Dunn's animadversions. *Exceptional Children* 56:357–361.

Kavanagh, J. and Mattingly, I. (eds.). 1972. *Language by Ear and by Eye.* Cambridge, MA: MIT Press.

Kenneweg, S. 1988. Meeting special learning needs in the Spanish curriculum of a college preparatory school. *In* B. Snyder (ed.). *Get Ready, Get Set, Go! Action in the foreign language classroom.* Columbus, OH: Ohio Foreign Language Association.

Kotsonis, M. and Patterson, C. 1980. Comprehension monitoring skills in learning disabled children. *Developmental Psychology* 16:541–542.

Larrivee, B. 1981. Modality preferences as a model for differentiating beginning reading instruction: A review of the issues. *Learning Disability Quarterly* 4:180–188.

Levine, M. 1987. *Developmental Variation and Learning Disorders.* Cambridge, MA: Educators' Publishing Service.

Liberman, I. 1982. A language-oriented view of reading and its disabilities. *In* H. Myklebust (ed.). *Progress in Learning Disabilities,* Vol. 5. New York: Grune and Stratton.

Liberman, I. 1987. Language and literacy: The obligation of schools of education. *In* W. Ellis (ed.). *Intimacy with Language: A forgotten basic in teacher education.* Baltimore, MD: Orton Dyslexia Society.

Liberman, I. and Shankweiler, D. 1979. Speech, the alphabet, and teaching to read. *In* L. Resnick and P. Weaver (eds.). *Theory and Practice of Early Reading,* Vol. 2. Hillsdale, NJ: Erlbaum.

Liberman, I. and Shankweiler, D. 1985. Phonology and the problems of learning to read and write. *Remedial and Special Education* 6:8–17.

Lundberg, I. 1987. Phonological awareness facilitates reading and spelling acquisition. *In* W. Ellis (ed.). *Intimacy with Language: A forgotten basic in teacher education.* Baltimore, MD: Orton Dyslexia Society.

Magee, P. and Newcomer, P. 1978. The relationship between oral language skills and academic achievement of learning disabled children. *Learning Disability Quarterly* 1:63–67.

Mann, V. and Liberman, I. 1984. Phonological awareness and verbal short-term memory. *Journal of Learning Disabilities* 17:592–599.

Mann, V., Shankweiler, D., and Smith, S. 1984. The association between comprehension of spontaneous sentences and early reading ability: The role of phonemic representation. *Journal of Child Language* 11:627–643.

Miller, K. 1990. Personal communication.

Morris, M. and Leuenberger, J. 1990. A report of cognitive, academic, and linguistic profiles for college students with and without learning disabilities. *Journal of Learning Disabilities* 23:355–361.

Myer, B., Ganschow, L., Sparks, R., and Kenneweg, S. 1989. Cracking the code: Helping students with specific learning disabilities. *In* D. McAlpine (ed.). *Defining the Essentials for the Foreign Language Classroom.* Lincolnwood, IL: National Textbook Company.

Newcomer, P. and Magee, P. 1977. The performance of learning (reading) disabled children on a test of spoken language. *The Reading Teacher* 30:896–900.

Oller, J. 1979. *Language Tests at School: A pragmatic approach.* London: Longman.

Oller, J. 1981. Research on the measurement of affective variables: Some remaining questions. *In* R. Anderson (ed.). *New Dimensions in Second Language Learning.* Rowley, MA: Newbury House.

Oller, J. and Perkins, K. 1978a. Intelligence and language proficiency as sources of variance in self-reported affective variables. *Language Learning* 28:85–97.

Oller, J. and Perkins, K. 1978b. A further comment on language proficiency as a source of variance in certain affective measures. *Language Learning* 28:417–423.

Orton, J. 1966. The Orton-Gillingham approach. *In* J. Money (ed.). *The Disabled Reader.* Baltimore, MD: The Johns Hopkins University Press.

Oxford, R. 1989. Use of language learning strategies: A synthesis of studies with implications for strategy training. *System* 17(2):235–247.

Oxford, R. 1990. Language learning strategies and beyond: A look at strategies in the context of styles. *In* S. Magnan (ed.). *Shifting the Instructional Focus to the Learner.* Middlebury, VT: Northeast Conference on the Teaching of Foreign Languages.

Perfetti, C. 1985. *Reading Ability.* New York: Oxford University Press.

Pimsleur, P. 1966. Testing foreign language learning. *In* A. Valdman (ed.). *Trends in Language Teaching.* New York: McGraw-Hill.

Pimsleur, P. 1966. *Pimsleur Language Aptitude Battery and Manual.* New York: Harcourt, Brace, and Jovanovich.

Pimsleur, P. 1968. Language aptitude testing. *In* A. Davies (ed.). *Language Testing Symposium: A linguistic approach.* London: Oxford University Press.

Pimsleur, P., Mosberg, L., and Morrison, A. 1962. Student factors in foreign language learning. *Modern Language Journal* 46(4):160–170.

Pimsleur, P., Sundland, D., and McIntyre, R. 1964. Underachievement in foreign language learning. *International Review of Applied Linguistics* 2:43–50.

Pompian, N. 1986. Like a Volvo lifted off my chest. *Undergraduate Bulletin* (Dartmouth College) 3:1–2.

Schumann, J. 1976. Social distance as a factor in second language acquisition. *Language Learning* 26:135–143.

Scovel, T. 1978. The effect of affect: A review of the anxiety literature. *Language Learning* 28:124–142.

Sinatra, G. 1990. Convergence of listening and reading processing. *Reading Research Quarterly* 25:115–130.

Slingerland, B. 1971. *A Multisensory Approach to Language Arts for Specific Language Disability Children: A Guide for Primary Teachers, Books 1–3.* Cambridge, MA: Educators Publishing Service.

Sparks, R. and Ganschow, L. 1991. Foreign language learning difficulties: Affective or native language aptitude differences? *Modern Language Journal* 75:3–16.

Sparks, R. and Ganschow, L. (in preparation). Foreign Language Screening Instrument—College (FLSI-C).

Sparks, R., Ganschow, L., and Javorsky, J. In press. Diagnosing and accommodating the foreign language learning difficulties of college students with learning disabilities. *Learning Disabilities: Research and Practice.*

Sparks, R., Ganschow, L., and Pohlman, J. 1989. Linguistic coding deficits in foreign language learners. *Annals of Dyslexia* 39:179–195.

Sparks, R., Ganschow, L., Javorsky, J., Pohlman, J. and Patton, J. 1991a. Identifying Native Language Difficulties among High and Low-Risk Foreign Language Learners in High School. Manuscript submitted for publication.

Sparks, R., Ganschow, L., Javorsky, J., Pohlman, J., and Patton, J. 1991b. Test comparisons among students identified as high-risk, low-risk, and learning disabled in high school foreign language courses. Manuscript submitted for publication.

Sparks, R., Javorsky, J., and Ganschow, L. 1990. Role of the service provider in helping students with learning disabilities with foreign language learning problems. *In* J. Vander Putten (ed.). *Reaching New Heights: Proceedings of the 1989 AHSSPPE Conference.* Columbus, OH: Association on Handicapped Student Service Programs in Postsecondary Education.

Stahl, S. 1988. Is there evidence to support matching reading styles and initial reading methods? *Phi Delta Kappan* 70:317–322.

Stanovich, K. 1986. Explaining the variance in reading ability in terms of psychological processes: What have we learned? *Annals of Dyslexia* 36:67–96.

Stanovich, K. 1988. Explaining the difference between the dyslexic and garden-variety poor reader: The phonological—core variable—difference model. *Journal of Learning Disabilities* 21:590–612.

Stanovich, K. 1990. Reading disability: Assessment issues. *In* H. L. Swanson (ed.). *Handbook on the Assessment of Learning Disabilities: Theory, research, and practice.* Austin, TX: Pro-Ed.

Stanovich, K., Cunningham, A., and Feeman, D. 1984. The relationship between early reading acquisition and word decoding with and without context. *Journal of Educational Psychology* 76:668–677.

Tarver, S. and Dawson, M. 1978. Modality preferences and the teaching of reading. *Journal of Learning Disabilities* 11:17–29.

Traub, N. and Bloom, F. 1975. *Recipe for Reading.* Cambridge, MA: Educators Publishing Service.

Vellutino, F. 1979. *Dyslexia: Theory and research.* Cambridge, MA: MIT Press.

Vellutino, F. 1987. Dyslexia. *Scientific American* 256:34–41.

Vellutino, F. and Scanlon, D. 1986. Linguistic coding and metalinguistic awareness: Their relationship to verbal memory and code acquisition in poor and normal readers. *In* D. Yaden and S. Templeton (eds.). *Metalinguistic Awareness and Beginning Literacy.* Portsmouth, NH: Heinemann.

Vickery, K., Reynolds, V., and Cochran, S. 1987. Multisensory teaching approach for reading, spelling, and handwriting, Orton-Gillingham based curriculum, in a public school setting. *Annals of Dyslexia* 37:189–200.

Vogel, S. 1974. Syntactic abilities in normal and dyslexic children. *Journal of Learning Disabilities* 7:103–109.

Vogel, S. and Adelman, P. 1990. Extrinsic and intrinsic factors in graduation and academic failure rates among LD college students. *Annals of Dyslexia* 40:119–137.

Wagner, R. and Torgesen, J. 1987. The nature of phonological processing and its causal role in the acquisition of reading skills. *Psychological Bulletin* 101:192–212.

Wallach, G. and Butler, K. 1984. *Language Learning Disabilities in School-Aged Children.* Baltimore: Williams and Wilkins.

Wesche, M., Edwards, H., and Wells, W. 1982. Foreign language aptitude and intelligence. *Applied Psycholinguistics* 3:127–140.

White, N. 1986. The effects of a simultaneous-multisensory alphabetic-phonic, direct instruction approach on the teaching of spelling. Ph.D. diss., University of San Francisco, San Francisco.

Wiig, E. and Fleischmann, N. 1980. Prepositional phrases, pronominalization, reflexivization, and relativization in the language of learning disabled college students. *Journal of Learning Disabilities* 13:45–50.

Wiig, E. and Semel, E. 1973. Comprehension of linguistic concepts requiring logical operations by learning disabled children. *Journal of Speech and Hearing Research* 16:627–636.

Wiig, E. and Semel, E. 1975. Productive language abilities in learning disabled adolescents. *Journal of Learning Disabilities* 8:578–586.

Wiig, E. and Semel, E. 1976. *Language Disabilities in Children and Adolescents.* Columbus, OH: Merrill.

Wiig, E. and Semel, E. 1980. *Language Assessment and Intervention for the Learning Disabled.* Columbus, OH: Merrill.

Wiig, E., Semel, E., and Crouse, M. 1973. The use of English morphology by high-risk and learning disabled children. *Journal of Learning Disabilities* 6:457–465.

Williams, J. 1987. Educational treatments for dyslexia at the elementary and secondary levels. *In* W. Ellis (ed.). *Intimacy With Language.* Baltimore, MD: Orton Dyslexia Society.

Wolf, M., Bally, H., and Morris, R. 1986. Automaticity, retrieval processes, and reading: A longitudinal study in average and impaired readers. *Child Development* 57:988–1,000.

Reading Program—
Remedial, Integrated, and Innovative

Susan R. Butler

University of Sydney
Sydney, Australia

An innovative integrated remedial reading program has been developed based on recent research findings. My longitudinal studies have revealed that poor reading compounds itself over the years. The majority of children with reading disabilities currently remain in regular classrooms with varying techniques being used depending upon individual school directives and current educational theory.

Despite current remedial techniques, the poorer reader tends to remain so throughout the school years. Innovative techniques must be developed in the hope of altering this pattern.

This paper presents one alternative strategy which can be used to upgrade reading skills and break the cycle of reading failure. The Reading Assistance Tutorial Pack (R.A.T. Pack) is a carefully sequenced series of activities that enables the learner to experience the motivating and reinforcing properties of success through all stages of phonetic and reading skills development.

It is a systematic, multidisciplinary remedial reading program based on sound behavior, psycholinguistic and cognitive theories of learning— incorporating listening, speaking, seeing, writing, thinking, and comprehension skills. The R.A.T. Pack demands a high percentage of on-task behavior and trains phonological processing strategies. Functional language use is promoted through enjoyable activities involving sentence construction, cloze passages, puzzles, games, and other creative manipulations of the surface features of languages. The program has proven successful in schools, homes, and clinics.

Longitudinal studies have revealed that poor reading compounds itself over the school years. An innovative remedial program which has

Annals of Dyslexia, Vol. 41, 1991.

altered this pattern is described. Several research studies are presented assessing its effectiveness.

Reading Competency

Although reading is one of the most valuable skills a child acquires, many find reading a great struggle and never achieve its mastery. A recent Australian longitudinal study of the skills of 392 children in kindergarten and their subsequent reading performance over the school years indicates that kindergarten language skills are strong predictors of subsequent reading ability in Grades 1, 2, 3 and 6 (Butler et al. 1985). Path analysis revealed that the long term influence of these kindergarten skills on later reading is primarily indirect through their effect on reading acquisition in Grades 1 and 2. This finding appears to be favorable for the long term success of an intervention program in reading. Since the characteristics found in kindergarten have no substantial direct influence on later reading achievement, it should be possible to override these by the influence of intervention programs. The fact that the poorer readers in Grade 1 tend to remain so through the school years points to our inability to provide the required remedial reading programs which would lead to these children becoming effective readers.

Schonhaut and Satz (1983) reviewed follow-up studies of children with early learning problems. They pointed out that the outlook for these children is poor unless they come from a high SES family and/or are exposed to an intensive method such as the Orton-Gillingham program. Badian (1988), in a longitudinal study to the end of the eighth grade, questioned why 45 percent of the children thought to be at risk at age four were still poor readers despite continuing help. She, too, suggested a treatment procedure such as Orton-Gillingham for such students.

The acquisition of reading skills is the primary cognitive task of the early school years. The major concern is to discover how reading competency can be increased. An innovative integrated remedial reading program has been suggested as one method of increasing reading competency. This program has been developed in keeping with current research findings.

Current Research Findings

Active Learning

Watson (1990) examined the development of conceptual reasoning, oral language, and reading across the first five years of school with a sample of children from Sydney, Australia. His findings call for a theory of reading which gives adequate place to the developing cognitive processes and maintains that children are active rather than passive agents in learning to read. A child's emerging developmental processes have their own momentum which strongly influences learning. Therefore a teacher needs to consider the child's active constructive role in learning when selecting instructional methods. Watson calls for greater emphasis on the development of strategy skills at both the micro level (e.g., phonological processing) and the macro level (specific application to functional tasks, e.g., cloze). Paris and Oka (1986) maintain that self-regulated learning should be an educational objective for handicapped children and unsuccessful students. They state that self-regulated learning combines cognitive skill and motivational will, so that students can select challenging tasks, apply effective learning strategies, and measure their success against personal standards. They further argue that self-regulated learning builds self confidence in children, enabling them to attack challenging problems and to persist in the face of difficulty. This work supports the view of Watson that learning to read is a problem-solving task in which the students are the active agents, not just passive respondents.

Strategies

Marie Clay (1984) has suggested that reading-disabled children have stopped making appropriate responses. Rather, they have specialized rigidly in particular types of responses. Further evidence for cognitive rigidity has been demonstrated in learning-disabled children by Lorsbach and Worman (1988).

Experimental psychologists have demonstrated the reality of learned helplessness in poor readers. Bristow (1985) discusses the well-documented passivity in poor readers which she believes is tied to inappropriate materials that frustrate the child, leading to learned helplessness from repeated failure. Learned helplessness results from reduced motivation and reduced ability to perceive success. Butkowsky and Willows (1980) suggest that this concept of learned helplessness may be explained by attribution theory. Generally, the poorer readers have lower expectations for success because they attribute their failure to internal stable causes such as lack of ability.

Metacognitive training is important for reading-disabled students to help them become autonomous and active learners, able to monitor their own performance and deployment of strategies (Wong 1987). Brown (1980) lists the principle strategic metacognitive components necessary for skilled reading as "predicting, checking, monitoring, reality testing, and coordination and control of deliberate attempts to study, learn, or solve problems" (p. 454).

The importance of phonological processing abilities in reading is well documented (Chall 1967; Morris 1982; Stanovich 1980; Williams 1980). A comprehensive review of this area was provided by Wagner (1986) who argues that research has demonstrated that phonological processing abilities can be measured, that such processing is directly related to the acquisition of reading skills, and that this relation is at least partially causal. If we acknowledge that the reading disabled are not a homogeneous lot in terms of their perceptual and processing skills, then the futility of a purely phonics-based program is all too apparent. A multidisciplinary approach is desirable, recognizing the fundamental importance of phonological processing abilities, but in tandem with other perceptual and cognitive abilities in the wider developmental context.

Picture Mnemonics

Ehri, Deffner, and Wilce (1984) note the effectiveness of using picture mnemonics in developing phonic awareness as a subskill in reading. They compare "the effectiveness of integrated picture mnemonics with the effectiveness of a control condition in which letter-sound relations were taught with pictures having the same names as the integrated pictures, but drawn differently so that the letter shapes did not form part of the drawings" (p. 882). A second experiment replicated these findings with a larger sample of letter-sound stimuli and included a no-picture control condition. They found that "children taught with integrated mnemonics learned more letter-sound associations and also more letter-picture associations than did the other two groups, which did not differ. Integrated pictures were effective because they linked two otherwise unconnected items in memory. The shape of letters included in pictures reminded the learners of previously seen pictures with those shapes whose names began with the relevant letter-sounds" (p. 880).

Program Use

The Reading Assistance Tutorial Pack (R.A.T. Pack) is one psycholinguistic and social semiotic approach to literacy (Butler 1990a). A direct linguistic experiential approach underlies this program through the use of story characters, poems, plays, riddles, and reading-together activities. A sequenced pattern of activities enables the learner to experience the motivating and reinforcing properties of success through all stages of reading skills development. It is a systematic, multidisciplinary remedial reading program based on current behavioral, psycholinguistic, and cognitive theories of learning. It incorporates listening, speaking, seeing, writing, thinking, and comprehension skills in the program content.

The R.A.T. Pack demands a high percentage of on-task behavior and directly trains phonological processing strategies. The lessons' tasks are sequenced to follow a developmental hierarchy of phonetic skills. Application of functional language is promoted through enjoyable activities involving sentence construction, cloze passages, crossword puzzles, game activities, and other creative manipulations of the surface features of language. It eschews a single process view of the development of reading skills in children. Behavioral, psycholinguistic, and cognitive approaches to learning are incorporated through multisensorial modalities and the development of language skills through multisensory manipulation. The building of a sight vocabulary is an essential component of the program because an immediate lexical store builds confidence.

Linguistic Awareness

Proficient attention-directed application of reading strategies is obtained through sequenced practice and activities designed to focus on linguistic awareness. The Neurological Impress/Paired Reading Method used in the R.A.T. Pack enables children to move from initial hesitant dependent oral reading styles to greater independence and fluency. The tutor and student are encouraged to point to the words to follow the reading of the material. Clay (1969) emphasizes the importance of pointing while reading out loud. She states that the child is using movement to make a correct word-for-word match between the spoken and the printed word. This can lead to self-correction and knowledge about word boundaries.

The R.A.T. Pack consists of twelve books varying in difficulty from early sounds through to vocabulary development and comprehension. The program can be used by any competent reader to help a student who is having difficulty with reading skills. It is preferable to move with the student through the series of books. However, there is a Butler (1990b) R.A.T. Pack Placement Test which can be used to identify the specific areas of difficulty and start the student at the appropriate lesson. The material is divided into lessons for ease of use.

An outline of the twelve books is provided in Table I. An alternate adult program is available for the more mature student, and a mathematical series will be available shortly. The program is available in research form. It is continually being tested and adapted as a result of research trials.

Table I
The R.A.T. Pack Books

Book 1	*Alphabet Soup (Different Sounds)*
Book 2	*The Littlest Words and Magical "e"*
Book 3	*Go Togethers (Consonant Crush)*
	(Two letters that make one sound, e.g., "sh")
Book 4	*Consonant Concoctions*
	(Blends at the Beginning of a Word)
	(Two letters that run together smoothly to make one sound (a blend), e.g., "br..")
Book 5	*Consonant Concoctions*
	(Blends at the Ending of a Word)
	(Two letters that run together smoothly to make one sound (a blend), e.g., "..st")
Book 6	*Consonant Salad*
	(Blending 3 individual sounds together, e.g., "spl")
Book 7	*Linking Letters (Part 1)*
	(Letters going together to make one sound, e.g., "ee")
Book 8	*Linking Letters (Part 2)*
	(Letters going together to make one sound, e.g., "ai")
Book 9	*Silent Letters*
Book 10	*Words on a Diet and Not So Slim Words*
	(Shortened words, e.g., "can't")
	(Compound words made up of two words, e.g., "butterfly")
	(Suffixes and Prefixes)
Book 11	*Vocabulary Building and Reference Skills*
Book 12	*Comprehension and Living Skills*

Research Testing

Over the past ten years, the program has been tested on learning-disabled students by teachers and students at the University of Sydney in its clinics and at local schools. Also, parents have been using it with their children.

Experiment 1

In 1980, University of Sydney undergraduate students used the program with Grade 4 students enrolled in three Catholic primary schools near the University of Sydney in Australia. The initial sample consisted of 152 students who were given the GAP (McLeod 1981), a silent group-reading comprehension test which employs "cloze procedure." The 40 students whose scores corresponded to the lowest quartile on this test were randomly assigned to experimental and control groups. Both of these groups received further testing using the Neale Analysis of Reading Test Form A, (1963) as well as the Stanford

Diagnostic Reading Test, Level 1 (Karlsen, Madden and Gardner 1966) which purports to assess the various subskills of reading. The University of Sydney students acted as tutors for eight weeks during the R.A.T. Pack for three 20-minute periods a week. At the end of the teaching sessions, the experimental and control children were retested on all earlier tests. Tests revealed that, on retest, the Experimental Group scored significantly higher than the Control Group on the Comprehension subtest of the Neale Analysis of Reading Test (t = 2.39; p. < .05) as well as on two subtests of the Standard Diagnostic Reading Test-Syllabication and Sound Discrimination. Syllabication was significant at the one percent level of chance (t = 2.80; p. < .01) and Sound Discrimination was significant at the five percent level (t = 2.09; p. < .05). A third subtest of the Stanford Diagnostic Reading Test—Blending almost reached significance (t = 1.96; p. > .05).

Experiment 2

In 1989, a study was carried out with a class of 22 reading-disabled boys (10 and 11 years of age) in grade 5 at St. Patrick's College in Strathfield, a suburb of Sydney, Australia. The students were tested on the Holborn Reading Test (Watts 1944) which is an assessment of ability to read sentences of increasing difficulty with respect to vocabulary, sentence structure and comprehension. The parents of twelve of the students volunteered to use the R.A.T. Pack at home. The other ten students acted as the Control Group. Most of the Experimental Group used the R.A.T. Pack from one to three times a week. Based on the R.A.T. Pack Placement Test, students in the Experimental Group started at the appropriate level of the R.A.T. Pack.

After four months, the Holborn Reading Test was readministered along with individual Butler R.A.T. Pack Reading Surveys, (1989) filled out by the students and the parents. The differences between the pre- and posttest results for both the Control and the Experimental groups were examined. There was a statistically significant difference between the groups' means, with the experimental group showing greater gains (t(20) = 3.289, p. < .01). On the R.A.T. Pack Reading Survey, all parents reported that they enjoyed using the program and that it had improved the students' reading. Eleven of these parents reported that their child had more confidence in reading and had improved comprehension. Nine of the parents reported improvement in word attack skills and fluency as well as a more positive attitude towards reading. The students themselves all reported that the program had helped and that they had enjoyed using it. Eleven of the students reported that they felt more confident in reading.

The adoption of the R.A.T. Pack was voluntary. The fact that the Experimental Group was self-selecting could bias results. Nevertheless, these results suggest positive trends in the effects of parental use of the program. Further investigation of this issue is underway.

Present Use

The program here described has been in use in various settings over time. Results suggest that it is useful in both the school and home situations. It is currently being used in hospitals in Australia and the United States. As a Fulbright Scholar in Pediatric Psychiatry at Sloan-Kettering Cancer Center in New York City in 1986, I began using the program with 18 children of varying ages from 5 to 16 who were in remission from leukemia. These children had various reading problems—but as a whole the program did effect a positive change when used in the home by the parents. The program continues to be used at the Center in the wards, and research data is being collected as to its effectiveness.

In 1990, the program is being used on a large scale as part of an extended parental tutoring program at St. Patrick's College, Sydney. The use of the program is being monitored in clinics and the state schools in Australia. As part of the program to integrate handicapped adults into the community, the adult program is being used in a six-month transition program.

Summary

The R.A.T. Pack provides an innovative, integrated multidisciplinary approach which develops linguistic awareness and strategy application through sequenced activity and reading modules. It offers a program that can be used in various settings by tutors with minimal training. At a time when we are faced with the urgency to upgrade reading standards, it is encouraging to have this tool available to help alter the cycle of deep seated reading disability.

References

Badian, N. A. 1988. The prediction of good and poor reading before kindergarten entry: A nine-year follow-up. *Journal of Learning Disabilities* 21:98–103.

Bristow, P. S. 1985. Are poor readers passive readers? Some evidence, possible explanations, and potential solutions. *The Reading Teacher* 39(3):318–325.

Brown, A. L. 1980. Metacognitive development and reading. In R. J. Spiro, B. B. Bruce and W. F. Brewer (eds.). *Theoretical Issues in Reading Comprehension* (pp. 453–481). Hillsdale, NJ: Lawrence Erlbaum Associates.

Butkowsky, I. S. and Willows, D. M. 1980. Cognitive-motivational characteristics of children varying in reading ability: Evidence for learned helplessness in poor readers. *Journal of Educational Psychology* 72(3):408–422.

Butler, S. R. 1989. *R.A.T. Pack Reading Survey*. Sydney: Remedial Action Pty. Ltd.

Butler, S. R. 1990a. *Reading Assistance Tutorial Pack (R.A.T. Pack)*. Sydney: Remedial Action Pty. Ltd.

Butler, S. R. 1990b. *R.A.T. Pack Placement Test*. Sydney: Remedial Action Pty. Ltd.

Butler, S. R., Marsh, H. W., Sheppard, M. I., and Sheppard, T. L. 1985. A seven-year longitudinal study of early prediction of reading achievement. *Journal of Educational Psychology* 77(3):349–361.

Chall, J. S. 1967. *Learning to Read: The great debate*. New York: McGraw-Hill.

Clay, M. M. 1969. Reading errors and self-correction behavior. *British Journal of Educational Psychology* 39:47–56.

Clay, M. M. 1984. *Reading; The patterning of complex behavior, 2nd Ed*. Auckland, New Zealand: Heinemann Educational Books.

Ehri, L. C., Deffner, N. D. and Wilce, L. S. 1984. Pictorial mnemonics for phonics. *Journal of Educational Psychology* 76(5):880–893.

Karlsen, B., Madden, R., and Gardner, E. F. 1966. *Stanford Diagnostic Reading Test*. New York: Harcourt, Brace and World.

Lorsbach, T. C. and Worman, L. J. 1988. Negative transfer effects in learning disabled children: Evidence for cognitive rigidity? *Contemporary Educational Psychology* 13:116–125.

McLeod, J. 1981. *GAP Reading Comprehension*. Sydney: Heinemann Educational Books.

Morris, J. M. 1982. New phonics for initial literacy. *Australian Journal of Reading* 5(2):52–60.

Neale, M. 1963. *Neale Analysis of Reading*. London: Macmillan.

Paris, S. G. and Oka, E. R. 1986. Self-regulated learning among exceptional children. *Exceptional Children* 53(2):103–108.

Schonhaut, S. and Satz, P. 1983. Prognosis for children with learning disabilities. A review of follow-up studies. *In* M. Rutter (ed.). *Developmental Neuropsychiatry*. New York: Guilford Press.

Stanovich, K. E. 1980. Toward an interactive-compensatory model of individual differences in the development of reading fluency. *Reading Research Quarterly* 16:32–71.

Wagner, R. K. 1986. Phonological processing abilities and reading: Implications for disabled readers. *Journal of Learning Disabilities* 19(10):623–630.

Watson, A. 1990. Cognitive skills in reading. *In* S. R. Butler (ed.). *The Exceptional Child: An introduction to special education*. Sydney: Harcourt Brace Jovanovitch.

Watts, A. F. 1944. *The Language and Mental Development of Children*. London: George G. Harrap.

Williams, J. P. 1980. Teaching decoding with an emphasis on phoneme analysis and phoneme blending. *Journal of Educational Psychology* 72:1–15.

Wong, B. Y. L. 1987. How do the results of metacognitive research impact on the learning disabled individual? *Learning Disability Quarterly* 10:189–195.

Nonverbal Learning Disabilities and Remedial Interventions

Jean M. Foss

Pine Ridge School
Williston, Vermont

Adolescents with nonverbal learning disabilities who enroll in private, special secondary schools consistently present a pattern of behaviors which prevents achievement of their potentials in academic areas and impedes their abilities to interact effectively with others. With weaknesses in the fine graphomotor skills for writing and poor organization at all levels, they produce limited written output and often fail to complete academic assignments. Their response to pressure to produce is to become less productive. These students perceive social situations inaccurately; they are not successful in their interactions, especially with peers. They have learned to resolve difficult situations by employing their relatively strong verbal skills to enlist parents and other adults in intervening for them. They have not developed the skills to intervene for themselves.

Effective remedial interventions include training the students in skills for planning and organizing, for studying, for written expression, and in social cognition and interpersonal communication. Students gain positive feelings of personal effectiveness through a process—at first verbally mediated, ultimately verbally self-directed—in which they are encouraged to plan, risk, and act on their own behalfs to resolve matters of personal concern.

The number of adolescents with deficits in nonverbal aspects of learning who apply for admission to independent special secondary schools has grown significantly in the past several years. Histories based on school records and parents' anecdotes indicate that there has been little understanding of the nature of the difficulties these young

Annals of Dyslexia, Vol. 41, 1991.

people have faced. Nor have they received instruction directed toward overcoming their areas of weakness. The limited research on this population indicates that the prognosis for success in adapting and functioning is poor. To change this, professionals must improve diagnostic skills in order to identify these individuals in a more timely way. We must devise and implement interventions to strengthen areas of weakness. We must also teach these young people strategies for adapting and coping when faced with expectations for performance which exceed their skills and abilities.

My purposes in this paper are these: 1) to describe such learners and their development sufficiently to promote earlier identification and intervention, and 2) to direct attention to the varied areas which can be strengthened through remedial intervention.

Processing Strengths and Weaknesses

The pattern of strengths and weaknesses in individuals with learning disabilities involving processing nonverbal information is characteristic and highly recognizable once we are sensitive to it. On the WISC-R or WAIS the verbal scale score often exceeds the performance score by 15 points or more. When subtest scores are grouped as suggested by Bannatyne (1974), the verbal conceptualization factor is usually the strongest, the spatial factor the weakest. Reading skills in word identification, phonetic analysis, and oral reading of passages usually surpass comprehension of implicit semantic relationships among words and of literal and inferrential meanings of passages. Spelling skills are strong, handwriting is poor, and other skills for organizing and producing written work are problematic. All areas of mathematics are weak relative to decoding and spelling. While these students perform arithmetic operations with some success because they can follow the formulae, they lack understanding of mathematics concepts and do not readily solve problems in mathematics.

Within the framework of an information processing model and a hierarchy of processes, we hypothesize that the weaknesses these individuals demonstrate in academic skills are rooted in deficits in perception and visual imagery. These deficits result in confusions in language processing and cognition (Johnson and Myklebust 1967). The confusions are manifest in difficulties in interpreting spatial, part-whole, and causal relationships and in expressing such relationships orally and/or in writing. These individuals do not form visual images readily and do not revisualize (see Figure 1). They also tend to focus on details and frequently fail to grasp the complete picture.

When asked to produce from memory the design in Figure 2 during administration of the Memory for Designs subtest of the Detroit Tests of Learning Aptitude (Baker and Leland 1935), dyslexic individ-

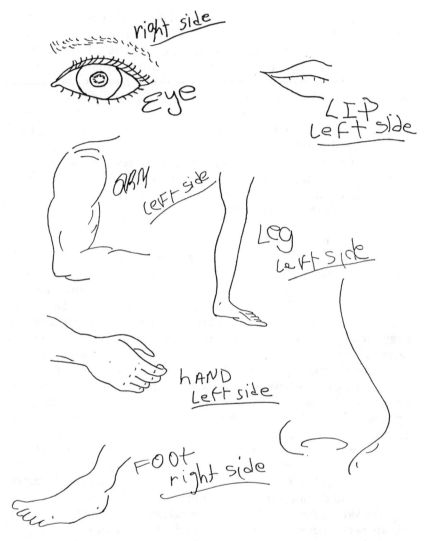

Figure 1. *Lack of ability to revisualize the most basic of spatial relationships is manifested in errors such as these on an informal task which requires labeling body parts as being on another person's left or right side.*

uals usually represent the gestalt and the relationships of the parts to the whole. Individuals with nonverbal learning disabilities usually fail to depict a unified whole, as seen in Figure 3. Even those products which appear to approximate the stimulus were constructed in a part-by-part fashion. Given their fundamental difficulty integrating discrete parts with a unifying whole, these individuals also have difficulty grasping classifications and classifying information.

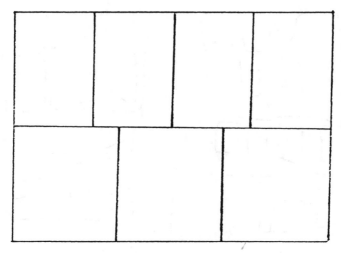

Figure 2. This design is to be drawn from memory following a five-second presentation.

Our first, most basic communications are nonverbal. It follows that breakdowns in processing nonverbal information have significant impact on perception and interpretation of social situations and on the behaviors which are responses to those perceptions and interpretations. The young people with whom we are concerned do not attend to nor interpret accurately the nonverbal messages inherent in interpersonal and social interactions. They derive little or no meaning from vocal tone and pitch, facial expressions, gestures, conventions governing touch and distance, nor from relationships implicit in the status and roles of participants and in the nature of an occasion. As a consequence they are likely to misinterpret interpersonal and social interactions and to interact in inappropriate ways. Further, they appear to have formed concepts of self which are based exclusively upon the verbal messages we give in response to them.

The histories of such students, as provided by their parents, contain many similarities. As young children these learners were considered precocious by parents and other adults because they were extremely verbal and used language in ways similar to adults. Although these youngsters were awkward and slow to acquire motor skills and did not "fit in" with other children, adults developed high expectations for them based on their verbal precocity.

In their early years in school, expectations that these youngsters would succeed in academics were reinforced by their diligent efforts to learn and eagerness to please. These efforts and attitudes diverted attention away from the nagging awareness that they had few or no

Figure 3.   *These drawings are attempts by individuals with nonverbal learning*
                disabilities to reproduce the stimulus design (Figure 2) from memory.

friends. They did not adjust their communications to the interests nor
the level of language of peers. They did not seem to share peers' developmental agenda. They did not apprehend fully the context of peer
interactions. Instead, they responded on the basis of highly literal in-

terpretations of the words used. Parents and teachers tended to minimize or ignore concerns about this lack of peer acceptance and to focus on the youngsters' academic achievements.

When academic demands shifted from rote learning of skills, facts, and procedures to more complex integrated learnings and applications, these individuals began to fail and to cease to try. Similarly, as opportunities increased for both structured and spontaneous social interactions with peers, these youngsters' communication difficulties became more evident. They were rejected, frequently and overtly, and became increasingly isolated and withdrawn.

Unless the strengths, weaknesses, and needs of these youngsters are recognized and appropriate interventions are initiated, the prognosis is poor for success in school, for accomplishing the goals of adolescence, and for making positive personal and social adjustments in their lives. Without appropriate interventions these students are likely to become passive and unproductive. They are at risk for becoming depressed, isolated, and for presenting many vague somatic complaints which obscure their underlying causes (Rourke 1989; Strang and Rourke 1985).

Interventions

Effective remedial interventions can be designed to help such students improve their understanding of and performance in many areas of concern. To be effective, interventions must address the problem areas directly and explicitly. They must also involve the student in planning to apply newly learned behaviors to similar tasks and situations beyond the training exercises. The most effective instructional procedures help the learner to associate verbal labels and descriptions with concrete objects, actions, and experiences. Instruction depends heavily upon verbal mediation and verbal self-direction, both for analyzing information and for organizing to perform a task. These processes are modeled by the instructor while the student learns to direct himself.

Clarifying language concepts

The type of learner described above interprets the language which describes space and spatial relationships in vague, confused, or rigid ways. Developing accurate and flexible interpretations of this vocabulary must be a priority for diagnostic remedial instruction. The educational therapist (tutor) continually assesses the student's understandings of spatial and directional concepts in varied contexts and provides explicit multisensory instruction to establish meaningful associations for the language of space and direction. An adolescent student whose responses to a design copying task are represented in Figure 4 reproduced the same designs with improved accuracy (Figure 5) following such training. It is important to note that the training did not include practices with the same or similar designs. Training involved establishing verbal labels for geometric forms and for direction in two and three dimensions. Instruction also involved making linear measurements and estimating distance. The student also practiced a systematic, verbal self-direction procedure for analyzing and reproducing designs, which he and his tutor devised together.

Developing verbal reasoning

While such students tend to be concrete and rigid in their thinking, many successfully perform such structured reasoning tasks as completing verbal analogies and can learn to do so with increased flexibility. Instruction must first focus on developing flexible concepts of similarity and difference, of classification and categorization, of part/whole relationships, of time order and cause-effect relationships, and of spatial relationships. Student and tutor then devise a sequence of steps which includes self-questioning and self-monitoring with regard to understanding the vocabulary, identifying the implicit relationship among the words presented, describing the anticipated definition of

Spatial Relationships

Reproduce these designs using the dots at the right of each as points

of reference.

Figure 4. Even with the stimulus design and points of reference provided, an adolescent student with a nonverbal learning disability shows great confusion and difficulty copying designs.

Spatial Relationships

Reproduce these designs using the dots at the right of each as points of reference.

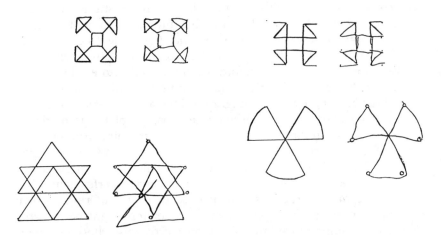

Figure 5. *The student whose initial efforts resulted in the designs shown in Figure 4 demonstrated improved performance as a result of multisensory instruction to establish/clarify concepts of space and direction.*

the target word, and retrieving a word to complete the analogy. Until he has internalized the procedure, the student refers to a list of the steps, verbalizing each step. The purpose and effects of such a procedure are to promote analysis and thought and to reduce impulsive responding which tends to be driven by verbal associations rather than understanding of the implicit relationships. For example, as a result of identifying and verbalizing the controlling relationship in the analogy foot:toes:: hand: _____ as being one of a whole to its part, this student provides "fingers." A highly predictable response, without using this procedure, would have been to answer "arm."

Increasing comprehension and written output

These students frequently and characteristically "shut down" when faced with academic pressures and performance demands which require more than they feel they will be able to do. We can avoid this, or at least minimize it, by recognizing that these youngsters may have much weaker comprehension skills than their grade-placement and decoding skills suggest and setting our expectations for them accordingly.

Consistent remedial efforts to help them to gain clear meanings for the many "empty" words they hear, read, and use certainly contribute to improving comprehension. Once these learners interpret words which express semantic relationships accurately, they benefit from being trained to search the text actively, paragraph by paragraph, to find words which signal the nature of the relationship which underlies the content. Working with text material which the student does not consider overwhelmingly difficult, the tutor and student together identify approaches to text which enhance the student's comprehension. Approaches and strategies which are often facilitative include discussing the subject matter before reading in order to establish a set based on the student's prior understanding, reading the selection aloud, prereading end-of-chapter questions and bold-face headings, and pausing at the end of each sentence or paragraph to summarize or paraphrase the information presented to that point. Students are trained to ask themselves questions which lead them to reflect upon their understanding as they read. Active verbalization or subvocalization appear to be important elements in improving performance. Depending upon the student's particular needs for monitoring his own comprehension, such questions as the following might be incorporated in a training procedure: "Are there words here whose meanings are unclear?" (If so, I must determine the appropriate meaning.) "Does this sentence/paragraph make sense in the context of what I have already read?" (If not, I should reread the sentence/paragraph to be sure I understand it. If I am still confused, I should go back to reread the conflicting material.) "Are there signal words here which indicate a relationship I should be thinking about?" (If so, I want to be sure I understand which ideas are connected by these signal words.)

The confusions which underlie comprehension difficulties also limit the student's ability to study efficiently and to produce written work of the quality expected of a high school student. To effect growth in these areas we must persist in clarifying semantic confusions and training the student to use the strategies for analyzing written information to identify patterns of organization. As the student develops clear meanings for classes of words which signal meaningful relationships, the tutor then provides many opportunities to practice using these words as a basis for organizing information and communicating in writing. The goals of these practices are to develop automaticity in using words which provide structure and organization and to extend the amount of information which the student will communicate in writing.

We must make accommodations in our expectations for the volume and quality of written products while the remedial and strategic trainings are in process. The most important of these accommodations is to set expectations for written output which match closely the student's demonstrated ability to produce such work with respect to quantity, quality, and time allowed. Time constraints and expectations regarding the size and scope of the product must be considered carefully. Some students will cease to perform at all if such pressures are felt to be excessive and overwhelming.

Improving cursive handwriting

Verbally mediated practices to improve cursive handwriting result in improvements in such aspects as letter formation, slant, spacing, alignment at the baseline, and in overall control and fluency.

Practices involve training the student to give verbal self-directions regarding posture, position of the paper, grasp of the pencil, as well as directions for forming individual letters, for starting at the baseline, etc. Procedures and practices are individually designed by tutor and student who analyze together the student's written products to identify aspects which they will work to improve.

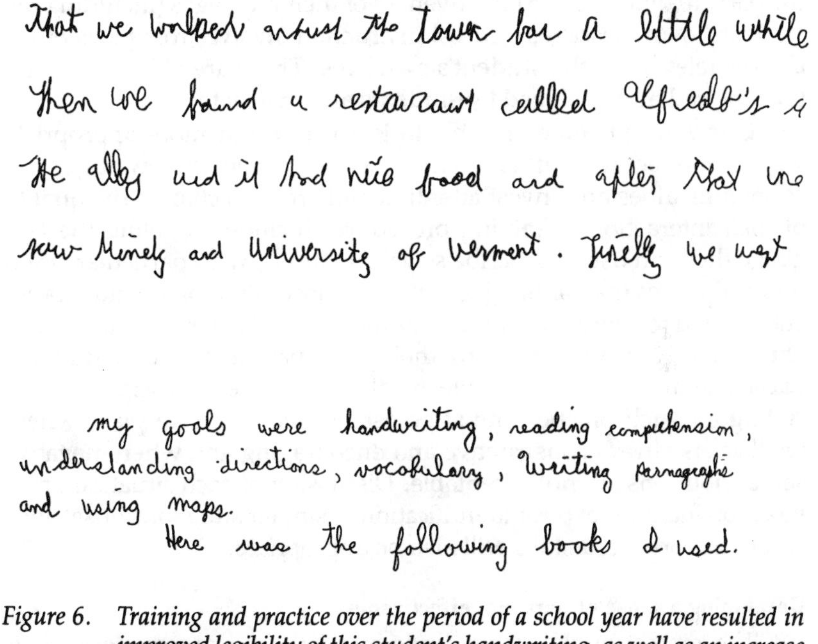

Figure 6. Training and practice over the period of a school year have resulted in improved legibility of this student's handwriting, as well as an increase in writing rate.

Improving Social Cognition

Effective interventions in the social realm also require direct and explicit instruction, practice in a controlled setting, and encouragement and feedback in the unstructured situations which occur in daily living. Our students benefit from direct instruction in which the elements of the communication act are made explicit. They do not apprehend the significance of the nonverbal cues which help to define social situations. Specific training and practice in attending to and interpreting such nonverbal aspects as facial expression, gestures, tone of voice, proximity and distance, status and roles of participants, grooming and use of dress and adornments, and the context of the communication result in improvements in perception and participation. Like the training procedures for developing other skills and understandings, this training depends heavily upon verbal mediation of social interactions and experiences. Young people who have fundamental difficulty labeling their own feelings and attitudes benefit from activities which establish verbally mediated associations for their own affective responses to various situations.

Once students understand the basic concepts involved in communication, they practice analyzing interpersonal and social interactions with respect to the nature of the situation, the roles and goals of the participants, and the effectiveness of their messages (including the students' own messages). Direct instruction involves role-plays of situations relevant to the student's own lives. These are videotaped and then viewed and analyzed by students and instructor.

Our young people are able to learn new and more appropriate ways to interact with others to the extent that they acknowledge their social difficulties and invest attention and effort to change the quality of their interactions. Training procedures include modeling the language they can use to describe social situations, with particular attention to the cues that define the context of those situations. Students are encouraged to express the outcomes they desire from their interactions with others, to plan and control their participation, and to modify that participation as a result of the feedback of other participants. The setting for such practices must be established as a safe place where feedback is always constructive and encouraging and where negative self-attributions are not acceptable. Discussion of each situation or interaction includes explicit identification of similar situations or settings where the practiced skills will also be appropriate.

Developing a sense of personal effectiveness.

The more completely we understand these learners, with their widely disparate abilities and weaknesses, the better able we will be to promote their feelings of self-esteem and attitudes of personal effectiveness. They have learned to use their verbal strengths with practiced skill to engage adults in "rescuing" them when demands for performance appear too great or when situations in which they find themselves seem too complex. "Rescuing" them does not foster in them feelings of personal competence and effectiveness. Rather, the result is to reinforce a sense of personal incompetence, while enhancing their view of the one who has "rescued" as being competent and effective. It is vital that we hold expectations for these young people which are commensurate with their demonstrated abilities across a continuum of tasks—receptive, integrative, expressive; verbal, nonverbal; perceptual, linguistic, cognitive. We must be honest and direct in helping them to understand and accept themselves as they are. Acting from these basic principles, we are able to help them to plan and then to act to achieve desired goals. This is true whether the goal is to improve language comprehension, fine motor skills, study skills, organization of ideas, or written composition; or if the goal is to interact with others in more satisfying ways. In addition to setting realistic goals and planning and acting to achieve those goals, they must also evaluate the outcomes of their efforts. If the outcomes of their efforts are not those which were sought, we engage the learner in identifying additional efforts which might improve the situation, while also acknowledging the positive aspects of the efforts they have already made. They must acknowledge their successes and attribute those successes to their own plans and efforts. All of these processes must be verbally mediated for and by these young people, toward the end that eventually they will become verbally self-directed.

Summary

There is a characteristic pattern of strengths and weaknesses in perceptual, linguistic, and cognitive abilities which may indicate a disability in nonverbal learning. Many individuals struggle with this disability without benefit of understanding of the reasons for their difficulties, and without appropriate help to overcome those difficulties. Instruction which directly addresses specific weaknesses can result in improvements. Elements which are common to effective interventions include explicit direct instruction, association of verbal and nonverbal aspects, and use of the relatively strong verbal skills to analyze and mediate the task or situation and to promote self-direction in completing a task or performing an action.

We must become more skilled in identifying these individuals and more responsive in providing the instruction which can make a difference in their lives.

References

Baker, H. J. and Leland, B. 1935. *Detroit Tests of Learning Aptitude*. Indianapolis: Bobbs-Merrill.

Bannatyne, A. 1974. Diagnosis: A note on recategorization of the WISC scaled scores. *Journal of Learning Disabilities* 7:272–274.

Johnson, D. and Myklebust, H. R. 1967. Nonverbal disorders of learning. *In Learning Disabilities Educational Principles and Practices*. New York: Grune and Stratton.

Rourke, B. P. 1989. *Nonverbal Learning Disabilities*. New York: Guilford Press.

Strang, J. D. and Rourke, B. P. 1985. Adaptive behavior of children who exhibit specific arithmetic disabilities and associated neuropsychological abilities and deficits. *In* B. P. Rourke (ed.). *Neuropsychology of Learning Disabilities*. New York: Guilford Press.

Part III
Recent Research Findings

Those who teach dyslexics and those who engage in research into the causes of and the most effective treatments for dyslexia, through mutual respect and understanding, can achieve much. Too often, these key individuals, immersed as they are in the demands each day presents, fail to make the critical links between theory and practice.

Through forums such as national and regional conferences, and through the scholarly and popular publications of several organizations, there is a continuing effort to forge those links. Recognizing that often the language of researchers is technical, nonetheless, those who select papers for this journal believe that you who choose to work with language-learning disabled students have a special responsibility to familiarize yourselves with current research studies in the field.

If we hope to persuade educational policy makers of the value of multisensory programs, we must be able to support our claims with more than anecdotal evidence. So, while we urge researchers never to lose sight of the individual behind the profile, we even more strongly urge practitioners to give thoughtful, critical eye to research studies reported in this and other professional journals.

In this section, there are topics to stretch your minds and to inspire your teaching or your future research.

In addressing the question of the life-long nature of dyslexia, Lefly and Pennington, in "Spelling Errors and Reading Fluency in Compensated Adult Dyslexics," note that some individuals appear to compensate sufficiently so that as adults they are no longer diagnosably dyslexic. They examine the characteristics of such people to determine the cause for the compensation. Implications for instruction may lie in the similarity of the compensated dyslexics with nondyslexics in all areas studied except for the automaticity with which they apply skills.

In "Early Identification of Dyslexia: Evidence from a Follow-up Study of Speech-language Impaired Children," Hugh W. Catts indicates that difficulty with semantics and syntax among speech-language

impaired children may be a useful predictor of poor reading performance. This study, however, cautions that preschool language impairment alone is not a sufficient indicator of later problems. When coexist-
ing with other problems in phonological processing, there appears to
be a greater risk of reading disabilities.

Steven G. Zecker compared reading-disabled and normally-
achieving children with respect to their orthographic code development. He reports his results in "The Orthographic Code: Developmental Trends in Reading-disabled and Normally-achieving Children."
Zecker found that reading-disabled children do develop an orthographic code, but that they do so at a much slower rate than their
normally-achieving peers.

The effect of phonological awareness training on a group of
severely dyslexic students is reported by Ann W. Alexander and her
colleagues in "Phonological Awareness Training and Remediation of
Analytic Decoding Deficits in a Group of Severe Dyslexics." They studied a group of older dyslexic children who participated in a program
which emphasized phonological awareness. These children showed
significant growth following the intervention program. Although the
authors recognize the limitations inherent in clinical studies, they offer
convincing evidence of the potential for improvement offered by training in phonological awareness.

Hollis Scarborough, in "Early Syntactic Development of Dyslexic
Children," examines the expressive and receptive syntactic abilities of
a group of preschoolers of comparable IQs, SES, and gender, some of
whom became normal readers and others disabled readers. He concludes that preschool language development is a significant factor in
later reading achievement, a conclusion with important implications
for early instructional intervention.

"Linguistic Profiles of Dyslexic and Good Readers" is the latest in a
series of studies undertaken by Nathalie Badian and her associates in
Massachusetts. This study of dyslexic, mildly dyslexic, average, and
good readers examined at kindergarten, grade 2, and grade 4, concludes that most strengths and weaknesses seen in kindergarten continue through the primary grades. The best kindergarten predictors of
later reading achievement were giving letter sounds and rapid naming.

In "Gestalt Imagery: A Critical Factor in Language Comprehension," Nanci Bell identifies the ability to create imaged wholes, or gestalts, as a major factor in language comprehension. Those who process
parts, rather than wholes, in response to verbal stimuli are subject to a
generalized language comprehension deficit. Bell proposes that those
with weak gestalt imagery be provided with special instruction involving sequential stimulation, reporting significant improvement in reading comprehension among those who have received such a program.

Spelling Errors and Reading Fluency in Compensated Adult Dyslexics

Dianne L. Lefly
Bruce F. Pennington

Univeristy of Denver
Denver, Colorado

Generally, a person who is diagnosed as dyslexic remains diagnosably dyslexic all his/her life. However, occasionally, an individual compensates for his/her difficulties in some way, and by adulthood is no longer diagnosably dyslexic. In what ways are these compensated dyslexics different from both dyslexics and nondyslexics? We compared IQ, achievement test, and spelling error scores in adult dyslexics, adult nondyslexics, and adult compensated dyslexics (N = 25) in the two studies reported here. The second study differed from the first in that the subjects were matched for age, education, IQ, and SES. In both studies, compensateds were significantly different from nondyslexics on the WRAT Spelling subtest and Reading Quotient scores. In the second study the compensateds differed from the nondyslexics in total raw score and average reading speed on Gray Oral Reading Test. On the other hand, they were different from dyslexics on all reading and spelling variables in both studies, except for PIAT Reading Comprehension in Study 2. Finally, in Study 2, the compensateds were different from both dyslexics and nondyslexics in average reading speed. In conclusion, it appears that compensation does not result from differences in IQ, education, or SES, though it may be influenced to some extent by sex. Compensateds appear very similar to nondyslexics in their reading and spelling skills; however, there appears to be a difference in the automaticity with which they apply these skills.

Annals of Dyslexia, Vol. 41, 1991.
ISSN 0736-9387

Much progress has been made in the past few years with respect to the cognitive phenotype of childhood dyslexia. However, few studies have focused on the adult outcomes of dyslexia. Those follow-up studies that have been done have usually focused on educational and occupational outcomes (Finucci 1986), or are studies that follow-up dyslexic children before they reach adulthood (DeFries and Baker 1983).

We have been studying families with a strong history of dyslexia for over ten years (Pennington et al. 1986; Pennington et al. 1987; Smith et al. 1983; Smith et al. in press). Much of our research has focused on adults. Judging by our work and that of others (Scarborough 1984), most dyslexics remain diagnosably dyslexic throughout their lives. Their reading and/or spelling skills as adults are deficient when compared to nondyslexic adults. However, there are a few adults who report clear histories of reading problems as children, but are not diagnosably dyslexic as adults. We call such adults "compensated dyslexics." Incidentally, a recent archival study validated adult self-reports of childhood reading problems against group achievement test results from childhood (Gilger in review). So we have evidence that indicates that compensated dyslexics were really dyslexic at some point and are not just over-reporters of childhood problems.

In our large study of familial dyslexia (Pennington et al. 1986), we reported data about adult familial dyslexics and compared them to other adult members of their extended families who did not have dyslexia. While investigating these differences, we also identified a group of individuals who reported a strong history of reading and spelling problems as children; however, when they were tested as a part of our study, they could not be clearly diagnosed as dyslexic.

Other reading researchers have identified similar small groups of apparently compensated adults in their work (Felton, personal communication 1990; Scarborough 1984). These samples were not ascertained from extended dyslexic families and consequently may have different etiologies for their disabilities.

Felton identified 51 individuals who were *severely* impaired in reading as children and who had been seen for treatment by June Orton. They were identified through self-report and school records. Her sample was predominantly male. Of the 51 subjects identified as severely reading disabled in childhood, only nine were female. These subjects were reevaluated as adults.

Felton's adult classification system was based on regression equation developed by Finucci et al. (1984). This equation was derived from the test results of 90 nondyslexic adults. Classification in this system is based on the deviation of a subject's observed scores from the scores predicted by the regression equation. If a subject's observed score is more than two standard errors of prediction (SEP) below the Finucci equation predicted score, he/she is classified as dyslexic. If the observed scored between 1 and 2 SEP below the predicted score, he/she is classified as borderline, and if the observed score is less than 1 SEP below the predicted score, he/she is considered in the normal range.

Of the 51 individuals identified for her study, 13 (11 males, 2 females) are now reading in the normal range (e.g., < 1 SEP below the predicted score), and an additional 13 (11 males, 2 females) were classified as a borderline group (1–2 SEP below). The remaining 25 subjects are still diagnosably dyslexic (more than 2 SEP below). Felton has not analyzed her data completely and, consequently, has not yet reported similarities and differences among the groups. Since the 13 adults now reading in the normal range were classified as severely reading disabled in childhood, we might call them "compensated adults." Felton's data provide a rough estimate of the rate of compensation, about 25 percent (13/51).

Through self-report alone, Scarborough identified 40 subjects (21 males and 19 females) who reported reading problems in elementary school. These subjects were recruited by a newspaper advertisement. These adults were the parents of Scarborough's high-risk longitudinal subjects (total sample 156 adults). Following the techniques used by Finucci et al. (1984) described above, she developed a regression equation based on the test results of a group of adult nondyslexic readers. She identified a "dyslexics" (n = 17; 10 males, 7 females) group, a "borderline" (n = 16; 7 males, 9 females) group, and an "indeterminate" (n = 9; 6 males, 3 females) group.

Adults in the borderline and indeterminate groups reported reading problems as children, but their reading levels were at or near expected levels as adults. The borderline group was described as a group of "recovered" dyslexics and the indeterminate group was described as having "recovered completely." If we think of the indeterminate group as "compensated adults," then the rate of compensation (9/40; 23 percent) is similar to that found by Felton.

Scarborough in her study tried to differentiate the test results of her borderline and indeterminate groups from her normal controls. Her results showed that: 1) self-reported previous reading problems were reliably associated with documented reading problems in adulthood; and 2) the indeterminate and borderline groups were significantly different from normal controls on almost all measures of reading and spelling. The two exceptions were that the borderline group was not different from normals on mirror-image reading and the indeterminate group was not different from normals on the spelling of orthographically regular pseudowords. She did not report comparisons between the two "recovered" groups and the dyslexic group.

We have also examined the rates of adult compensation in the Colorado Family Reading Study Sample—CFRS (Letwitter, DeFries, and Elston 1980). This was a sample of 133 nuclear families identified through an affected child. This sample comes close to being a representative population sample of reading-disabled (RD) families because probands were identified in two school districts rather than in clinics and appear to have been representative of all the RD children in the school. Both parents of each proband were tested for RD and also answered a single item questionnaire about childhood reading problems. Of those adults answering positively to this question, 22 percent did not test positive for RD and can be considered compensated. (The test criterion used here was the Specific Dyslexia Algorithm, the same as used in the present study and described below.) The sex ratio in this group of compensateds is 12 males/16 females, compared to 27 males/10 females in the parents who were positive on both history and test results (Pennington et al. in review).

In summary, the compensation rates across these three studies are quite similar, between 22 and 25 percent, despite different ascertainment procedures and diagnostic definitions. In the first two studies in which the adults were probands, there is the usual excess of males found in referred samples.

If some residual effects of prior dyslexia remain identifiable in compensated individuals, studying them can provide converging evidence as to the primary cognitive deficit in dyslexia, since the most persistent features of a disorder are often core or primary features (Pennington in press). In this context, the work of Campbell and Butterworth (1985) is interesting.

Campbell and Butterworth examined the reading and writing skills of an intelligent (WAIS IQ of 123) 23-year-old female college student, R.E. She had a history of early reading and spelling problems, but at the time she was evaluated as an adult, she read and spelled as well as her undergraduate classmates. However, in spite of her overall average ability to read and spell, she had great difficulty reading even the simplest nonwords, made phonetically inaccurate spelling errors, and classified a number of written nonwords as real words. Campbell and Butterworth stated that her problem seemed to be in accessing phonological representations of speech that she read or heard for the purpose of matching, repeating or segmenting. They concluded that R.E. was "phonologically dyslexic and dysgraphic with a developmental etiology." Had they not given her a nonword reading test, her phonological coding problem probably would have gone undetected. If R.E. were to be considered a "compensated dyslexic," clearly she still gave evidence of a deficit in phonological coding, since she could not decode even simple nonwords. Other evidence from both cross-sectional,

reading level match studies and behavior genetic studies indicates that
a deficit in phonological coding is at the core of dyslexia (Pennington
1990).

Studies like these raise questions about adult reading outcome
that have rarely been addressed systematically:

1. Are compensated dyslexic adults different from both dyslexic
   adults who have not compensated and from nondyslexic adults?
2. If residual deficits remain, are these convergent with the primary deficits found in other studies of dyslexia?
3. Why are some people able to compensate for dyslexia while
   others are not?

The purpose of the following studies is to attempt to address these
three questions systematically. We have a large three-generation family
sample in which to compare compensated, dyslexic, and nondyslexic
adults. An extended family sample such as ours allows us to compare
these groups in a more homogeneous sample than would be provided
by usual ascertainment procedures.

The research reported here did not take into account remediation
strategies, if any, to which these individuals were subjected, nor was it
possible to evaluate the individual compensatory strategies each of
them employed.

The purpose of Study 1 was to compare compensated adults to the
dyslexic and nondyslexic adults in our sample on demographic, IQ,
achievement, and spelling variables.

Study 1

Methods

Subjects. The subjects for this study are from our large extended
family sample (N = 360). Three groups were studied: compensated
adults (N = 25), nondyslexic adults (N = 56), and dyslexics adults
(N = 57). The nondyslexic and dyslexic comparison groups in this
study are subsets of all the adult nondyslexic (total N = 101) and dyslexic (total N = 87) subjects in our extended family sample.

In our family study, diagnosis was based on self-reported history
of reading problems and on achievement test performance. To be classified as a dyslexic, an individual had to meet two criteria: a self-
reported history of reading and spelling problems as a child, and test
results indicative of adult reading and/or spelling problems. To be diag-

nosed as a compensated adult, an individual had to have a positive history, but negative test results. To be classified as a nondyslexic, an individual had to be negative on both criteria, history and test results.

Reading history data was collected in two ways:

1. An interview was conducted with each member of an extended family. During this interview each person was asked to provide reading history information about himself as well as about other members of his family. This latter portion of the interview provided cross validation for individual reading problems within a family.
2. A reading history questionnaire (RHQ) was developed that was based on the one used by Finucci in her research (Finucci et al. 1982). In the early part of our research only interview information was gathered. The RHQ was developed later and administered to individuals along with the interview to establish its validity and reliability.

The RHQ allowed subjects to respond to questions about difficulty learning to read, repeating grades, failure in high school and college courses, attitude toward reading, spelling ability, and current amount of magazine, newspaper and/or book reading. On most items, three or four responses were allowed. The most favorable response was scored as zero and the least favorable was scored three. For example, the question about spelling ability allows for the following responses and scores: above average (0), average (1), below average, not very good (2), and poor, terrible (3).

Each person's RHQ score was the ratio of total points/total possible number of points on the questionnaire. The resulting ratio was then analyzed by diagnostic group (dyslexic vs. nondyslexic) to determine mean values. The overall means for dyslexics (N = 47) and nondyslexics (N = 65) in our sample were .52(.16) and .28(.11), respectively. These means were significantly different (p < .001).

To qualify as having positive test results, an individual had to meet at least one of these two test criteria:

1. He/she had to have a reading quotient (RQ) of .80 or below; (The reading quotient (RQ) compares the individual's observed reading and spelling scores with those expected of an individual the same age with the same amount of education);
2. He/she had to meet the requirements of the Specific Dyslexia Algorithm (SDA) on the Peabody Individual Achievement Test (PIAT). (To meet the SDA an individual's PIAT Reading Recognition and/or Spelling standard scores must differ from his/her

Math and/or General Information standard scores by at least
one standard deviation [15 points]).

Beyond diagnosis, there were two criteria for inclusion in one of
the comparison groups for Study 1. One criterion was whether or not
an individual's WRAT Spelling Test had been evaluated by our computerized Spelling Error Evaluation Program (SEEP) program described below. The second was that each subject have at least ten misspelled words on the WRAT Spelling Test. The number of errors is a
cutoff used in our previous work (Pennington et al. 1986; Pennington
et al. 1987), and was used in order to be consistent with our previous
research.

Not all adult subjects in our family study have had their spelling
errors analyzed by the SEEP program. Those whose spelling was analyzed were not chosen from their respective diagnostic groups in any
systematic way, but were the adults whose results were available for the
previous studies mentioned above. New subjects have since been
added to the family study, but their results have not been analyzed at
this time.

We felt it was important to limit the overall analyses to those whose
spelling errors had been evaluated by SEEP so that the same individuals would be included in all analyses. However, we wanted to be sure
that these subsets were representative of their respective diagnostic
groups. To this end, analyses were performed to compare included
dyslexic and nondyslexic subjects to those who were not included
within each diagnostic group on demographic, IQ, and achievement
variables.

There were no significant differences between the dyslexic groups,
and only one difference was discovered between the nondyslexic
groups. The nondyslexic controls who were included in the study (Grp
1; N = 57) had a lower mean PIAT Reading Recognition score than those
who were not included (Grp 2; N = 33) (Grp 1: M = 105.7 (8.6); Grp 2:
M = 111.9(9.1)). Since there were no systematic biases in the selection of
Grp 1, nor any differences in age, education, or IQ between Grp 1 and
Grp 2, the reason for this result was not clear. However, it was not
viewed as a confound, though it was considered in the analyses discussed below.

Procedures and Materials.   All subjects were administered the Peabody Individual Achievement Test (PIAT), the Spelling subtest of the
Wide Range Achievement Test (WRAT), and the Raven's Matrices (a
nonverbal IQ measure). These tests were administered in the standard
fashion. In addition, detailed reading history information was collected from each person as described above.

The WRAT spelling test responses for each individual were coded according to the system described in earlier papers (Pennington et al. 1986; Pennington et al. 1987). Only a brief description of this system will be provided here.

All the different spelling errors for each word were transcribed onto a master computer file for scoring. Errors were not identified by subject group in this file. Error codes were established and are described in detail in Pennington et al. (1986). Each error was scored by the first and second authors according to the coding system described below. Two main dimensions of spelling accuracy, phonological and orthographic, were examined at two levels of complexity.

SPA. A simple phonologically accurate misspelling (SPA) was defined as follows. The consonant structure of the whole string was examined to see whether all the consonant sounds and only the consonant sounds of the target word were present in the correct order. Vowel errors were ignored since correct vowel representation is a more complex and later attainment in the development of phonological accuracy. A target consonant sound could be represented by a different grapheme(s) than that in the target word, as long as these grapheme(s) had the target sound in some English word. A subject's SPA score is the percentage of his total errors that preserved consonant phonology.

CPA. In contrast to the SPA score, the complex phonological accuracy (CPA) code required accurate representation of both vowels and consonants. The raters had to agree that the subject's reading of the misspelling matched exactly the phonology of the target word. It was also permissible for words in this category to be orthographically illegal (e.g., "cwantity" for quantity). A subject's CPA score is the percentage of his total errors that preserved a word's complete phonology.

SOA. The simple orthographic accuracy (SOA) code required that a string have both the initial and final letters of the target word correct and not have any orthographically illegal letter sequences. Orthographically illegal was defined in the strong sense that such a letter sequence does not occur in any position in any English word within a morpheme (e.g., "angziaty" for anxiety, where the sequence *ngz* is orthographically illegal). Although a given misspelling might contain more than one of these simple orthographic inaccuracies, misspellings were only counted once in a subject's total of non-SOA words. A subject's score is the percentage of total errors that received a SOA score.

COA. Complex orthographic accuracy (COA) was defined as the correct spelling of four patterns within words, each of which represents a departure from a direct phoneme to grapheme translation and requires knowledge of more subtle or complex spelling regularities. The four patterns were single consonant alternation, vowel clusters, geminate consonants, and analogy words.

Single consonant alternations reflect the fact that most consonant graphemes can represent more than one phoneme, depending on context. For instance, the "c" in necessity represents the phoneme /s/, while in cat the "c" represents the phoneme /k/. There are 23 examples of this pattern on the WRAT II list which was given to all adults.

Vowel clusters involve digraphs or letter clusters which usually represent one phoneme; hence, the grapheme-phoneme correspondence is complex because it is a many-to-one correspondence. For instance, the "iou" in precious represents the single phoneme /u/. There are 14 vowel clusters on the WRAT II list.

Geminate consonants involve a consonant doubling (e.g., exaggerate), usually for reasons of affixation in the etiology of the word. There are 11 geminate consonants on the WRAT II list.

Analogy words contain letter groups whose basis is usually morphological, but which cannot be derived from simple phoneme-grapheme correspondence rules. For analogy words there is a "family resemblance" or analogy to other morphologically related words, either in the base morpheme (e.g., the *phys*-portion of *phys*ician, *phys*ical, and *phys*ics), or in a suffix morpheme (e.g., *-shion* in fa*shion*). There are 21 analogies on the WRAT II list.

To ensure that we were tapping a subject's specific knowledge of these complex orthographic patterns, only spelling errors were scored. We reasoned that the best test for the subject's knowledge of a given pattern was his ability to use it correctly in a word of which he was unsure and in which he misspelled other portions.

The basic percentage score for each of these patterns was the number of times a subject spelled that pattern correctly in a word which was otherwise misspelled divided by the total number of patterns of that type in the words he misspelled. The scores for the four patterns were analyzed separately and were also combined into an overall complex orthographic accuracy (COA) score.

Results

There are two levels of analyses in this study. The main analyses compare the groups on overall achievement variables. The second level of analyses focuses more closely on reading and spelling variables.

All analyses discussed in this section reflect comparisons between the compensated group and each comparison group independently.

Demographic Variables

There were no significant differences between the groups on age or IQ (Table I). It should be noted here that there are seven compen-

Table I
Mean (SD) of Age, Education, RHQ, IQ and Achievement Scores in
Study One

	Compensated Adults (N = 25)	Nondyslexic Adults (N = 56)	Dyslexic Adults (N = 57)
Sex			
M	7	24	38**
F	18	32	19
Age	44.68 (13.04)	40.26 (12.37)	39.03 (13.88)
Education	15.86 (2.80)	15.33 (2.32)	14.21 (2.37)**
			1 > 3
RHQ	0.44 (.13)	0.29 (.11)***	0.54 (.13)*
			3 > 1 > 2
IQ	120.89 (8.13)	118.22 (7.72)	115.89 (12.20)
SES	2.16 (1.11)	2.35 (1.17)	3.97 (1.08)**
			1 > 3
PIAT			
Math	104.04 (14.47)	107.91 (9.75)**	103.50 (12.27)
RRec	104.00 (12.39)	105.66 (8.64)	90.14 (11.79)***
			1 & 2 > 3
RComp	109.39 (11.10)	111.30 (8.11)	96.98 (13.25)***
			1 & 2 > 3
Spelling	104.96 (13.92)	110.39 (11.18)	80.30 (11.37)***
			1 & 2 > 3
Gen Info	108.00 (13.26)	106.29 (12.80)	106.50 (12.24)
WRAT Sp	105.00 (9.23)	109.21 (7.82)*	88.69 (13.74)***
			2 > 1 > 3
RQ	.99 (.08)	1.05 (.10)*	.76 (.14)***
			2 > 1 > 3

*p < .05   **p < .01   ***p < .001

sated adults, fourteen dyslexics, and fifteen nondyslexic individuals who do not have IQ results. To ensure that IQ was not a factor in the results, separate analyses within groups were carried out between those who had IQ results and those who did not. No significant differences were found in the results.

To be sure that the difference on PIAT Reading Recognition (RRec) between those nondyslexics included in this study and those who were not, discussed above, did not lead to spurious results between nondyslexics and compensateds on that variable, an analysis was performed that compared all nondyslexics to compensateds on RRec. The result was not significant.

On the Reading History Questionnaire, the Study 1 sample revealed significant differences among the three groups (Table I). The dyslexics reported the strongest histories of reading difficulties (.54), followed by the compensates (.44) and nondyslexics (.29).

Additionally, between the compensated group and the dyslexic group there were significant differences on SES, as evaluated by the Hollingshead Inventory, and total years of education (Table I); the compensateds had signficantly more education and higher SES. An analysis of covariance was performed on all variables using education and SES as covariates. The main effect of diagnosis, as discussed below, remained constant on all variables.

There was a significant sex difference between the compensated group and the dyslexic group ($X^2(1) = 10.49$; $p<.01$); but not between the compensated group and the nondyslexic ($X^2(1) = 1.61$; NS). Because of these sex differences, we used ANCOVAs to control for sex in the analyses reported below. Results showed a main effect for sex in the analysis of RQ between the compensateds and both comparison groups, and in the analysis of WRAT Spelling between the compensateds and the dyslexic group. All other significant results indicated no main effect for sex.

Achievement Variables

On the Piat Individual Achievement Test, there were no differences between any of the groups on Math or General Information. The only differences on the PIAT occurred between the dyslexic group and the other two groups on Reading Recognition, Reading Comprehension, and Spelling subtests. As expected, the dyslexics' scores were significantly lower than those of the other groups on these measures (Table I).

On the WRAT Spelling Test, the compensated group's mean was different than either comparison group. While their mean was in the average range, it was significantly lower than the nondyslexic group mean, but significantly higher than the dyslexic group mean. It would appear that the compensateds are not totally normal spellers, though they are much closer to being normal than are the adult dyslexics.

The spelling error pattern results revealed no significant differences between the compensated adults and the nondyslexic comparison group (Table II). The compensated adults' spelling was very similar to that of nondyslexics on these patterns. The mean score for CPA was slightly lower, but there were no significant differences.

When compared with the dyslexics, on the other hand, the compensated adults appear quite different on the two complex error variables, CPA and COA (Table II). The compensated adults were significantly

Table II
Mean (SD) of Spelling Variables in Study One

	Compensated Adults (N = 25)	Nondyslexic Adults (N = 56)	Dyslexic Adults (N = 57)
SPA	.73 (.17)	.77 (.17)	.64 (.16)*
			2 > 3
CPA	.47 (.24)	.56 (.23)	.31 (.18)**
			1 & 2 > 3
SOA	.96 (.01)	.97 (.02)	.96 (.02)
COA	.63 (.06)	.65 (.10)	.57 (.12)*
			1 & 2 > 3

*p < .05   **p < .01   ***p < .001

better than the dyslexic adults in both their complex phonological and orthographic knowledge.

Discussion

Our results are different from those of Scarborough discussed above. She found differences on almost all reading and spelling variables between the indeterminate and borderline groups and the nondyslexic controls. We found few such differences. This may be due all or in part to different diagnostic methods or to our subjects being from a more homogeneous population. Our subjects were all from extended dyslexic families all with an apparent autosomal dominate pattern of transmission. Moreover, few of the adult subjects were probands, since these kindreds were identified through affected children. In contrast, all of Scarborough's subjects were probands, and so there may have been a selection bias toward severity. In addition, the sex ratio in Scarborough's compensated group was about equal, whereas, 72 percent of our group was female.

In summary, it would appear that compensated dyslexics are quite different than the dyslexic adults in our sample. Possibly confounding the issue is the difference between the two groups in socioeconomic status and education. Is this difference responsible for compensation, or does compensation result in obtaining more education and, as a result, higher socioeconomic status? In an effort to address this more specifically, Study 2 compares compensateds, nondyslexics, and dyslexics who are matched for age, socioeconomic status, IQ and education. Once these confounding variables are controlled, the more specific questions about compensation can be addressed.

Study 2

Methods

Subjects. Three groups were studied: compensated adults (N = 25), nondyslexic adults (N = 24), and dyslexic adults (N = 25). The non-dyslexic and dyslexic subjects for this study are subsets of the diagnostic groups analyzed in Study 1. The only selection criteria beyond those in Study 1 were that they be matched on age, SES, IQ, and education.

Procedures. The subjects are a subset of the entire sample described above, and as such, were administered the same tests. All of these individuals had their spelling errors evaluated by the SEEP program described in Study 1 and had at least ten spelling errors on the WRAT Spelling Test. In this study, the results of the Gray Oral Reading Test are also discussed. This test was added to the battery late, and, consequently, it was not administered to all subjects in our original family study. For the purposes of this study, the Gray Oral was administered to 20 compensated adults, 19 nondyslexic adults, and 20 dyslexic adults.

The Gray Oral Reading Test is a timed oral reading test made up of 13 passages of increasing difficulty and complexity. This test is designed for administration to all ages from beginning readers through adults. However, not all subjects read the same passages. To assure that each subject reads at his/her appropriate level, a basal score is established for each individual. The basal is the last passage read without a single error of any kind. A ceiling score is obtained when a subject reads two consecutive passages with at least seven errors in each. A raw score is obtained for each individual based on the individuals reading speed and the number of errors for each passage completed. The usual method of scoring yields a grade-equivalent score based on the raw score obtained. We did not think that a grade-equivalent score would yield results sensitive enough to compare the subtle differences among our three groups. We devised a method of scoring we thought would yield results more meaningful for our purposes. This method of scoring is discussed below.

Results

As in Study 1, there are two levels of analyses in this study. The main analyses compare the groups on overall achievement variables. The second level of analyses focuses more closely on reading and spelling variables.

All analyses discussed in this section reflect comparisons between the compensated group and each control group independently.

Demographic Variables

As expected, there were no significant differences between the groups on age, SES, education, or IQ (Table III). It should be noted here that there were six compensated adults and one nondyslexic individual who did not have IQ results. To ensure that IQ was not a factor in the

Table III
Mean (SD) of Age, Education, IQ and Achievement Scores in Study Two

	Compensated Adults (N = 25)	Nondyslexic Adults (N = 56)	Dyslexic Adults (N = 57)
Sex			
M	7	13*	17**
F	19	11	8
Age	44.68 (13.04)	42.28 (12.07)	43.56 (13.52)
Education	15.86 (2.80)	15.73 (2.41)	14.99 (2.76)
RHQ	0.44 (.13)	0.34 (.09)*	0.52 (.13)
			1 & 3 > 2
IQ	121.00 (7.79)	118.70 (7.40)	119.60 (7.59)
SES	2.16 (1.11)	2.48 (1.27)	2.78 (1.17)
PIAT			
Math	104.04 (14.47)	107.63 (10.55)	107.36 (12.07)
RRec	104.00 (12.39)	107.54 (7.98)	95.04 (10.49)**
			1 & 2 > 3
RComp	109.39 (11.10)	111.04 (8.71)	102.92 (13.37)*
			2 > 3
Spelling	104.96 (13.92)	106.63 (10.71)	84.96 (10.82)***
			1 & 2 > 3
Gen Info	108.00 (13.27)	107.46 (13.43)	110.83 (11.67)
WRAT Sp	105.00 (9.23)	109.79 (7.02)*	93.08 (11.47)**
			2 > 1 > 3
RQ	.99 (.08)	1.03 (.08)*	.77 (.13)***
			2 > 1 > 3
Gray Oral	(N = 20)	(N = 19)	(N = 20)
Raw Score	87.00 (11.3)	96.6 (9.4)*	69.0 (20.1)***
			2 > 1 > 3
			2 > 1 > 3
Average Time/	36.23 (9.9)	29.21 (4.04)**	48.17 (20.58)*
Last 3 Passages			2 > 1 > 3
Completed (secs)			
Average Errors	3.87 (1.8)	3.02 (1.7)	5.85 (1.91)**
Last 3 Passages			1 & 2 > 3
Completed			

*p < .05   **p < .01   ***p < .001

results, separate analyses within groups were carried out between those who had IQ results and those who did not. No significant differences were found in the results as a consequence.

There were significantly more women in the compensated group than in either of the other groups ($X^2(1) = 3.86$; p<.05; comp v. dys $X^2(1) = 8.63$; p<.01). For this reason, sex was covaried in all of the following analyses. Results of the ANCOVAs indicate that sex was a factor in only two of the significant results reported here. Results showed a main effect for sex in the analysis of RQ between the compensateds and both comparison groups, and in the analysis of WRAT Spelling between the compensateds and the dyslexic group. All other significant results indicated no main effect for sex.

The Study 2 sample revealed a significant difference between the nondyslexic adults and both the compensated and dyslexic adults on the Reading History Questionnaire (Table III). The compensateds and dyslexics reported strong histories of reading difficulties, while the nondyslexics did not.

Achievement Variables

On the Piat Individual Achievement Test, the results are identical to those in Study 1. There were no differences between any of the groups on Math, or General Information. The only differences on the PIAT, again, occurred between the dyslexic group and the other two groups on Reading Recognition, Reading Comprehension, and Spelling subtests with the dyslexics being lower on all three variables (Table III).

On the WRAT Spelling Test, the compensated group's mean was different than either comparison group. While their mean was in the average range, it was significantly lower than the nondyslexic group mean, and higher than the dyslexic group mean, as it was in Study 1.

The Gray Oral Reading Test was administered to a subset of the sample as discussed above. The compensated adults differed significantly on total raw score points from both the dyslexic and nondyslexic controls (Table III), falling between these two groups. Since the raw score is based on both time and number of errors, it was not clear why the compensateds were different from both control groups. For this reason, we devised a more qualitative method of scoring.

The Gray Oral Reading Test is a test of oral reading accuracy and fluency. It is constructed so that each subject begins with a paragraph he/she reads without error, and proceeds until the subject is making seven or more errors per passage. Similarly, a subject's speed of reading is more rapid at the beginning because the words used are more familiar. As the test proceeds, the words used become less familiar, and, hence, the individual's reading time increases because time and effort must be expended to decode and pronounce unfamiliar words.

This is true regardless of where one begins the test. Typically, a non-dyslexic reader begins at a higher level and proceeds further on the test than does a dyslexic. Nonetheless, the most difficult passages for each individual are those just prior to ceiling, or in the case of many non-dyslexics, those at the end of the test.

Besides the raw score obtained using the standard scoring method, two other scores were used: 1) a fluency score was obtained by averaging the time it took each person to complete the last three passages he/she read, and 2) an error score obtained by averaging the number of oral reading errors made on the same last three passages.

The results were quite interesting (Table III). The compensateds' average reading speed on the last three passages was significantly slower than the nondyslexic controls and significantly faster than the dyslexic controls. At the same time the compensateds did not make significantly more errors than the nondyslexics, and made significantly fewer than the dyslexic controls on the same passages. While the compensateds read more slowly than the nondyslexics, they were nearly as accurate in their reading. They were able to decode unfamiliar words just as well as nondyslexics; however, they just did it with less automaticity.

The spelling error pattern results revealed no significant differences between the compensated adults and the nondyslexic comparison group (Table IV). The compensated adults' spelling was very similar to that of nondyslexics on these patterns. The compensateds' mean scores were all a little lower, but there were no significant differences.

When compared with the dyslexics, on the other hand, the compensated adults were different on the two complex error variables, CPA and COA (Table II). The compensated adults were significantly better

	Table IV		
	Mean (SD) of Spelling Variables in Study Two		
	Compensated Adults	Nondyslexic Adults	Dyslexic Adults
	(N = 25)	(N = 24)	(N = 25)
SPA	.73 (.17)	.77 (.18)	.66 (.15)
			.30 (.16)**
CPA	.47 (.24)	.53 (.21)	1 & 2 > 3
SOA	.97 (.01)	.97 (.02)	.96 (.02)
			.57 (.13)*
COA	.63 (.06)	.64 (.05)	1 & 2 > 3

*p < .05   **p < .01   ***p < .001

than the dyslexic adults in their complex phonological and orthographic knowledge, as was true in Study 1.

Discussion

Our results in this study are also quite a bit different from those of Scarborough (1984). Again, we found fewer differences between the compensateds' and nondyslexic controls' reading and spelling variables. As discussed earlier, the reasons for the differences between our findings and hers are not clear.

Scarborough reportedly found no differences in reading speed. Our results showed that the compensateds read at a speed significantly faster than that of the dyslexics, but significantly slower than the nondyslexics. So while these compensateds have "caught up" with the nondyslexics on almost every reading and spelling task in terms of accuracy, they remain slower oral readers and are more similar to the dyslexics in this area. Perhaps they still have some subtle phonological processing deficit that affects oral reading speed.

We have no way of knowing what compensatory processes these people used, but because they had been dyslexic at one time, we know that their decoding skills were probably much weaker, and it is possible that some subtle phonological decoding problems play a part in their slower reading speed.

On the WRAT spelling test, the compensateds are clearly more knowledgeable about complex spelling rules than are the dyslexics. Their knowledge of the spelling rules that are evaluated by our computer program is very similar to that of the nondyslexics. However, because their overall test scores on the WRAT are clearly not as good as nondyslexics with the same IQ level and educational experience, there must be some more subtle deficit that our coding system is not sensitive enough to pick out. An alternate hypothesis might be that, because of their slower reading speed, the compensateds have had less print exposure and fewer trials to memorize the correct spellings of these words.

In summary, the results of Study 1 and Study 2 are consistent. Study 1 suggested that SES and education may be involved in the differences between dyslexics and compensateds. However, when these variables are controlled, the differences between dyslexics and compensateds remain the same, as do the results between the compensateds and the nondyslexics. Thus, education and SES alone do not cause compensation, rather compensation may lead to higher education and SES.

Returning to the questions we raised above:

1. Are compensated dyslexic adults different from both dyslexic adults who have not compensated and from nondyslexic adults?

    Compensated dyslexics appear to be quite similar to non-dyslexics in most reading and spelling skills. However, their oral reading speed is more similar to that of dyslexics.

    It would appear that compensated dyslexics do not completely overcome their prior dyslexia. There are some interesting similarities between them and the dyslexic control group. Further, it appears there are subtle differences between true non-dyslexics and compensateds.

2. If residual deficits remain, are these convergent with the primary deficits found in other studies of dyslexia?

    Our previous research (Pennington et al. in press) has indicated that adult dyslexics have persistent problems with phoneme awareness skills. This, no doubt, has an impact on their ability to decode unfamiliar words. It is quite possible that this is reflected in the compensateds' slower oral reading speed. There is less automaticity in decoding and, hence, slower reading.

    It would be very interesting to compare phoneme awareness and related phonological skills in a homogeneous group of dyslexics, compensated dyslexics, and nondyslexics such as those in this study to explore whether or not compensated dyslexics have subtle deficits in this area. If such deficits were found, it would add strength to the position that phoneme awareness is the core deficit in dyslexia.

3. Why are some people able to compensate for dyslexia while others are not?

    The answer to this question is not completely clear. What is clear is that it does not appear to be solely based on intelligence. It is very interesting that females in our study are so much more likely to compensate than males. The sex ratios in Felton's and Scarborough's work do not so clearly favor females. Again, this may be due to different methods of ascertainment. The high rate of female compensation in our study, assuming a genetic etiology, indicates a sex difference in penetrance in the genes causing dyslexia.

Clinic samples such as those of Felton and Scarborough tend to be made up of a preponderance of males. Family samples do not show this preponderance. Our research and that of others (DeFries et al. in press) has found the sex ratios in familial samples such as ours are about 1.5–1.8 males to one female. Shaywitz et al. (1990) found the sex ratio for reading disability in school-aged children is one male to one female. The Shaywitz study was based on children only, and the family studies are based on both children and adults. Perhaps the differences in sex ratios between the Shaywitz et al. study and the DeFries study result from more compensation by females (Pennington in press). Further research will be required to help us better to understand why some individuals compensate while others do not, and why females appear so much more likely to compensate.

References

Campbell, R. and Butterworth, B. 1985. Phonological dyslexia and dysgraphia in a highly literate subject: a developmental case with associated deficits of phonemic processing and awareness. *The Quarterly Journal of Experimental Psychology* 37A:435–475.

DeFries, J. C. and Baker, L. 1983. Colorado family reading study: longitudinal analysis. *Annals of Dyslexia* 33:153–162.

DeFries, J. C., Olson, R. K., Pennington, B. F., and Smith, S. D. In press. Colorado reading project: an update. *In* Gray, D.B. and Duane, D. (eds.). *The Reading Brain: The biological basis of dyslexia*. York Press: Parkton, MD.

Felton, R. 1990. Personal Communication.

Finucci, J. M., Gottfredson, L. S., and Childs, B. 1986. A follow-up study of dyslexic boys. *Annals of Dyslexia* 35:117–136.

Finucci, J. M. 1986. Follow-up studies of developmental dyslexia and other learning disabilities. *In* S. Smith (ed.). *Genetics and Learing Disabilities* San Diego: College-Hill Press.

Finucci, J. M., Isaacs, S., Whitehouse, C., Childs, B. 1982. Empirical validation of reading and spelling quotients. *Developmental Medicine and Child Neurology* 24:733–744.

Finucci, J. M., Whitehouse, C. C., Isaacs, S. D., and Childs, B. 1984. Derivation and validation of a quantitative definition of specific reading disability for adults. *Developmental Medicine and Child Neurology* 26:143–154.

Gilger, J. W. In review. Using self-report and parental-report survey data to assess past and present academic achievement of adults and children.

Letwitter, F. I., DeFries, J. C., and Elston, R. C. 1980. Genetic models of reading disability. *Behavior Genetics* 10:9–30.

Pennington, B. F. 1990. Annotation: the genetics of dyslexia. *Journal of Child Psychiatry* 31:193–201.

Pennington, B. F. In press. Learning Disorders in Children: Differential diagnosis and treatment. New York: Guilford.

Pennington, B. F., McCabe, L. L., Smith, S. D., Lefly, D. L., Bookman, M. O., Kimberling, W. J., and Lubs, H. A. 1986. Spelling errors in adults with a form of familial dyslexia. *Child Development* 57:1001–1013.

Pennington, B. F., Lefly, D. L., Van Orden, G. C., Bookman, M. O., and Smith, S. D. 1987. Is phonology bypassed in normal or dyslexic development? *Annals of Dyslexia* 35:62–89.

Pennington, B. F., Van Orden, G. C., Smith, S. D., Green, P. A., and Haith, M. M. In press. Phonological processing skills and deficits in adult dyslexics. *Child Development*.

Pennington, B. F., Gilger, J., Pauls, D., Smith, S. A., Smith, S. D., and DeFries, J. C. In review. Evidence for dominant transmission of developmental dyslexia.

Scarborough, H. S. 1984. Continuity between childhood dyslexia and adult reading. *British Journal of Psychology* 75:329–348.

Shaywitz, S. E., Shaywitz, B. A., Fletcher, J. M., and Escobar, M. D. 1990. Prevalence of reading disability in boys and girls. *Journal of the American Medical Association* 264:998.

Smith, S. D., Kimberling, W. J., Pennington, B. F., and Lubs, H. A. 1983. Specific reading disability: Identification of an inherited form through linkage and analysis. *Science* 219:1345–1347.

Smith, S. D., Pennington, B. F., Kimberling, W. J., and Ing, P. S. In press. Familial dyslexia: Use of genetic linkage data to define subtypes. *Journal of the American Academy of Child Psychiatry.*

Early Identification of Dyslexia: Evidence from a Follow-Up Study of Speech-Language Impaired Children

Hugh W. Catts

University of Kansas
Lawrence, Kansas

A group of speech-language impaired children was administered a battery of standardized language tests and measures of phonological processing in kindergarten. Performance on these language measures was then compared to reading ability in first grade. Results indicated that children with semantic-syntactic language deficits had more difficulties in reading than did children with primarily speech articulation impairments. In addition, phonological processing measures were found to be good predictors of reading achievement. Results are discussed in terms of their implications for the early identification of developmental dyslexia.

For some time, researchers and practitioners have been interested in the early identification of developmental dyslexia (e.g., Badian 1982; Jansky and de Hirsch 1972). Progress in this area has been limited, however, by traditional conceptualizations or definitions of the disorder (e.g., Critchley 1970). These definitions generally have relied on

This research was supported by a grant from the Department of Education (HO24U8001). The author would like to thank the administrators, speech-language pathologists, teachers, and children from the Lawrence and Topeka Public Schools for their cooperation in this project. Much appreciation is also expressed to Linda Swank, Laurie Stewart, Amy Larsen, Shaunna McIntosh, Karen Wiggins, Chiehfang Hu, and Janet Marquis for their assistance in data collection and analysis.

Annals of Dyslexia, Vol. 41, 1991.
ISSN 0736-9387

the presence of a specific reading disability as the primary symptom of the disorder. As a result, practitioners have often delayed identification until children have begun school and have experienced significant problems in learning to read.

Recently, a more comprehensive conceptualization of dyslexia has been proposed (Catts 1989a; Chasty 1985; Kamhi and Catts 1989; Liberman and Shankweiler 1985; Scarborough 1990). According to this view, many cases of dyslexia are best characterized as instances of a developmental language disorder, a disorder that is present early in life and manifests itself in different ways during development. Besides a specific reading disability, a prominent manifestation of the disorder is the occurrence of oral language difficulties. These problems are often present in the preschool years and may continue into later childhood, adolescence, and even adulthood (e.g., Johnson and Blalock 1987; Scarborough 1990; Wolf and Obregon 1989). This conceptualization of dyslexia, thus, provides for the opportunity to identify the disorder early in development on the basis of oral language problems.

Research in the last 10–15 years has sought to specify more clearly the nature of the early language problems associated with dyslexia. One area of research that is particularly relevant is the study of children with developmental speech-language impairments, that is, children with significant delays in the acquisition of speech and/or language abilities (see Aram and Hall, 1989 and Weiner 1985 for a review of the literature). Practitioners working with speech-language impaired children have for years noted that these children often experience difficulties in learning to read upon entering school. Longitudinal or follow-up studies have also been undertaken to investigate the academic difficulties associated with preschool speech-language impairments (Aram and Nation 1980; Bishop and Adams 1990; Levi et al. 1982; Padget 1988; Silva, McGee, and Williams 1983; Stark et al. 1984; Tallal, Curtiss, and Kaplan 1989; Wilson and Risucci 1988). This work has documented that many, but not all, speech-language impaired children have difficulties learning to read.

The above research also provides some preliminary suggestions concerning which speech-language impaired children are most at risk for reading problems. A number of studies, for example, indicate that preschool children with semantic-syntactic impairments, or what are more generally referred to as language impairments, have a higher risk of subsequent reading disabilities than do children with primarily speech articulation problems (Bishop and Adams 1990; Hall and Tomblin 1978; Levi et al. 1982; Shriberg and Kwiatkowski 1988). Investigators have also considered whether the common distinction between receptive (comprehension) and expressive (production) language impairments is related to later reading difficulties. In this regard, several studies have reported that preschool receptive language impairments are more often associated with later reading disabilities than are expressive language problems (Tallal, Curtiss, and Kaplan 1989; Wilson and Risucci 1988). Others, however, have provided evidence that expressive language abilities/deficits are also good predictors of reading outcome in speech-language impaired children (Bishop and Adams 1990; Magnusson and Naucler 1990).

The present study was undertaken to further examine the relationship between preschool speech-language impairments and reading disabilities. In an on-going study, a group of speech-language impaired children were identified in kindergarten and are being followed through the primary grades. This paper reports on data collected through the end of first grade. In kindergarten, children were given a battery of standardized tests that evaluated receptive and expressive language abilities as well as speech articulation skills. In addition, a battery of experimental language tasks that measured phonological awareness, phonological recoding in lexical access, and phonetic coding in working memory was administered. Measures of these latter abilities, often referred to as *phonological processing abilities*, have been shown to be highly related to early reading development in a large number of studies involving wide cross sections of children (see Catts 1989b; Jorm and Share 1983; Wagner and Torgesen 1987 for review). Phonological processing abilities, however, have seldom been investigated in longitudinal studies of speech-language impaired children (Magnusson and Naucler 1990; Tallal, Curtiss, and Kaplan 1989). Thus, the inclusion of phonological processing measures in this study may help clarify the relationship between early speech-language impairments and later reading disabilities.

Method

Subjects

Forty-one speech-language impaired (S-LI) children participated in this investigation. At the beginning of the study, the subjects were in kindergarten and were an average age of 6 years, 4 months. There were 32 males and 9 females. Each of the children had been referred for a speech-language evaluation in one of two Midwest public school districts. In addition to the evaluation the children received in the schools, a battery of standardized speech and language tests was administered for this investigation. This battery included three measures of receptive semantic or syntactic abilities; *Peabody Picture Vocabulary Test-Revised, Token Test for Children,* Grammatical Understanding subtest of the *Test of Language Development-2,* and three measures of expressive semantic or syntactic abilities; *Expressive One-Word Picture Vocabulary Test, Structured Photographic Expressive Language Test-II*, combined performance on the Sentence Imitation and Grammatical Closure subtests of the *Test of Language Development-2*, and a measure of speech articulation; *Goldman-Fristoe Test of Articulation*. In addition, the combined score from the Block Design and Picture Completion subtests of the *WPPSI* (or *WISC-R* for children older than 6½ years) served as a measure of nonverbal ability.

The results of the standardized testing indicated that 28 of the 41 S-LI subjects demonstrated a language impairment and are subsequently referred to as the language-impaired (LI) subgroup. A language impairment was operationally defined as performance of at least 1 SD below the mean on at least two of three receptive language measures and/or two of three expressive language measures. The remaining 13 subjects did not meet the above criterion for a language impairment but demonstrated a mild to moderate speech articulation impairment and/or were enrolled in articulation therapy during the kindergarten school year (referred to as the speech-impaired (SI) subgroup). Several SI subjects had received articulation therapy throughout the school year and had resolved the majority of their speech problems by the spring when this investigation was undertaken. However, given the limited number of speech-impaired children available in the spring of kindergarten, placement in articulation therapy was considered a sufficient criterion for inclusion in the SI subgroup. All S-LI subjects further demonstrated normal non-verbal ability. School records also indicated that these children had hearing within normal limits and no history of emotional disorders.

Thirty children without a history of speech-language impairments or a referral for such impairments also participated in this study. These children served as a comparison group to evaluate the performance of the S-LI subjects on the measures of reading ability. The control subjects were enrolled in the same classrooms or schools as the S-LI subjects and were approximately the same age (6 years, 1 month at the beginning of the study). There were 18 males and 12 females in this group. Each of these children performed within normal limits on the battery of speech-language tests and the measure of nonverbal ability.

Procedures and Materials

The subjects were first evaluated in the spring of their kindergarten school year. At that time, each subject was administered the battery of standardized speech-language tests listed above. In addition, subjects were given a battery of experimental language tasks measuring phonological processing abilities. These included two measures of phonological awareness, three measures of phonetic recoding in lexical access, and one measure of phonetic coding in working memory.

Phonological awareness. Phonological awareness is the explicit awareness of the sound segments in words (Liberman and Shankweiler 1985). Two tasks were employed to assess subjects' phonological awareness. The *DELETION* task, which was adapted from Rosner (1971), required the subject to delete the initial syllable or phoneme from a word and say the remaining sound sequence. The child was introduced to the task by the use of three picture plates. The first plate displayed a picture of a cow and a boy. The child was instructed to say "cowboy." The investigator then covered the picture of the cow and said, "Now, say cowboy without the cow." The same procedures were used with picture plates displaying a cup and a cake and a tooth and a brush. Following these training trails, 20 stimulus items were administered, without the use of pictures to assist the subjects. Test items progressed from syllable deletion of compound words (e.g., *base*ball, *rail*road) and two syllable words (e.g., *ba*by, *per*son) to phoneme deletion in monosyllabic words (e.g., *s*it, *t*all). In all cases, the sound sequence remaining after segment deletion was a high frequency word. Corrective feedback was given for the first five errors and testing was stopped after eight consecutive incorrect responses.

The *BLENDING* task required the subject to blend together and pronounce syllables or phonemes. A hand puppet was used during training and stimulus presentation. Subjects were told that the puppet did not speak correctly, but rather "said words one sound at a time." Subjects were instructed to listen carefully and to say the word "the right way." The investigator illustrated the correct response to the puppet's pronunciation of *rein deer*. This was followed by the practice items *bed room*, *suit case*, and *snow man*. Twenty-one test items followed. These progressed from the blending of words/syllables (e.g., *birth day*, *mo ther*) to onset and rimes (e.g., *f un*, *s ing*) and finally to phonemes (e.g., *f i sh*, *s oa p*). Corrective feedback was provided for the practice items and the first five errors. No ceiling was employed.

Phonetic recoding in lexical access. Phonetic recoding in lexical access refers to the ability to retrieve the name or phonological code corresponding to a written word or a pictured item (Wagner and Torgesen 1987). Phonetic recoding ability has frequently been assessed by rapid naming tasks (e.g., Denckla and Rudel 1976; Wolf 1984). Three rapid naming tasks were employed in this study. The *RANOBJ* and the *RAN-COL* were similar to those used by Denckla and Rudel (1976) and Wolf (1984). In these tasks, subjects rapidly named a series of common objects (RANOBJ) or colors (RANCOL) displayed on 11 × 14 inch stimulus charts. Each chart contained 50 stimulus items consisting of five objects or five colors repeated randomly in five horizontal rows of ten items each. Prior to beginning, all subjects demonstrated their ability to name each of the five objects or colors in isolation. Subjects were then instructed to name as quickly as possible each item on the chart, preceding left to right, row by row. A stopwatch was used to measure (in 0.1 seconds) the total time necessary to name all 50 items on the chart.

A similar format was employed in the *RANAN* task. In this task, subjects rapidly named a series of colored animals presented on an 8 × 11 inch chart. There were a total of 24 stimulus items consisting of three animals (cow, pig, horse) randomly displayed in one of three colors (black, blue, red) and randomly repeated in four rows of six items each. Subjects were required rapidly to name each of the items (e.g., red pig, blue cow) on the stimulus chart. Again, the total duration to name all 24 items was measured.

Phonetic coding in working memory. Phonetic coding in working memory refers to the use of a sound-based code to hold information in memory. Research indicates that a phonetic code is the primary code for storing verbal information in working memory (Baddeley 1986; Conrad 1964). The sentence memory or *SENMEM* task was employed as an index of phonetic coding ability. In this task, subjects were required to repeat up to 14 sentences varying in length from 4 to 13 words. Each sentence was read aloud by the examiner and the subject was instructed to be a "copy cat" and say exactly what the examiner had said. A subject's score was the number of sentences repeated correctly. The repetition of a sentence was considered correct if all the lexical items were produced in the correct order. Because subjects displayed speech-language impairments, sentence repetitions containing phonological or morphological alterations were not considered to be in error. Testing was discontinued after three consecutive sentence repetitions produced in error.

Reading measures. In the spring of first grade, all subjects were administered tests of reading ability. These included the Word Identification (Word Id) and Word Attack subtests from the *Woodcock Reading Mastery Tests-Revised*. In the Word Id subtest, children were required to read a series of words in isolation. The Word Attack subtest, on the other hand, required children to read a list of pseudowords and provided an index of their knowledge and use of grapheme-phoneme correspondence.

Results

Table I displays the normal control and S-LI groups' mean standard scores (and standard deviations) on the Word Id and Word Attack

Table I
Mean standard scores (and standard deviations) on the Word Identification
and Word Attack subtests for the normal control and S-LI groups, as well as
for the LI and SI subgroups within the S-LI group.

	Normal N = 30	S-LI N = 41	LI N = 28	SI N = 13
Word Id	110.4 (15.4)	97.1 (18.4)	91.5 (17.7)	109.2 (14.8)
Work Attack	99.1 (14.2)	87.3 (14.7)	83.7 (14.4)	95.0 (12.8)

tasks administered in first grade. As can be observed, the control subjects performed above the test norm for the Word Id task, but scored
approximately equal to the norm on the Word Attack subtest. As a
group, the S-LI subjects were reading more poorly than the control
subjects on each of the reading tasks. Further analyses, however, indicated that these group differences were primarily the result of the poor
performance by the children with semantic-syntactic deficits (i.e., LI
subgroup) within the S-LI group. A 2 (reading test) × 3 (group) multivariate analysis of variance and preplanned follow-up comparisons indicated that the LI subgroup performed significantly more poorly than
the normal control group on the Word Id task ($t = 4.4, p < .001$) and
Word Attack task ($t = 4.0, p < .001$). The children with primarily
speech articulation impairments (i.e., SI subgroup), on the other hand,
demonstrated mean reading scores within the normal range and did
not differ significantly from the control group on the Word Id ($t = .24,$
$p > .05$) or Word Attack tasks ($t = .87, p > .05$).

   In order to examine the relationship between S-LI subjects' reading abilities in first grade and their language abilities in kindergarten,
Pearson product-moment correlation coefficients were calculated between the first grade reading tasks and the standardized language
tests and measures of phonological processing. In this analysis, standardized language tests were partitioned into those measuring receptive language abilities and those concerned with expressive language
abilities. Subjects' performances on each of the receptive language
tests were converted to z-scores and added together to create an overall
estimate of receptive language ability (RECL). Similar procedures were
employed to derive an estimate of expressive language ability (EXPL).
As can be seen in Table II, both RECL and EXPL were found to have a
low-moderate correlation with the Word Id task; but only EXPL was
significantly related to the Word Attack task. Most of the phonological
processing measures also proved to be related to reading outcome.
This was particularly true for the DELETION task which demonstrated

Table II

Pearson product-moment correlation coefficients between standardized and experimental language tasks administered in kindergarten and reading abilities measured in first grade.

	Word Id	Word Attack
RECL	.48**	NS
EXPL	.48**	.58**
DELETION	.60**	.61**
BLENDING	.48**	.57**
RANAN[a]	.58**	.46*
RANOBJ	.57**	.40*
RANCOL	.52**	NS
SENMEM	.43*	.54**
NVIQ	NS	NS

[a]Pearson r for rapid naming tasks are expressed in absolute values.
*p < .05
**p < .01

the strongest relationship to reading ability among the standardized and experimental language measures. Nonverbal ability, on the other hand, was unrelated to reading abilities in first grade.

A multiple regression analysis was undertaken to assess the relative contributions of the standardized language tests and the measures of phonological processing in predicting reading outcome in the S-LI subjects. Again in this analysis, the standardized language tests were divided into receptive and expressive measures (i.e., RECL, EXPL) and entered into the regression analysis along with the phonological processing measures and the measure of nonverbal ability. As was expected on the basis of the zero-order correlation coefficients, the DELETION task accounted for the most variance in the Word Id ($r^2 = .36$) and Word Attack ($r^2 = .37$) subtests. After the DELETION task was entered into the regression model for Word Id, only the RANOBJ task accounted for additional variance. Together, the DELETION and RANOBJ tasks accounted for 50 percent of the variance in Word Id performance. In the case of the Word Attack subtest, the SENMEM task accounted for an additional 8 percent of the variance beyond that accounted for by the DELETION task (combined $r^2 = .45$).

To further examine the effectiveness of the kindergarten language measures in predicting reading outcome, a discriminant analysis was performed. For this analysis, S-LI subjects were divided into good and poor readers on the basis of their combined performances on the Word Id and Word Attack measures. Poor readers were defined as those subjects whose combined reading scores fell at least 1 SD below the mean combined reading score of the normal control group. Subjects not meeting this criterion were considered to be good readers. These procedures led to the identification of 19 poor readers among the S-LI group, which included 17 from the LI subgroup (60 percent) and 2 from the SI subgroup (15 percent).[1] Each of the language measures used in the previous analyses was entered separately in the discriminant analysis. Table III presents the F-values and the percentages of correct classification of reading group membership for each of these variables. As can be seen in Table III, good and poor reading groups were found to be significantly different on each of the language measures, with the greatest difference occurring in the case of the DELETION task. The RECL, DELETION, RANAN, and SENMEM measures each separately provided for 75–78 percent correct classification of subjects into reading groups. As a classification variable, the DELETION task tended to over identify poor readers. Most S-LI subjects who became poor readers performed poorly on this task (89.5 percent), but so did some children who later became good readers (36.4 percent). Children who performed well on this task, however, almost always became good readers (87.5 percent). Similar results were obtained in the case of the

Table III

F-values and percentages of correct classification of reading group membership for each of the language measures.

Variable	F-values	Percentage Correct Classification
RECL	13.2**	78.1%
EXPL	13.1**	61.0%
DELETION	17.7**	75.6%
BLENDING	8.8**	70.7%
RANAN	9.6**	75.6%
RANOBJ	4.6*	51.2%
RANCOL	9.3*	70.7%
SENMEN	10.3*	75.6%

*$p < .05$
**$p < .01$

---

[1]The poor reader performance criterion of at least 1 SD below normal was chosen to assure sufficient numbers of poor readers for data analysis purposes. Some subjects satisfying this criterion might not meet more stringent criterion often associated with developmental dyslexia (i.e., at least 1½ or 2 SD below normal). However, research suggests that moderately poor readers differ from severely poor readers in a quantitative rather than qualitative manner (Ellis 1985; Olson et al. 1985; Seidenberg et al. 1985; Stanovich, 1988). Therefore, data obtained employing a more lenient criterion for the classification of poor readers should also have implications for severely impaired readers.

SENMEM task. Kindergartners who performed well on this task were predominately in the good reader group (83.3 percent), whereas subjects who performed less well became both poor readers (84.2 percent) and good readers (31.8 percent). The RANAN task, on the other hand, showed a more even classification of readers. For both subjects who scored well, and those who scored less well, the RANAN task correctly classified about 75 percent. Finally, the results indicated that taken together the DELETION and RANAN tasks were the best combination of predictors of reading group membership, resulting in 82.9 percent correct classification.

Discussion

The results of this study are consistent with previous research that demonstrates that young children with speech-language impairments are at risk for developing reading problems upon entering school. Many of the S-LI subjects in this study had begun, by the spring of first grade, to fall behind their normal peers in the development of reading abilities. As a group, the S-LI children performed significantly more poorly than the normal control subjects on tests of reading ability.

Although group differences were observed between the normal and S-LI groups, there was much variability among S-LI subjects in reading outcome. Whereas many S-LI children displayed reading problems, some showed reading abilities within the normal range. Variability in reading outcome proved to be related, in part, to the type of speech-language impairment experienced by the subjects. As in previous studies, children with deficits in semantic-syntactic language abilities more often had reading difficulties than did children whose primary problems were in speech articulation. The latter children generally displayed reading abilities within the normal range and as a group did not differ significantly from normal control subjects. These findings, together with those of earlier investigations (Bishop and Adams 1990; Hall and Tomblin 1978; Levi et al. 1982; Shriberg and Kwiatkowski 1988), demonstrate that speech articulation problems by themselves are not an early indicator of a reading disability.

The relationship of receptive and expressive language impairments to reading outcome was also considered. Results showed that both receptive and expressive language deficits were linked to reading problems, but in general, neither type of language impairment appeared to be more closely related to reading outcome than the other. Both receptive and expressive language ability were significantly related to performance on the Word Id task, but only expressive language ability was significantly correlated with Word Attack performance. Receptive language ability, however, was a better predictor of reading group membership than was expressive language ability. Recall that previous research has also reported somewhat equivocal results concerning the relationship between the receptive/expressive nature of language problems and reading disabilities. Perhaps it is the presence of a language impairment and not the receptive/expressive nature of the impairment that is the important risk factor for reading disabilities (Scarborough 1991). On the other hand, it is possible that receptive and expressive language impairments have not been examined closely enough to provide an adequate test of their relationship to reading development. This may be particularly true in the present study in which rather global measures were employed. Perhaps as studies examine the receptive/expressive nature of language impairments more closely, a clearer relationship will emerge. In addition, it will be necessary to consider the relationship of these problems to reading comprehension as well as word recognition abilities.

Children's performances on measures of phonological processing were also found to be significantly related to reading outcome. The best predictor of reading ability among the phonological processing measures was the DELETION task. This task accounted for the most variance in Word Id and Word Attack performances. The DELETION task also proved to be among the best tasks at differentiating good and poor readers. Kindergarten children's performance on this task, which only took approximately five minutes to administer, led to a 75.6 percent correct classification of reading group membership. It should be noted, however, that the DELETION task was most accurate in identifying good readers. Kindergartners who scored well on this task almost always were average or above average readers in first grade.

Recall that the DELETION task is a measure of subjects' explicit awareness of the sound structure of language or what is referred to as phonological awareness. Over the last ten years, a large body of research involving predominately children without speech impairment has established that measures of phonological awareness are among the best early predictors of reading development (see Catts 1989b; Stanovich 1988; Wagner and Torgesen 1987). These measures, administered to preschool and kindergarten children, have been shown to be strongly related to reading in the early grades (Bradley and Bryant 1985; Lundberg 1987; Mann and Liberman 1984; Share et al. 1984; Stanovich, Cunningham, and Cramer 1984). In a recent study in Sweden, Magnusson and Naucler (1990) also found that measures of phonological awareness were related to reading development in speech-language impaired children. Thus, the present results and those of Magnusson and Naucler suggest that phonological awareness measures may also be good indicators of reading outcome in speech-language impaired children.

Besides phonological awareness tasks, tasks measuring phonetic recoding in lexical access and phonetic coding in working memory also were found to be related to reading ability. The RANOBJ task combined with the DELETION task to account for the most variance in the Word Id subtest, whereas the RANAN and DELETION tasks were the best combination of measures for predicting reading group membership. The phonetic coding task, SENMEM, combined with the DELETION task to best predict performance on the Word Attack subtest. By itself, the SENMEM task was also a good predictor of reading group membership. But like the DELETION task, this task more accurately predicted good readers than poor readers.

Others have also found that measures of rapid naming or phonetic coding ability are related to early reading development. In speech-language impaired children, Tallal, Curtiss, and Kaplan (1989) reported a low but significant correlation between rapid naming ability at age 6 and reading at age 8. In the more general population, Wolf (1984; 1986), Felton and Brown (1989), and Blachman (1984) have demonstrated that rapid naming tasks administered in kindergarten are good predictors of reading in the primary grades. Also working with children with no speech-language impairment, Mann (1984), Mann and Liberman (1984), and Badian (1988) have shown that tasks measuring phonetic coding in working memory are predictive of reading ability.

Finally, the present study has implications for the early identification of developmental dyslexia. Recall that according to recent theories, many cases of dyslexia are argued to be the result of a developmental language disorder. The results of this study suggest that a speech-language impairment, specifically one involving the semantic-syntactic aspects of language, may be an early manifestation of the developmental language disorder associated with dyslexia. As an early manifestation, a preschool language impairment could thus serve as an early indicator of dyslexia.

Whereas a preschool language impairment may be an early indicator of dyslexia, this study, combined with previous research, suggests that such an impairment is not a sufficient or necessary indicator of the disorder. An early semantic-syntactic impairment does not appear to be a sufficient indicator because not all children with such impairments go on to have the reading disabilities associated with dyslexia. In this study, 40 percent of the children in the LI subgroup did not have reading problems in the first grade (at least not in word recognition). Other longitudinal studies have reported similar percentages of unimpaired readers among language-impaired children (Aram, Ekelman, and Nation 1984; Garvey and Gorden 1973; Padget 1988; Tallal, Curtiss, and Kaplan 1989; Wilson and Risucci 1988). The present results, however, do suggest that the significance of an early language impairment as an indicator of dyslexia increases when the impairment co-occurs with other language problems, specifically, problems in phonological awareness, phonetic recoding in lexical access, and phonetic coding in working memory. S-LI subjects displaying deficits in these aspects of phonological processing proved to be at a greater risk for reading disabilities than did those without such difficulties.

A preschool language impairment also does not appear to be a necessary indicator of dyslexia. Not all children with reading disabilities have been found to have a history of semantic-syntactic impairments. Scarborough (1990; 1991) has reported that subtle syntactic problems may be present in many children who later become dyslexic, but research and clinical observations in general, suggest that many dyslexic children do not have histories of significant semantic-syntactic language impairments (Badian et al. 1990; Kamhi et al. 1989; Rutter and Yule 1975). Some of these children, however, may still have a developmental language disorder; one that manifests itself in other domains than semantics or syntax. Again, the domain of phonological processing appears to be a likely candidate. As reviewed above, a large number of studies have shown that problems in phonological awareness, phonetic recoding in lexical access, and phonetic coding in working memory are prevalent in wide cross sections of children who later demonstrate reading disabilities, including many children without semantic-syntactic language deficits. Thus, future research into the early identification of dyslexia will need to consider other language deficits in addition to semantic-syntactic difficulties.

References

Aram, D., Ekelman, B., and Nation, J. 1984. Preschoolers with language disorders: 10 years later. *Journal of Speech and Hearing Research* 27:232–244.

Aram, D. and Hall, N. 1989. Longitudinal follow-up of children with preschool communication disorders: Treatment implications. *School Psychology Review* 18:487–501.

Aram, D. and Nation, J. 1980. Preschool language disorders and subsequent language and academic difficulties. *Journal of Communication Disorders* 13:159–179.

Baddeley, A. 1986. *Working Memory.* New York: Oxford University Press.

Badian, N. 1982. The prediction of good and poor readers before kindergarten entry: A four-year follow-up. *Journal of Special Education* 16:309–318.

Badian, N. 1988. The prediction of good and poor readers before kindergarten entry: A nine-year follow-up. *Journal of Learning Disabilities* 21:98–103.

Badian, N., McAnulty, G., Duffy, F., and Als, H. 1990. Prediction of dyslexia in kindergarten boys. *Annals of Dyslexia* 40:152–169.

Bishop, D. and Adams, C. 1990. A prospective study of the relationship between specific language impairment, phonological disorders and reading retardation. *Journal of Child Psychology and Psychiatry* 30:1027–1050.

Blachman, B. 1984. Relationship of rapid naming ability and language analysis skills to kindergarten and first-grade reading achievement. *Journal of Educational Psychology* 76:610–622.

Bradley, L. and Bryant, P. 1985. *Rhyme and reason in reading and spelling*. International Academy for Research in Learning Disabilities Monograph Series, No. 1. Ann Arbor, MI: University of Michigan Press.

Catts, H. 1989a. Defining dyslexia as a developmental language disorder. *Annals of Dyslexia* 39:50–64.

Catts, H. 1989b. Phonological processing deficits and reading disabilities. *In* A. Kamhi and H. Catts (eds.). *Reading Disabilities: A developmental language perspective*. Austin, TX: Pro-ed.

Chasty, H. 1985. What is dyslexia? A developmental language perspective. *In* M. Snowling (ed.). *Children's Written Language Difficulties: Assessment and management*, 11–28. Windsor: NFER-Nelson Publishing Co.

Conrad, R. 1964. Acoustic confusions in immediate memory. *British Journal of Psychology* 5:75–84.

Critchley, M. 1970. *The Dyslexic Child*. Springfield, IL: Thomas Publishing Company.

Denckla, M. and Rudel, R. 1976. Rapid automatized naming (R.A.N.): Dyslexia differentiated from other learning disabilities. *Neuropsychologia* 14:471–479.

Ellis, A. 1985. The cognitive neuropsychology of developmental (and acquired) dyslexia: A critical survey. *Cognitive Neuropsychology* 2:169–205.

Felton, R. and Brown, I. 1989. Phonological processes as predictors of specific reading skills in children at risk for reading failure. *Reading and Writing: An Interdisciplinary Journal* 2:3–23.

Garvey, M. and Gorden, N. 1973. A follow-up study of children with disorders of speech development. *British Journal of Communication Disorders* 8:17–28.

Hall, P. and Tomblin, J. 1978. A follow-up study of children with articulation and language disorders. *Journal of Speech and Hearing Disorders* 43:227–241.

Jansky, J. and de Hirsch, K. 1972. *Preventing Reading Failure: Prediction, diagnosis, intervention*. New York: Harper and Row.

Johnson, D. and Blalock, J. 1987. *Adults with Learning Disabilities: Clinical studies*. New York: Grune and Stratton.

Jorm, A. and Share, D. 1983. Phonological recoding and reading acquisition. *Applied Psycholinguistics* 4:103–147.

Kamhi, A. and Catts, H. 1989. *Reading Disabilities: A developmental language perspective*. Austin, TX: Pro-ed.

Kamhi, A., Catts, H., Mauer, D., Apel, K., and Gentry, B. 1989. Phonological and spatial processing abilities in language- and reading-impaired children. *Journal of Speech and Hearing Disorders* 53:316–327.

Levi, G., Capozzi, F., Fabrizi, A., and Sechi, E. 1982. Language disorders and prognosis for reading disabilities in developmental age. *Perceptual and Motor Skills* 54:1119–1122.

Liberman, I. and Shankweiler, D. 1985. Phonology and the problems of learning to read and write. *Remedial and Special Education* 6:8–17.

Lundberg, I. 1987. Phonological awareness facilities reading and spelling acquisition. *In* W. Ellis and R. Bowler (eds.). *Intimacy with Language*. Baltimore: The Orton Dyslexic Society.

Magnusson, E. and Naucler, K. 1990. Reading and spelling in language-disordered children—linguistic and metalinguistic prerequisites: report on a longitudinal study. *Clinical Linguistics and Phonetics* 4:49–61.

Mann, V. 1984. Longitudinal prediction and prevention of reading difficulty. *Annals of Dyslexia* 34:117–136.

Mann, V. and Liberman, I. 1984. Phonological awareness and verbal short-term memory. *Journal of Learning Disabilities* 17:592–599.

Olson, R., Kliegl, R., Davidson, B., and Foltz, G. 1985. Individual and developmental differences in reading disability. *In* T. Waller (ed.). *Reading Research: Advances in theory and practice.* London: Academic Press.

Padget, Y. 1988. Speech- and language-impaired three and four year olds: A five year follow-up study. *In* R. Masland and M. Masland (eds.). *Preschool Prevention of Reading Failure.* Parkton, MD: York Press.

Rosner, J. 1971. *Phonic Analysis Training and Beginning Reading Skills.* Pittsburgh: University of Pittsburgh Learning Research and Development Center Publication Series.

Rutter, M. and Yule, W. 1975. The concept of specific reading retardation. *Journal of Child Psychology and Psychiatry* 16:181–197.

Scarborough, H. 1990. Very early language deficits in dyslexic children. *Child Development* 61:1728–1743.

Scarborough, H. 1991. Early syntactic development of dyslexic children. *Annals of Dyslexia* 41.

Seidenberg, M., Bruck, M., Fornarolo, G., and Backman, J. 1985. Word recognition processes in poor and disabled readers. Do they necessarily differ? *Applied Psycholinguistics* 6:161–180.

Share, D., Jorm, A., MacLean, R., and Mathews, R. 1984. Sources of individual differences in reading acquisition. *Journal of Educational Psychology* 76:1309–1324.

Shriberg, L. and Kwiatkowski, J. 1988. A follow-up study of children with phonologic disorders of unknown origin. *Journal of Speech and Hearing Disorders* 53:144–156.

Silva, P., McGee, R., and Williams, S. 1983. A longitudinal study of children with developmental language delay at age three: Later intelligence, reading, and behavior problems. *Developmental Medicine and Child Neurology* 29:630–640.

Stanovich, K. 1988. The right and the wrong places to look for the cognitive locus of reading disability. *Annals of Dyslexia* 38:154–180.

Stanovich, K., Cunningham, A., and Cramer, B. 1984. Assessing phonological awareness in kindergarten children: Issues of task comparability. *Journal of Experimental Child Psychology* 38:175–190.

Stark, R., Bernstein, L., Condino, R., Bender, M., Tallal, P., and Catts, H. 1984. Four-year follow-up study of language impaired children. *Annals of Dyslexia* 34:49–68.

Tallal, P., Curtiss, S., and Kaplan, R. 1989. The San Diego longitudinal study: Evaluating the outcomes of preschool impairment in language development. Final Report, NINCDS.

Wagner, R. and Torgesen, J. 1987. The nature of phonological processing and its causal role in the acquisition of reading skills. *Psychological Bulletin* 101:192–212.

Weiner, P. 1985. The value of follow-up studies. *Topics in Language Disorders* 5:78–92.

Wilson, B. and Risucci, D. 1988. The early identification of developmental language disorders and the prediction of the acquisition of reading skills. *In* R. Masland and M. Masland (eds.). *Preschool Prevention of Reading Failure.* Parkton, MD: York Press.

Wolf, M. 1984. Naming, reading, and the dyslexias: A longitudinal overview. *Annals of Dyslexia* 34:87–136.

Wolf, M. 1986. Rapid alternating stimulus naming in the developmental dyslexias. *Brain and Language* 27:360–379.

Wolf, M. and Obregon, M. 1989. 88 children in search of a name: A five year investigation of rate, word-retrieval, and vocabulary in reading development and dyslexia. Paper presented at the biennial meeting of the Society for Research in Child Development, Kansas City, MO.

The Orthographic Code:
Developmental Trends in Reading-Disabled
and Normally-Achieving Children

Steven G. Zecker

Northwestern University
Evanston, Illinois

An auditory rhyme detection task was employed to examine orthographic code development in 27 reading-disabled (RD) and 27 normally-achieving (NA) children ranging in age from 7-0 to 11-5. The amount of orthographic facilitation (that is, the reduction in response latencies for orthographically similar as opposed to orthographically dissimilar rhyme pairs) was recorded for each subject. Results indicated that RD children exhibit significantly less facilitation overall than NA children and that RD children do not demonstrate comparable orthographic facilitation effects to NA children until they are about two years older than their NA peers. It is concluded that children with a reading disability have a lessened ability to access automatically and make available stored lexical information relating to orthography.

The development of spelling proficiency in normally-achieving and learning-disabled children has been a surprisingly little-researched area. In examining the literature one is struck by the much greater historical focus on research examining reading than spelling. Given that so many theorists have stated their beliefs that development of and disabilities in spelling and reading are so closely related (Boder 1973; Johnson and Myklebust 1967), this lack of research is even more surprising.

Annals of Dyslexia, Vol. 41, 1991.
ISSN 0736–9387

An important issue in examining spelling development concerns the ability of young spellers to access and use stored orthographic information when spelling. While it is quite clear that good adult spellers rely extensively on orthographic representations of words to aid in spelling (Frith 1985; Laxon, Coltheart, and Keating 1988), evidence for the use of orthographic structure in young spellers is quite limited. Currently there is more evidence in support of the use of orthographic information in early reading development than there is in the development of spelling (Frances 1984; Goswami 1986; Goswami and Bryant 1986; Reitsma 1983). This work has typically shown that even children as young as seven years of age can use orthographic analogies in reading. While it is unclear whether such young children are able easily to generalize orthographic information to new instances (Reitsma 1983), there can be little doubt that at least some seven-year-old children are aware of the importance of orthographic analogy in reading.

Not only is the role of orthographic information in the development of spelling a less-researched area than in reading, the results of the studies that have been conducted are equivocal. For example, Marsh and his colleagues (Marsh et al. 1980; Marsh et al. 1981) argue that children do not use orthographic analogy in spelling until rather late in development, at a point following the successful use of analogy in reading. However, Goswami (1988) has pointed out that the words used in the two Marsh et al. studies were quite difficult; it is possible that the youngest subjects (seven-year-olds) did not know how to spell the words that formed the bases for the orthographic analogies to be effectively used. Thus, it is difficult to conclude from this work that the use of orthographic analogies emerges at such a late developmental stage.

Campbell (1985) found evidence suggesting that some children as young as nine years of age could use orthographic knowledge to spell nonwords. However, some qualification of Campbell's results is also needed, as only proficient young spellers were able to use orthographic knowledge. The poorer spellers in her study relied on sub-word segments rather than a full and complete orthographic representation of the word. Thus, Campbell's results implicate both spelling ability (and, presumably, corresponding knowledge of phoneme-grapheme correspondence rules) and chronological age as being important determinants of a child's ability to use orthographic information in spelling.

In contrast to the Marsh et al. and Campbell studies, which suggested that young children cannot use orthographic knowledge effectively, support for the idea that even beginning readers and spellers retrieve and use orthographic information comes from several sources. Ehri (1980) demonstrated that children as young as seven years could acquire orthographic information and use it when spelling. In Ehri's

study children learned a series of nonwords printed in one of two phonetically identical ways. Following the learning of these nonwords,
children were asked to spell them. Examination of the children's written responses indicated that they consistently used the particular
orthography that they had learned earlier. Even misspellings of nonwords maintained the previously-learned orthography. Ehri's results
thus suggest that acquisition and use of orthographic information occur quite a bit earlier than do the results of Campbell (1985) and Marsh
et al. (1980, 1981).

    Consistent with Ehri's conclusion are the results of Goswami
(1988) who showed that beginning spellers (seven-year-olds) were able
to make orthographic analogies from a clue word to new words. In a
second experiment Goswami further showed that seven-year-old children could make orthographic analogies from stored knowledge, a situation more like actual spelling. However, these children did not vary
their use of orthographic analogies in situations where the spelling-
sound relations of the learned words varied in consistency, suggesting
that their use of orthographic analogy was not yet fully developed.

    Thus, as this brief review of the literature indicates, while there is
agreement that the use of stored orthographic knowledge is important
in learning to spell proficiently, there is a lack of consensus as to when
young children are able to use this knowledge. Some researchers suggest that children as young as seven years of age are able to use orthographic knowledge in spelling (Ehri 1980; Goswami 1988); others hold
that such use does not occur until at least nine years of age (Campbell
1985); while still others (Marsh et al. 1980, 1981) believe that children
must reach an age of eleven years before achieving proficiency in the
use of orthographic knowledge. Differences in the tasks and subjects
employed in these studies undoubtedly have contributed to the differing conclusions; however, these differences cannot be easily evaluated
so as to make their findings fully compatible.

    The situation with respect to developmental differences between
normally-achieving and learning-disabled children on the ability to
store and use orthographic information is even less clear. Historically,
many theorists have held that the spelling errors of dyslexics are qualitatively different from those of normally-achieving children (Bannatyne
1971; Critchley 1975; Farnham-Diggory 1978; Johnson and Myklebust
1967; Orton 1937). While the studies reviewed previously here used
nondisabled children as subjects, implicit in several of them was the
notion that learning-disabled children would differ from the nondisabled children on tasks measuring the use of orthographic knowledge.
However, qualitative differences between the two groups, if any, were
not predicted. Only Campbell (1985) contrasted good and poor spellers
in any way; as mentioned previously, her skilled seven-year-olds demon-

strated an ability to use orthographic analogy in spelling, while her poor spelling seven-year-olds were unable to do so. Recently, research examining the performance of learning-disabled and normal spellers on various spelling tests (Bruck 1988; Gerber 1984; DeMaster, Crossland, and Hasselling 1986; Moats 1983) suggests that disabled spellers are not qualitatively different in their use of underlying processes from their younger, normally-achieving peers. Thus, these studies suggest that disabled spellers lag developmentally behind their normally-achieving counterparts, but that they spell by using the same processes as younger spellers and do not typically resort to bizarre or idiosyncratic approaches. A reasonable prediction from this research, then, might be that a similar result would be noted for tasks measuring the use of orthographic knowledge: some learning-disabled spellers would use such knowledge, but in a manner more like that of younger children.

The researchers discussed thus far employed a variety of tasks in order to examine the development of orthographic knowledge. Such tasks as dictated spelling of real words (Gerber 1984; Goswami 1988), dictated spelling of nonwords (Bruck 1988; Laxon, Coltheart, and Keating 1988) and spelling in context (DeMaster, Crossland, and Hasselling 1986) have been used in these and other studies. Often extensive analyses of errors have accompanied these tasks and have provided a window on the processes used by spellers of varying ages and ability levels. These tasks (as well as others in which subjects are asked, in some way, to produce a spelled product) have all provided valuable information to researchers. Data addressing the development of spelling ability, the processes underlying spelling ability, and differences in spelling ability and spelling processes between various groups of subjects (including dyslexics and children with learning disabilities) have relied extensively on tasks of this type. However, these tasks by no means exhaust the list of techniques available to experimenters examining the spelling process. Recently, a very different task has shown promise as a means of examining the process underlying spelling: the rhyme detection task.

While the ability to create and recognize rhymes has been considered strongly related to (or perhaps a causal agent in) reading and writing (Bradley and Bryant 1983, 1985; Lundberg, Olofsson, and Wall 1980), the tasks used generally provided only gross information concerning accuracy. While such data have proven informative, they did little to enlighten us about the underlying processes involved. However, by modifying a typical rhyme recognition task considerably more data are observable and inferences can be drawn about underlying processes.

Seidenberg and Tanenhaus (1979) first used this rhyme detection task in a study where college subjects were asked to listen to a string of auditorially presented words and determine (by pressing a button) when a word (the target) which rhymed with the initial (cue) word was heard. The remaining words in the list were foils. Seidenberg and Tanenhaus recorded the reaction time (in msec) for each response. Of critical importance in their study was the orthographic relationships between the rhyming word pair. One-half of all rhyme pairs were orthographically similar (e.g., COAT-BOAT), while the other half were orthographically dissimilar (e.g., VOTE-BOAT).

The major finding obtained in this study was that the orthographically similar rhymes were detected significantly faster than the orthographically dissimilar rhymes. That is, decisions for the orthographically similar pairs were facilitated in the shared orthography in that condition. This finding of a "visual" effect on a task which could be performed entirely via an acoustic analysis of the spoken words was counterintuitive and sparked considerable related work. Seidenberg and Tanenhaus pointed out that their results were analogous to the similarly counterintuitive phonological effects observed on a visual lexical decision task by Meyer, Schvaneveldt, and Ruddy (1974); that is, lexical decisions to phonologically similar word pairs (e.g., POUCH-COUCH) were faster than to phonologically dissimilar word pairs (e.g., TOUCH-COUCH). Both Seidenberg and Tanenhaus, Schvaneveldt, and Ruddy (1974) and Meyer (1979) proposed similar explanations for their results: that hearing or reading the first word of the pair resulted in lexical access which automatically made available multiple lexical codes, among them the codes for orthography and phonology. It was further presumed that such lexical information spread (via a process such as "Spreading activation," as proposed by Collins and Loftus (1975) to other lexical entries sharing the same code information. This activation "primes" the lexical entries and results in facilitation (a lessening of response latency) when such an entry is a target word.

The orthographic effect is defined as the amount of facilitation, that is, the difference in response latency between the orthographically similar and orthographically dissimilar rhyme conditions. The presence of an orthography effect is interpreted as providing evidence that the subject is capable of automatically accessing, using, and integrating orthographic and phonological lexical information. Research has shown that the orthography effect is lateralized in the left cerebral hemisphere (Zecker et al. 1986), that it occurs only for words and not nonwords (Zecker and Nicklaus 1984), and that the magnitude of the effect correlates with spelling ability (Zecker 1989).

While the orthographic effect is not large (typically it is observed to be about 75 to 125 msec), it is robust when obtained with literate young adults. The present study seeks to extend previous findings with college-age subjects to normally-achieving and learning-disabled

children, so as to observe both developmental trends and possible differences between the two groups. Of particular interest will be the
comparison between young normally-achieving children and their
older reading-ability and spelling-ability matched learning-disabled
peers. This comparison has the potential to provide evidence concerning the similarities or differences between the two groups in terms of
the orthographic processes underlying spelling which they use.

Method

Subjects

A total of 54 subjects ranging in age from 7-0 to 11-5 participated in
this study. Of this total, 27 subjects were reading-disabled and 27 were
normally-achieving. Within the RD and NA groups, one-third (nine
subjects) fell into each of three age groups: young (7-0 to 8-5), middle
(8-6 to 10-0), and older (10-1 to 11-5). All subjects were of at least normal
intelligence, had no uncorrected deficits of sensory processes, and had
not experienced significant cultural or educational disadvantage. Subjects were obtained from a university learning disabilities clinic and
suburban public schools.

All children in the reading-disabled (RD) group were significantly
underachieving in reading, as determined by a discrepancy of at least
one standard deviation between their potential (as measured by a standardized intelligence test) and their score on a standardized measure
of reading decoding, the Wide Range Achievement Test-Revised
(WRAT-R, Jastak and Wilkinson 1984). All subjects in the normally-
achieving (NA) group were decoding (also as measured by the WRAT-R)
at a level commensurate with their overall potential.

An examination of the characteristics of the subjects, as indicated
by Table I, shows that the NA and RD groups differed by only two
points in their mean IQs, by two months in chronological age, and by
less than one month in grade placement. These differences between
the groups were all nonsignificant, $t < 1$ in each case. The two groups
did differ significantly on reading level, with subjects in the NA group
averaging 2.3 grade levels higher than subjects in the RD group ($t_{(52)} =$
3.58, $p < .05$).

Caution was used in selecting participants to assure that all subjects were unimpaired in other respects. No subject in the study possessed a neurological problem, sensory impairment, physical disability, or environmental disadvantage. Screening for these exclusionary
criteria was done by referring to available records or by discussion with
teachers. Although a precise determination of socioeconomic status was
not possible, virtually all subjects fell within the middle-SES range.

Table I
Characteristics of the subjects in the two groups used in this study

	Age			
	7–0 to 8–5	8–6 to 10–0	10–1 to 11–5	Total
Reading Disabled				
Number	9	9	9	27
Mean IQ	102.5	101.2	97.1	100.5
Mean Age	7–8	9–3	10–8	9–2
Mean Grade	2.6	3.9	5.2	3.9
Mean Reading Level	1.3	2.5	3.0	2.36
Group				
Normally Achieving				
Number	9	9	9	27
Mean IQ	99.5	104.2	104.0	102.5
Mean Age	7–11	9–5	10–6	9–4
Mean Grade	2.7	4.1	5.1	4.0
Mean Reading Level	3.1	5.0	5.8	4.6

Stimuli

An experimental session consisted of 128 trials, each trial consisting of a pair of words. On one-half of the trials the two words rhymed (a "yes" response) while the other one-half of the word pairs were nonrhymes. Of the 64 rhyming pairs, 32 formed orthographically similar rhymes (e.g., BUM-GUM), while the other 32 pairs formed orthographically dissimilar rhymes (e.g., THUMB-GUM). The 64 nonrhyming pairs were created by using the same words from the rhyming condition; however, by taking one word from each of two rhyming pairs, a nonrhyme pair was created (e.g., BUM-BIRD).

All words were high frequency, monosyllabic words and were selected so that all would be in the receptive vocabulary of even the youngest subjects. A set of eight practice trials preceded the 128 experimental trials. None of the words used in the practice trials was used in the experimental trials.

Procedure and apparatus

The stimuli were recorded by a male speaker on a stereo cassette recorder. Subjects listened to the stimuli with stereo headphones. A Gerbrands electronic voice key received the output from the tape recorder. A Lafayette digital reaction timer connected to the voice key was activated when the second word of each stimulus pair was initiated.

The 128 trials consisted of a random ordering of pairs from all conditions. In an attempt to reduce fatigue and/or boredom effects, a two-minute rest break was provided to all subjects after the 64th word pair. Each trial consisted of a spoken word followed 1-sec later by a second word. An approximately 7-sec pause separated the trials. Subjects were instructed that their task was to indicate whether the words formed a rhyme (a "yes" response) or a nonrhyme (a "no" response). Subjects were instructed to respond as quickly as possible without making errors. Decisions about whether the word pairs were rhymes were indicated by pressing the appropriate telegraph key. The hands used to indicate the responses were counterbalanced across subjects. Both response latencies (in msec) and accuracy were recorded for each trial.

Results

Analysis of response errors indicated that even subjects as young as seven years of age find the rhyme decision task to be quite easy. Across all trials and all subjects, errors occurred on only 4.41 percent of all word pairs. Although infrequent, more errors were observed for the RD group (mean of 7.0 out of 128 trials or 5.4 percent) than for the NA group (mean of 4.2 errors out of 128 trials or 3.3 percent), $t(52) = 3.10$, $p < .05$. In general, there was a trend toward making more errors on "no" trials (that is, calling a nonrhyming pair a rhyming pair) than on "yes" trials, although this difference was not statistically significant. Similarly, a nonsignificant trend was noted for age, with subjects in the youngest group making more errors (mean of 6.1 percent) than those subjects in the middle (mean of 3.7 percent) or older (mean of 3.4 percent) age groups. These error patterns could not be explained in terms of a speed-accuracy trade-off, since overall subjects in the RD group responded significantly more slowly than subjects in the NA group $(F_{(1,48)}, 6.10, p < .056)$. Similarly the youngest group of subjects was significantly slower to respond than the middle age group, which in turn was slower than the oldest subjects $(F_{(2,48)} = 5.54, p < .05)$. Thus, those subjects who made the most errors (the RD and young subjects) also were the slowest responders, ruling out any speed-accuracy trade-off.

In analyzing the response latency data, only latencies for correct responses were used. Since errors were infrequent, little data were excluded from the analysis. Examination of the distribution of the response latency data for each subject within each treatment combination revealed that in many cases the data were positively skewed. Thus, median latencies were used rather than means for all latency analyses. The latency data were analyzed separately for the rhyming pairs and the nonrhyming pairs.

The analysis of the latency data for the rhyming pairs was carried out using a 2 (Groups) × 3 (Age) factorial analysis of variance (ANOVA). The amount of facilitation due to orthographic similarity (that is, the median latency for the orthographically similar rhyme pairs) was considered the dependent variable. The decision to use the amount of facilitation as the dependent variable rather than treating orthographic similarity (similar vs. dissimilar) as a repeated measures factor within the ANOVA design was made due to concerns about meeting the additional assumptions required with a mixed-model ANOVA. Specifically, the apparent lack of compound symmetry would have mandated a much more conservative Geisser and Greenhouse (1958) F-test be used (Marascuilo and Serlin 1988). By using as the dependent variable a value which represents the difference between the levels of the potential third factor, the use of this overly conservative test was avoided.

The ANOVA on the amount of orthographic facilitation observed on the "yes" (rhyming) trials indicated that the main effects for both age ($F_{(2,48)} = 9.01, p < .05$) and group ($F_{(1,48)} = 8.08, p < .05$), as well as the age × group interaction ($F_{(2,48)} = 11.01, p < .05$) attained significance. Examination of the amount of orthographic facilitation observed (see Table II) indicates that subjects in the RD group shows less facilitation than NA subjects and that younger subjects show less facilitation than older subjects. Examination of the interaction shows that RD subjects show little in terms of a facilitation effect until beyond ten years of age, while NA subjects show facilitation (although in differing amounts) at all three age levels.

Follow-up tests indicated that the age main effect was obtained because the youngest subjects showed significantly less facilitation than either the middle or older students, $p < .05$ in both cases. The means for the middle and older subjects were not significantly different, $p > .05$. A follow-up test examining the age × group interaction indicated that subjects in the NA group demonstrated significantly more orthographic facilitation than RD subjects for the youngest ($p < .05$) and middle ($p < .01$) age groups, while the NA and RD subjects did not differ in the oldest age group $p > .05$.

Analysis of the "no" data (for nonrhyme pairs) examined only overall latencies, since no contrast between orthographically similar

Table II
Amount of orthographic facilitation (in msec) by age level for the normally-achieving and reading-disabled groups.

	Age			
	7–0 to 8–5	8–6 to 10–0	10–1 to 11–5	Total
Reading Disabled Group	−6	19	63	28.7
Normally Achieving	38	106	85	76.3
Mean	16	62.5	79	52.5

and orthographically dissimilar nonrhymes was designed. Analysis of the responses to nonrhymes indicated significant main effects for both group ($F_{(1,48)}$ = 6.69, p < .05) and age ($F_{(2,48)}$ = 5.12, p < .05, but a non-significant interaction of group and age ($F_{(2,48)}$ = 2.17, p > .05). Examination of means indicated that RD subjects were slower (by 124 msec) than NA subjects and that the youngest subjects were slower than the middle and older subjects (by 124 and 151 msec, respectively). Since further examination or analysis of the nonrhyming data is not relevant to the present examination of the development of the orthographic code, additional treatment of the data was not performed.

Discussion

The results of this study indicate that the rhyme detection task can be used successfully with children as young as seven years of age to provide evidence about the lexical code processes underlying spelling. The subjects in this study found the task to be interesting, and the results demonstrated that the task was well within their ability level. Error rates were low for subjects in both groups and across all three age levels.

Moreover, the task demonstrated its ability to show developmental trends and group differences in the access, use, and integration of orthographic information. Analysis of the data for rhyming pairs indicated that the normally-achieving children showed some effect of orthography at all three age levels, although only subjects in the two oldest groups (that is, those over an age of 8-6) showed an amount of facilitation comparable to that observed in older subjects. Thus, these results suggest that the ability to use orthographic information automatically occurs quite early in terms of age and/or reading ability, and that changes from age 8-6 up to the college years are not great.

A rather striking finding not apparent from examining the group means presented in Table II concerns the consistency of the orthography effects as observed in NA subjects. For example, all nine of the NA subjects in the older group showed an orthographic facilitation effect greater than 45 msec, as did seven of the nine subjects in the middle age group. Thus, the robust nature of the effect for orthography as observed with college-age subjects (Seidenberg and Tanenhaus 1979; Zecker et al. 1986) is also observed with much younger children. While the subjects in the youngest NA group did demonstrate a small orthography effect, they did so in a much less consistent manner than did the subjects in the two older groups. Only three subjects out of nine had orthographic facilitation effects larger than 45 msec, and three had effects with a magnitude of less than ten msec. Thus, it appears that some of the youngest subjects showed evidence of a rudimentary orthographic code, while others had not yet begun to demonstrate any such process.

In contrast to the NA subjects, children in the RD group showed an effect of orthography only at the oldest age level. While this effect of 63 msec was significant, it was nonetheless of a lesser (although non-significant) magnitude than for the same age subjects in the NA group. Subjects in the youngest RD groups showed no evidence of having the ability to access and use orthographic information; in fact, not one subject of the nine demonstrated an orthographic facilitation effect larger than 33 msec. Five subjects actually had negative values for their facilitation effects, clearly demonstrating that they were unable to use stored orthographic information to help them in making the rhyme decisions. Similar results were observed for the middle RD group; the comparison between these subjects and their same age NA peers shows how differently the orthographic code develops in the two groups.

Thus, the results clearly support the notion that the orthographic code develops at different rates in normally-achieving and reading-disabled children. It is quite clear that age, while related to the magnitude of the orthographic effect, is not the primary determining factor for automaticity of use of the orthographic code. Across all subjects there was a correlation of .30 between chronological age and amount of orthographic facilitation. This correlation was higher for NA subjects (.36) than for RD subjects (.20). While statistically significant, the magnitude of the relationship is small and accounts for less than ten percent of the total variability in the effect of orthography.

Reading level, on the other hand, appears to be more strongly related to amount of orthographic facilitation observed. Reading level correlates more highly with amount of facilitation for all subjects combined (.52) as well as for the NA and RD groups separately (.56 and .48, respectively). Thus, one might conclude that the ability to decode single printed words in an efficient and accurate manner is in some way strongly related to the ability to make available and use stored orthographic information automatically when provided with a spoken word. Intuitively this relationship is appealing since both decoding and rhyme detection are cross-modal tasks: decoding requires a phonological representation to be generated from a visual stimulus (the printed word), while demonstrating an orthography effect necessitates a generation of a visually-based orthographic representation when given an auditory stimulus. Although overly simplistic, decoding and rhyme detection might be thought of as requiring similar pairs of processes operating in opposite directions.

However appealing the idea that decoding ability strongly relates to the ability to access and use orthographic information, there must be more involved. The correlation between decoding ability and amount of facilitation suggests that only 25 percent of the variability in the amount of orthographic facilitation can be explained by decoding ability. Further, the oldest group of RD subjects decoded at a third-grade level, virtually an identical level to the youngest NA subjects, yet the older RD subjects averaged 25 msec more facilitation than the young NA subjects. Although not statistically significant this difference suggests that there are factors in addition to decoding that influence the automatic access and use of orthographic information. A comparison of the middle and older RD subjects makes this point even more strongly. Although these two age groups differed by only one-half grade level in decoding ability, the older RD subjects demonstrated more than three times as much orthographic facilitation, a statistically significant difference. This result suggests that either reading level has a very strong and sudden influence on orthographic code use between second and third grade (an unlikely possibility), or else some additional factor is influencing the amount of facilitation observed.

One possible explanation is that it is not ability per se that is the determining factor in demonstrating an orthography effect, but rather previous experience in reading and spelling, in combination with ability, that determines whether an orthography effect is obtained and in what magnitude. Orthography effects are felt to be due to unconscious, automatic lexical processes. Automaticity is known to result from repeated experiences with a task or process. Thus, it may be reasonable to speculate that children who have had greater exposure to the printed word and to spelling tasks (e.g., ten- and eleven-year-olds reading at a third-grade level) would have somewhat greater automaticity as a sheer result of experience than those with less experience (e.g., seven- and eight-year-olds also reading at a third-grade level or eight- and nine-year-olds reading at a mid-second-grade level).

This notion that orthography effects are due to an interaction of exposure to reading and spelling along with some minimal reading level is consistent with ideas such as Stanovich's (1986) concerning what he termed Matthew effects, whereby those who possess better reading skills read more than their peers who do not possess such skills, and, as a result, realize added benefits in a variety of areas related to reading. Stanovich and West (1989), after examining individual differences in exposure to print, concluded that orthographic processing skills appear to be linked to print exposure. Stanovich has used this argument to explain why the gap between normally-achieving and learning-disabled children in reading-related ability tends to grow as the children grow older and the discrepancy in the amount of reading activities between these groups increases. However, it would seem that such a hypothesis could also apply when, for example, comparing reading-disabled subjects nearly two years different in age, but reading within one-half grade level of each other, as was the case with the middle and older groups in the present study. Not only do the older subjects have a slightly higher decoding ability, but they also have benefited from substantially more experience with reading that may have allowed the automaticity of certain processes underlying reading (one being the code for orthography) to develop.

At the beginning of this paper, it was noted that there is considerable disagreement among researchers concerning whether learning-disabled and normally-achieving children spell via similar mechanisms, or whether learning-disabled children tend to resort to bizarre or idiosyncratic strategies. The results of this study seem to suggest that while the code for orthography develops at a much slower rate in learning-disabled children, such children will eventually demonstrate an effect of orthography equal to that of their normally-achieving peers. Thus, LD children beyond the age of about ten would appear to possess the underlying lexical code for spelling.

Much less clear, however, are the implications of the results of the younger learning-disabled children who showed little, if any, evidence of an orthographic code. It seems clear that they are unable to access automatically and make available orthographic information to help them to spell. However, it is unknown how these children do attempt to spell words; just because they lack automaticity of orthographic activation does not mean that they must resort to unusual, idiosyncratic processes when they spell. After all, their young normally-achieving peers also lack automaticity of activation of orthographic information, yet they are able to spell in a generally consistent, rule-governed manner that ultimately results in the creation of the underlying code for orthography. Thus the present results, while suggesting that older LD children do possess an underlying code for orthography, do not necessarily mean that younger LD without such a code do not have the ability to spell by using conventional strategies.

In summary, the rhyme detection task is a promising alternative technique for allowing a window into the processes underlying spelling in children. While the present study employed a relatively small number of subjects and items across a relatively narrow age span, it was nonetheless possible to observe both clear developmental trends and between-groups differences. Future work with this task can more carefully determine the ages at which automaticity of orthographic access takes place and provide further evidence about those areas of achievement and underlying processes most strongly related to the effect. By expanding the total number of word pairs and including multiple examples of particular orthographic patterns (for example, pairs made from the words *toe, hoe, foe, bow, low,* and *mow* or perhaps *face, lace, pace, base,* and *case*) would allow researchers to see whether certain orthographic combinations are acquired earlier developmentally, or conversely whether some patterns are particularly problematic for children with learning disabilities.

References

Bannatyne, A. 1971. *Language, Reading and Learning Disabilities.* Springfield, IL: Charles Thomas.

Boder, E. 1973. Developmental dyslexia: A diagnostic approach based on three atypical reading-spelling patterns. *Developmental Medicine and Child Neurology* 15:663–687.

Bradley, L. and Bryant, P. E. 1983. Categorizing sounds and learning to read—A causal connection. *Nature* 301:419–421.

Bradley, L. and Bryant, P. E. 1985. *Rhyme and reason in reading and spelling.* IARLD Monographs No. 1. Ann Arbor, MI: The University of Michigan Press.

Bruck, M. 1988. The word recognition and spelling of dyslexic children. *Reading Research Quarterly* 22:51–69.

Campbell, R. 1985. When children write nonwords to dictation. *Journal of Experimental Child Psychology* 40:152–180.

Collins, A. M. and Loftus. E. F. 1975. A spreading activation theory of semantic processing. *Psychological Review* 82:407–428.

Critchley, M. 1975. Specific developmental dyslexia. *In* E. H. Lenneberg and E. Lenneberg (eds.). *Foundations of Language Development: A multidisciplinary approach.* Vol. 2 New York: Academic Press.

DeMaster, V. K., Crossland, C. L., and Hasselling, T. S. 1986. Consistency of learning disabled students' spelling performance. *Learning Disability Quarterly* 9:89–96.

Ehri, L. 1980. The development of orthographic images. *In* U. Frith (ed.). *Cognition Processes in Spelling.* London: Academic Press.

Farnham-Diggory, S. 1978. *Learning Disabilities.* Cambridge, MA: Harvard University Press.

Frances, H. 1984. Children's knowledge of orthography in learning to read. *British Journal of Educational Psychology* 54:8–23.

Frith, U. 1985. The usefulness of the concept of unexpected reading failure. Comments on reading retardation revisited. *British Journal of Experimental Psychology* 54:8–23.

Geisser, S. and Greenhouse, S. W. 1988. An extension of Box's results on the use of the F-distribution in multivariate analysis. *The Annals of Mathematical Statistics* 29:885–891.

Gerber, M. 1984. Orthographic problem-solving ability of learning-disabled and normally-achieving children. *Journal of Learning Disabilities* 7:157–164.

Goswami, U. 1986. Children's use of analogy in learning to read: A developmental study. *Journal of Experimental Child Psychology* 42:72–83.

Goswami, U. and Bryant, P. E. 1986. Rhyming, analogy, and children's reading. Paper presented at the Conference on Early Reading Acquisition, Centre for Cognitive Science, March 1986, University of Texas-Austin.

Goswami, U. 1988. Children's use of analogy in learning to spell. *British Journal of Developmental Psychology* 6:21–33.

Jastak, S. and Wilkinson, G. S. 1984. *Wide Range Achievement Test-Revised.* Wilmington, DE: Jastak Associates, Inc.

Johnson, D. J. and Myklebust, H. R. 1967. *Learning Disabilities: Educational principles and practice.* New York: Grune and Stratton.

Laxon, V., Coltheart, V., and Keating, C. 1988. Children find friendly words friendly too: words with many orthographic neighbors are easier to read and spell. *British Journal of Educational Psychology* 58:103–119.

Lundberg, I., Olofsson, A., and Wall, S. 1980. Reading and spelling skills in the first school years predicted from phonemic awareness skills in kindergarten. *Scandinavian Journal of Psychology* 21:159–173.

Marascuilo, L. A. and Serlin, R. C. 1988. *Statistical Methods for the Social and Behavioral Sciences*. New York: W. H. Freeman.

Marsh, G., Friedman, M. P., Welch, V., and Desberg, P. 1980. Development of strategies in learning to spell. *In* U. Frith, (ed.). *Cognitive Strategies in Spelling*. London: Academic Press.

Marsh, G., Friedman, M. P., Desberg, P., and Saterdahl, K. 1981. Comparison of reading and spelling strategies in normal and reading disabled children. *In* M. P. Friedman, J. P. Das, and N. O'Connor (eds.). *Intelligence and Learning* (pp. 363–367). New York: Plenum.

Meyer, D. E., Schvaneveldt, R. W., and Ruddy, M. G. 1974. Functions of graphemic and phonemic codes in visual word recognition. *Memory and Cognition* 2:309–321.

Moats, L. C. 1983. A comparison of the spelling errors of older dyslexic and second-grade normal children. *Annals of Dyslexia* 33:121–139.

Orton, S. T. 1937. *Reading, Writing and Speech Problems in Children*. New York: W. W. Norton and Company.

Reitsma, P. 1983. Printed word reading in beginning readers. *Journal of Experimental Child Psychology* 36:321–339.

Seidenberg, M. S. and Tanenhaus, M. K. 1979. Orthographic effects in rhyme monitoring. *Journal of Experimental Psychology: Human Learning and Memory* 5:546–554.

Stanovich, K. 1986. Matthew effects in reading: some consequences of individual differences in the acquisition of literacy. *Reading Research Quarterly* 21:360–407.

Stanovich, K. and West, R. 1989. Exposure to print and orthographic processing. *Reading Research Quarterly* 24:402–433.

Zecker, S. G. 1989. Orthographic code development in normal and reading disabled children. At the Orton Dyslexia Society Conference, November 1989, Dallas, TX.

Zecker, S. G. and Nicklaus, K. 1984. *Lexical access and orthographic priming*. At the Eastern Psychological Association Convention, April 1984, Baltimore, MD.

Zecker, S. G., Tanenhaus, M. K., Alderman, L., and Siqueland, L. 1986. Laterality of lexical codes in auditory word recognition. *Brain and Language* 29:372–389.

Phonological Awareness Training and Remediation of Analytic Decoding Deficits in a Group of Severe Dyslexics

Ann W. Alexander
Helen G. Andersen
Patricia C. Heilman

The Morris Center
Gainesville, Florida

Kytja K. S. Voeller

University of Florida
Gainesville, Florida

Joseph K. Torgesen

Florida State University
Tallahassee, Florida

The goal of the present study was to evaluate the effectiveness of the Auditory Discrimination in Depth Program (ADD) in remediating the analytic decoding deficits of a group of severe dyslexics. A group of ten severely dyslexic students ranging in age from 93 to 154 months were treated in a clinic setting for 38 to 124 hours (average of 65 hours). Pre- and post-treatment testing was done with the Woodcock Reading Mastery Test and the Lindamood Auditory Conceptualization to assess changes in phonological awareness and analytic decoding

Annals of Dyslexia, Vol. 41, 1991.
ISSN 0736–9387

skills. Results revealed statistically significant gains in phonological awareness and analytic decoding skills.

Although the concept of developmental dyslexia, or specific reading disability, continues to be a focus of controversy (Coles 1987), there is an emerging consensus on at least two conclusions about the disorder. First, most would accept the idea that there may be a number of different causes for specific reading disabilities. Second, there is wide agreement that the greatest reading problem for dyslexic children involves difficulty acquiring accurate and fluent word identification skills (Stanovich 1982; 1988). Most dyslexic children have great difficulty learning to apply the "alphabetic principle" to take advantage of grapheme-phoneme regularities in reading unfamiliar words. They are often unable to attain fully alphabetic (Frith 1985) reading skills. Not only does this problem limit their ability to read independently, but it may also prevent subsequent development of more sophisticated orthographic word reading strategies (Frith 1985).

An interesting case study of a child with this type of reading disorder was recently presented by Snowling and Hulme (1989). When originally tested at the age of 8 years, 5 months, JM had a WISC-R IQ of 123, but only reached the 7-year level on the Neal Analysis of Reading Ability. Further study of his reading skills showed that his sight vocabulary was equivalent to that of a group of 7-year-olds with normal reading skills, but his ability to pronounce nonwords was seriously impaired in comparison with them. He had essentially no skills in arriving at word pronunciation through an analysis of phonological structure as represented by letters. Following this intitial testing, JM was placed in a residential school that specialized in teaching dyslexic children. The educational program was multisensory and emphasized training in grapheme-phoneme correspondences, use of English spelling patterns and conventions, and other content designed to promote alphabetic reading skills.

After 45 months of training, at the age of 12 years, JM's reading skills were reexamined. His word reading accuracy had increased between 26 and 31 months, while his comprehension scores had improved by 53 months. Almost all of the improvement in reading accuracy occurred because of growth in his sight vocabulary. For example, when compared with a group of 10-year-olds who had a similar overall reading level, he read familiar words almost as well. However, on a set of single-syllable nonwords that the normal readers read with 91 percent accuracy, JM attained a score of only 26 percent. In fact, his reading skills for nonwords were still one standard deviation below that of the normal 7-year-olds to whom he had been compared earlier!

The most widely accepted current explanation for the difficulties dyslexic children experience in attaining alphabetic reading skills involves a dysfunction "in the phonological component of their natural capacity for language" (Liberman, Shankweiler, and Liberman 1989, p. 1). This difficulty in processing the phonological features of language can be shown on a variety of non-reading tasks that assess either: 1) awareness of the phonological structure of words; 2) ability to represent phonological information in memory; or, 3) subtle speech perception and production skills (Wagner and Torgesen 1987). Either singly or together, these processing deficits are frequently associated with reading difficulties similar to those described in the case study in that they are especially difficult to remediate.

For example, a recent follow-up study of children with severe phonological representation problems showed that these children made almost no progress over a ten-year span in improving their analytic decoding skills (Torgesen in press). These children had received regular instruction in a program for learning-disabled children, and their math skills had reached high school levels. In a study of different subtypes of reading-disabled children, Lyon (1985) found that two subgroups with phonological processing disabilities were among those who made almost no reading progress in a program that involved explicit instruction in phonic strategies for reading.

More recently, Lovett, Benson, and Olds (in press) reported a study in which dyslexic children were randomly assigned to one of three treatment conditions providing training in word recognition and decoding skills, oral and written language, or classroom survival skills. The word recognition and decoding program produced the greatest treatment gains. However, Lovett, Benson, and Olds observed that their subjects improved due to a greater reliance on a whole word reading approach rather than on a phonological decoding approach. These authors suggested that dyslexic children may be incapable of acquiring effective phonological decoding skills. Other programs which have reported effective intervention with heterogeneous samples of reading-disabled children (Ogden, Hindman, and Turner 1989), report much less success with older children who are more severely impaired.

Although it is clear that dyslexic children with phonological processing difficulties can make significant progress in reading through the development of their sight vocabularies and comprehension skills, helping them to acquire better alphabetic reading skills remains a desirable educational goal. Alphabetic reading skills take advantage of the generative qualities of English orthography, and they open to the reader important clues to word identity so that tens of thousands of words can be read independently (Liberman 1987). One important new intervention technique to improve the alphabetic reading skills of dyslexic children is suggested by research on their phonological processing deficits. Specifically, this research has investigated phonological awareness as it relates to the acquisition of early reading skills.

Phonological awareness can be defined as one's sensitivity to, or explicit awareness of, the phonological structure of words in one's language (Liberman, Shankweiler, and Liberman 1989). It can be conceptualized as a kind of understanding or awareness that allows children to see the connections between written and oral language. There are large individual differences in phonological awareness among young children, and children with reading disabilities continue to show difficulties in this area even at older ages (Bradley and Bryant 1978; Gough and Tunmer 1986). Not only is performance on phonological awareness tasks in kindergarten predictive of later reading difficulties (Lundberg, Olofsson and Wall 1980; Stanovich, Cunningham, and Feeman 1984), but also there is beginning evidence that early training in phonological awareness may facilitate the acquisition of word reading ability in young children (Bradley and Bryant 1985; Lundberg, Frost, and Peterson 1988).

These latter studies raise the possibility that phonological awareness training may also be a useful part of educational interventions for many dyslexic children. In fact, one early study (Williams 1980) did show that the analytic decoding skills of learning-disabled children in first grade could be improved significantly by a program of phonics instruction that contained explicit training in phonological awareness. However, this study did not continue long enough to test the limits of awareness training with these children, nor did it focus specifically on reading-disabled children with phonological processing problems. The purpose of the present paper is to report a clinical training study that applied in-depth training in phonological awareness as part of a program to remediate the alphabetic reading deficiencies of a group of older dyslexic children. Although this study did not employ a control group design, the magnitude and consistency of the treatment effects, in light of earlier reported training difficulties in this area, allow us to conclude that the training method employed has substantial promise for dyslexic children.

Method

Subjects

The subjects were ten Caucasian children selected from a larger clinic population on the basis of discrepancies between their general intelligence and their word reading and phonological awareness skills. The children came from homes in the middle to upper-middle SES range, were all attending private schools or receiving special reading help in the public schools at the time of referral, and all attained a Full

Scale Intelligence score above 85. Their average age was 129 months, with a range from 93 to 154, and they were equally divided by sex. Their phonological awareness skills were assessed with the Linda-mood Auditory Conceptualization Test (LAC) (Lindamood and Linda-mood 1979), which tests awareness of individual phonemes in words as well as the ability to manipulate the phonemes in various ways. Standard scores are not available for this test, as the distribution of scores is bimodal at the age of our subjects. All subjects in our sample attained scores on the LAC that were substantially below the level expected for children of their age and IQ. Furthermore, nine of the ten displayed a discrepancy of at least 1.5 SD between their full scale IQ and their scores on the Word Identification subtest of the Woodcock Reading Mastery Test (Woodcock 1973). One of the lower IQ subjects did not have a discrepancy this large, but had a Word Identification score more than 2 SD below that expected for her age. Although two subjects had previously been treated with Ritalin, none was receiving pharmacological treatment at the time of the study. Descriptive characteristics for each subject are provided in Table I.

Procedure

The pretest measures included the LAC, and the Word Identification and Word Attack subtests from the Woodcock Reading Mastery Test (Woodcock 1973). The word analysis test requires children to read a series of increasingly difficult phonologically regular nonwords, and provides a sensitive measure of alphabetic reading skills (Frith 1985). Following administration of the pretests, all children were provided training with the Auditory Discrimination in Depth (ADD) program developed by Charles and Patricia Lindamood (Lindamood and Lindamood 1975). The training was provided in one hour sessions four

Table I
Characteristics of Individual Children in Treatment Group

Subject	Age (mos)	Sex	FS IQ	Parent Education/Occupation
1	144	M	101	M-Master's, F-some college
2	142	F	126	M & F College Degree
3	130	M	89	M & F College Degree
4	154	F	105	M-teacher, F-1 yr. college
5	145	F	86	M & F Teachers
6	93	M	96	M-Ph.D. Cand., F-B.A. deg.
7	132	F	108	M-R.N., F-M.D.
8	107	M	115	M-R.N., F-M.D.
9	103	M	133	M-Nurse Anesth., F-M.D.
10	136	F	108	M-1 yr. college, F-B.A. deg

times a week for seven subjects; and intensively (four hours per day for six weeks) for three of the subjects. The training was provided in the school setting for three subjects and at the Morris Center for seven of the subjects. Number of hours training varied between 38 and 124, with an average of 64 hours. Training was concluded when the child had finished all levels of the program.

Description of Training Program

The Auditory Discrimination in Depth (ADD) Program is a highly structured, scripted program that develops oral and phonological awareness. It was used as outlined in the manual. All students followed the same training sequence. The training sequence included oral and phonological awareness training and generalization of the training to spelling and reading.

Subjects were first trained in oral awareness. The ADD Program uses a multisensory approach to learning. The auditory elements of speech sounds are not separated from the more basic oral motor activity that produces them. The subjects learned to use sensory information from the ear, eye and mouth to identify, classify, and label sounds. For example, 16 individual speech sounds, or phonemes (/p/, /b/, /t/, /d/, /k/, /g/, /f/, /v/, /th/, /th/, /s/, /z/, /sh/, /zh/, /ch/, /j/), were categorized into eight voiced/unvoiced pairs or cognates. The pairs were labeled according to their distinctive oral motor characteristics. The students discovered, by observing their mouth movements in a mirror, that /p/ and /b/ are made by closing the lips and then allowing the air to explode or "pop out" of the mouth. The label "lip popper" was chosen to describe the salient oral motor characteristics of the bilabial plosives. The /p/ was identified as the quiet (unvoiced) lip popper.

After discovering, describing, and labeling the oral motor characteristics of 39 speech sounds, the student selected a mouth form picture that pictorially represented each speech sound. Criterion for completion of oral awareness training was 100 percent accuracy on the check out task requiring the student to describe the oral motor characteristics, and identify the label and mouth form picture for each speech sound.

A basic assumption of the ADD program is that using sensory feedback from the eye, ear, and mouth in identifying, classifying, and labeling the consonant and vowel sounds leads to a deeper perception of the sounds. Each sound emerges as a distinct entity because the nature of its contrast to other sounds is experienced consciously. The labels which describe the salient motor characteristics of the speech sounds facilitate the development of metalinguistic ability. After establishing conscious awareness of the distinctive oral motor characteristics of speech sounds, the task of associating the sounds with their corresponding alphabet symbols was introduced.

Following oral awareness and sound/symbol association training, all subjects received phonological awareness training. Phonological awareness training provided experience at a level prior to where most phonics or reading programs begin. Tracking sounds via a concrete medium is one of the keys to the ADD Program. In a series of problem-solving exercises, the students used mouth form pictures and then colored blocks to represent speech sounds. By arranging and manipulating pictures or blocks (encoding), the students indicated the number, order, and sameness or difference of sounds they felt/heard.

Figure 1 provides examples of the problem types presented during this phase. As in the example, the sounds were first presented as isolated units. In the next phase, the subjects were taught to represent the sequences of sounds when they were pronounced as a single syllable. As students gained experience in tracking and representing sequences of speech sounds with a concrete medium (pictures and blocks), the skill was generalized to representing sequences of speech sounds with letter symbols. Students practiced spelling and reading phonetically regular pseudowords of increasing complexity. As reading and spelling pseudowords stabilized, real words were introduced and phonics rules were explored.

Results

The dependent variables that were used to assess effects of the training procedures were scores on the LAC, and Word Identification and Word Attack scores from the Woodcock Reading Mastery Test. Pre- and posttest scores on each of these measures, as well as number of hours of training for each subject, are reported in Table II.

A score of 100 on the LAC is a perfect score. All the children improved substantially in their performance on the LAC, and all but one attained a perfect score at the conclusion of treatment. Both the size and consistency of these effects allow us to conclude that the ADD program provided very effective instruction in phonological awareness for the subjects in this sample.

In terms of its effects on reading, the program produced significant gains on both measures. Not only were the changes significant for the group as a whole (Word Identification, $t(9) = 7.5$, $p < .001$, Word Attack, $t(9) = 5.4$, $p < .001$), but they were very consistent across subjects. Furthermore, performance on the Word Attack subtest was "normalized" in the sense that the achievement of all subjects was now in

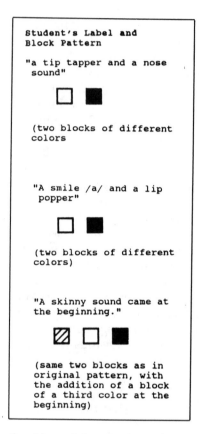

Figure 1. Examples of problem solving exercises using colored tiles to represent sounds (Lindamood and Lindamood, 1975, pp. 9 and 10).

the average range. Only two subjects failed to improve their performance substantially on both reading tests. These were highly intelligent students who had been included in the sample because of a discrepancy between their Full Scale IQ and their reading scores, but who had been reading in the average range prior to treatment.

The normalization of scores on the Word Attack subtest suggests that, at the conclusion of treatment, the children had available to them a powerful new strategy for reading words. In order to examine possible changes in their reading strategies between the pre- and posttests, we examined the kinds of errors they made on the Word Identification subtest. We borrowed an error analysis scheme from Snowling, Stackhouse, and Rack (1986) that is designed to elucidate movement from a logographic, or whole word/visual reading strategy, to a more alphabetic one. We coded errors in four categories: 1) logographic—error shares more than 50 percent of its letters with its target, and is always a

Table II
Performance on Phonological Awareness and Reading Measures

Subject	Hours of Treatment	LAC		Word Ident		Word Attack	
		Pre	Post	Pre	Post	Pre	Post
1	57	70	100	75	85	63	97
2	47	88	100	78	85	80	97
3	124	58	100	60	78	68	99
4	84	33	100	57	65	83	103
5	57	45	100	68	85	62	92
6	78	31	100	74	86	83	98
7	47	63	99	80	98	72	96
8	67	51	100	90	99	97	99
9	38	64	100	96	102	99	100
10	53	76	100	73	93	70	103
Mean	65.2	57.9	99.9	75.1	87.6	77.7	98.4

real word (e.g., pint/paint, lettuce/letter); 2) lexical-sounding—error shares less than 50 percent of letters with target, is always a real word, thought to reflect partial use of grapheme-phoneme skills (e.g., hatch/ ham, sausage/salt); 3) unsuccessful sound attempts—errors reflect greater dependence on alphabetic strategy, are always nonwords, but share significant phonological elements with target word (e.g., urgent/ urgruent, prudent/purden); 4) alphabetic—acceptable phonic readings of irregular words (e.g., said/sade).

Unfortunately, pretest errors were available for only seven of the subjects, as three had been pretested in another clinic and actual responses were not available. Table III presents a categorization of all sub-

Table III
Types of Errors Made on the Word Identification Subtest

Subject	Logographic		Lexical-Sound		USA		Alphabetic	
	Pre	Post	Pre	Post	Pre	Post	Pre	Post
1	4	2	2	0	1	4	0	2
2	6	2	1	0	4	6	0	1
3	7	0	5	0	1	8	0	3
4	–	1	–	1	–	19	–	1
5	3	2	2	0	3	4	0	2
6	–	1	–	0	–	10	–	0
7	6	5	0	0	5	3	0	0
8	–	2	–	0	–	2	–	0
9	9	5	3	0	4	6	0	0
10	5	3	3	0	4	3	0	1

jects' posttest errors as well as pretest errors made by the seven subjects for whom complete data were available.

For purposes of analysis, the two categories reflecting primarily a logographic strategy were combined, as were the two categories reflecting a greater reliance on alphabetic strategies. Furthermore, analysis was restricted to the seven subjects for whom complete data were available. At pretest, 72 percent of the errors were logographic, while at posttest, only 30 percent were. This represents a significant, $X2 = 23.5$, $p < .001$, change in the type of error, and it suggests that the subjects had a greater tendency to use an alphabetic strategy at the posttest than at the pretest.

Discussion

The purpose of this study was to assess the effects of extensive training in phonological awareness as part of an intervention program for older dyslexic children with word identification difficulties. All of the children in the sample also showed either moderate or severe performance problems on a pretest of phonological awareness. The results of the study provide at least three sources of evidence about the effectiveness of the program.

First, the program was clearly effective in dramatically altering the level of phonological awareness of all the children in the study. All subjects received perfect, or near perfect, scores on the LAC at posttest. Because of the ceiling effect represented by these perfect scores, we cannot conclude that the awareness skills of the children in our sample were fully equivalent to those of their age peers. However, evidence from previous research with the LAC (Lindamood and Lindamood 1979) suggests that, at the conclusion of training, the trained students had a level of awareness that could no longer be considered a limiting factor in their acquisition of alphabetic reading skills.

A second source of evidence about the effectiveness of the ADD program is found in the posttest standard scores on the Word Attack subtest. Not only was there an improvement of more than 1⅓ standard deviations in standard score from pre- to posttest, but also the final scores were clearly in the normal range for children of this age. These results are very different from other studies cited in the introduction that have followed the progress of dyslexic children through intervention programs designed to increase their alphabetic reading skills.

Finally, there was convincing evidence that students in the study generalized their newly acquired alphabetic reading skills to a test in which they were required to read real words accurately. Although the students were still frequently unsuccessful in applying these skills to difficult words, they did show evidence of trying to apply new, and potentially more productive, strategies to the task. If these strategies are applied in other reading situations, they should provide the children a much broader range of independent reading skills than they previously possessed.

As in any clinical training study of this type, our results are clearly limited in important ways. First, this initial investigation needs to be followed up with a more extensive study using a control group design. We are currently planning, and seeking funding, for such a study.

Second, the ADD program is very complex, so that it is not clear which of its many elements was most important in producing the training effects we obtained. It is our clinical impression that the early phases of training, in which the ADD is unique from most other phonological awareness training programs, were very helpful for the severely impaired childen in this study. Many of the children had little sensitivity to the kinesthetic cues associated with the production of different phonemes, and the names that were assigned to phoneme groups helped to make these distinctive articulatory features concrete. These names also made it easier to discuss student errors on the various exercises (encoding, decoding). Subsequent investigations may demonstrate that the early phases of training are necessary only for more severely impaired children. Certainly, a number of programs without these features have successfully improved the level of phonological awareness in samples of younger children (Bradley and Bryant 1985; Ball and Blachman 1988; Lundberg, Frost, and Peterson 1988). However, all of these studies have reported only average effects on performance, so that it is not clear if these overall average improvements are masking the failure of some children to improve at all. One recent study that did report individual effects (Torgesen and Morgan 1990) indicated that, although average training effects were significant, 30 percent of a sample of kindergarten children did not profit from the phonological awareness training at all. Perhaps these children are the type that might profit from the more extensive training activities that make up the early phases of the ADD program.

Finally, this study leaves unanswered many important questions about the ultimate reading outcomes for children in the study. Although the alphabetic reading skills of our sample were normalized in terms of accuracy, we did not measure fluency of word identification processes. It is likely that our students had not attained fully automatic, or fluent use of these skills in their reading. Thus, their rate of decoding individual words was probably slower than their age peers. Given other data reported for children with phonological processing problems (Torgesen et al. 1987), it is possible that these dyslexic children will be unable to attain normal levels of fluency, even with extensive practice of their skills. However, it is also true that few other samples of dyslexic children have attained levels of accuracy for alphabetic reading skills as high as those reported in this study, so that future improvements in fluency must remain an open question.

We also did not obtain measures of reading comprehension for our sample, as the intervention was targeted on word reading skills alone. However, there is ample evidence that decoding accuracy and fluency are closely tied to comprehension levels (Perfetti 1985; Roth and Beck 1987), so that we can reasonably expect reading comprehension increases to be the eventual result of improvements in decoding accuracy. In this case, more complete data from one of the subjects in the present study may be instructive. In addition to being dyslexic, this child also had a severe expressive language disorder, including marked verbal dyspraxia, which had been diagnosed at age 2½. He had received extensive speech and language therapy, special education training, and private tutoring with a reading disabilities tutor since preschool. At pretest for this study, when he was 10 years, 10 months old, his scores on the Word Identification and Word Attack subtests were 60 and 68, respectively, and his score on the Comprehension subtest was 58. Over the next five months, he received therapy with the ADD program on a 1:1 basis for a total of 124 hours. At the conclusion of training, his standard scores on Word Identification, Word Attack, and Comprehension, were 78, 99, and 81, respectively. For this child, at least, improvements in his alphabetic reading skills were accompanied by significant improvements in reading comprehension.

Although the nature of this study allows only tentative conclusions about the effectiveness of phonological awareness training for older dyslexic children, the study does underline the need for further research in this area. In addition to its practical and immediate benefits, this research should help us to increase our understanding of the basic disorder. Studies that powerfully manipulate levels of phonological awareness should contribute important information about relationships among different kinds of phonological processing problems, as well as clarify the relative importance of these different kinds of limitations in producing the reading symptoms.

References

Ball, E. W. and Blachman, B. A. 1988. Phoneme segmentation training: Effect on reading readiness. *Annals of Dyslexia* 38:208–225.

Bradley, L. and Bryant, P. E. 1978. Difficulties in auditory organization as a possible cause of reading backwardness. *Nature* 221:746–747.

Bradley, L. and Bryant, P. 1985. *Rhyme and Reason in Reading and Spelling*. Ann Arbor: University of Michigan Press.

Coles, G. S. 1987. *The Learning Mystique:* A critical look at "learning disabilities." New York: Pantheon.

Frith, U. 1985. Beneath the surface of developmental dyslexia. *In* K. Patterson, J. Marshall, and M. Coltheart (eds.). *Surface Dyslexia* (pp. 301–330). London: Erlbaum.

Gough, P. and Tunmer, W. 1986. Decoding, reading, and reading disability. *Remedial and Special Education,* 7:6–10.

Liberman, I. Y. 1987. Language and Literacy: The obligation of the Schools of Education. *In* R. F. Bowler (ed.). *Intimacy with Language* pp. 1–9. Baltimore, MD: The Orton Dyslexia Society.

Liberman, I. Y., Shankweiler, D., and Liberman, A. M. 1989. The alphabetic principle and learning to read. *In* D. Shankweiler and I. Y. Liberman (eds.). Phonology and Reading Disability: Solving the reading puzzle. Ann Arbor, MI: University of Michigan Press.

Lindamood, C. H. and Lindamood, P. C. 1979. *Lindamood Auditory Conceptualization Test.* Allen, TX: DLM/Teaching Resources.

Lindamood, C. H. and Lindamood, P. C. 1975. *Auditory Discrimination in Depth.* Allen, TX: DLM/Teaching Resources.

Lovett, M. W., Benson, N. J., and Olds, J. In press. Individual difference predictors of treatment outcome in the remediation of specific reading disability. *Learning and Individual Differences.*

Lundberg, I., Frost, J., and Peterson, O. 1988. Effects of an extensive program for stimulating phonological awareness in pre-school children. *Reading Research Quarterly* 23:263–284.

Lundberg, I., Olofsson, A., and Wall, S. 1980. Reading and spelling skills in the first school years predicted from phonemic awareness skills in kindergarten. *Scandinavian Journal of Psychology* 21:159–173.

Lyon, G. R. 1985. Educational validation studies. *In* B. P. Rourke (ed.). *Neuropsychology of Learning Disabilities.* pp. 228–253. New York: Guslford Publications, Inc.

Ogden, S., Hindman, S., and Turner, S. D. 1989. Multisensory programs in the public schools: A brighter future for LD children. *Annals of Dyslexia* 39:247–267.

Perfetti, C. A. 1985. *Reading Ability.* New York: Oxford University Press.

Roth, S. F. and Beck, I. L. 1987. Theoretical and instructional implications of the assessment of two microcomputer word recognition programs. *Reading Research Quarterly* 22:197–218.

Snowling, M. and Hulme, C. 1989. A longitudinal case study of developmental phonological dyslexia. *Cognitive Neuropsychology* 6:379–401.

Snowling, M., Stackhouse, J., and Rack, J. 1986. Phonological dyslexia and dysgraphia—a developmental analysis. *Cognitive Neuropsychology* 3:309–339.

Stanovich, K. E. 1982. Individual differences in the cognitive processes of reading I: word decoding. *Journal of Learning Disabilities* 15:485–493.

Stanovich, K. E. 1988. Explaining the differences between the dyslexic and the garden-variety poor reader: The phonological-core variable-difference model. *Journal of Learning Disabilities* 21:590–604.

Stanovich, K. E., Cunningham, A. E. and Feeman, D. J. 1984. Relation between early reading acquisition and word decoding with and without context: A longitudinal study of first grade children. *Journal of Educational Psychology* 76:668–677.

Torgesen, J. K. In press. Cross-age consistency in phonological processing. *In* S. Bradey and D. Shankweiler (eds.). *Phonological Processes in Literacy: A tribute to Isabelle Y. Liberman.* Hillsdale, NJ: Lawrence Earlbaum Assoc.

Torgesen, J. K. and Morgan, S. 1990. The effects of two types of phonological awareness training on word learning in kindergarten children. Manuscript submitted for publication, Florida State University, Tallahassee, FL.

Torgesen, J. K., Rashotte, C. A., Greenstein, J., Houch, G., and Portes, P. 1987. Academic difficulties of learning disabled children who perform poorly on memory span tasks. *In* H. L. Swanson (ed.). *Memory and Learning Disabilities: Advances in Learning and Behavioral Disabilities.* pp. 305–333. Greenwich, CT: JAI Press.

Wagner, R. K. and Torgesen, J. K. 1987. The nature of phonological processing and its causal role in the acquisition of reading skills. *Psychological Bulletin* 101:192–212.

Williams, J. P. 1980. Teaching decoding with an emphasis on phoneme analysis and phoneme blending. *Journal of Educational Psychology* 72:1–15.

Woodcock, R. W. 1973. *Woodcock Reading Mastery Tests.* Circle Press, MN: American Guidance Service.

Early Syntactic Development of Dyslexic Children

Hollis S. Scarborough

Brooklyn College
City University of New York

The syntactic development of preschoolers who later became disabled readers was compared to that of children who were similar to the dyslexics in sex, socioeconomic status, and IQ, but who became normal readers. Expressive and receptive syntactic abilities were examined longitudinally from age 30 to 60 months. The dyslexic group was poorer than the control group on all measures until the age of five, at which time both groups exhibited similar syntactic proficiency. The etiological relation of language development to reading disabilities is discussed.

The notion that dyslexia is fundamentally a developmental language disorder has been entertained for decades (Jansky and deHirsch 1972; Orton 1937), and has recently received renewed interest in the wake of numerous demonstrations that oral language processing problems in the late preschool years often precede and contribute to subsequent reading disabilities (e.g., Bowey and Patel 1988; Bryant et al. 1989; Butler et al. 1985; Catts 1989; Mann and Ditunno, 1990; Scarborough 1989; Share et al. 1984; Stuart and Coltheart 1988). The present

This research was supported by grants from the National Institute of Child Health and Human Development and the March of Dimes Birth Defects Foundation. The author would particularly like to thank Maria Hager, Janet Wyckoff, Wanda Dobrich, and Gail Emery for their assistance with data collection and analysis.

Address for correspondence: Department of Psychology, Brooklyn College-CUNY, Brooklyn, NY 11210

Annals of Dyslexia, Vol. 41, 1991.
ISSN 0736-9387

study provides further support for that hypothesis through an examination of the development of oral syntax in dyslexic and nondyslexic children when they were two to five years of age.

Language is a multifaceted human faculty, the development of which begins very early in life. Thus to hypothesize that dyslexia is a language-based disability leaves open many questions about how broadly impaired the dyslexic child's language abilities may be, about when during development such linguistic problems may emerge, and about the etiological relation of language problems to reading difficulties. One widely held current view is that the phonological capabilities of children at the time they begin learning to read are most critically important for discovering the sound-letter correspondences necessary to the successful decoding of print, and thus that failures in primary reading acquisition may largely be attributable to this specific weakness in the phonological component of language during the late preschool years (e.g., Brady and Fowler 1988; Catts 1989; Jorm and Share 1983; Liberman and Shankweiler 1980; Stanovich 1988).

This "phonological hypothesis" about the relation between oral language and reading disability may be incomplete in several respects. Regarding the breadth of the oral language problem associated with dyslexia, there is evidence that syntactic and morphological abilities of dyslexic schoolchildren are also substantially impaired (e.g., Byrne 1981; Feagans and Short 1984; Fletcher, Satz, and Scholes 1981; Leong 1989; Siegel and Ryan 1984). To some extent, these nonphonological deficits may merely be consequences of the cognitive, instructional, and emotional sequelae to early reading failure (Stanovich 1986, Share and Silva 1987). However, recent demonstrations that kindergarteners and younger preschoolers who later develop reading disabilities exhibit syntactic as well as phonological deficits (Bishop and Adams 1990; Bowey and Patel 1988; Butler et al. 1985; Morice and Slaghuis 1985; Scarborough 1990b; Share et al. 1984) are more difficult to explain in these terms.

With respect to the onset of differences between dyslexic and nondyslexic children, there is growing evidence that the oral language problems of children who become disabled readers often emerge long before any reading instruction typically begins. Retrospective reports by parents of dyslexic schoolchildren have often included mention of early speech and language problems (e.g., Ingram, Mason, and Blackburn 1970; Lyle 1970; Rutter and Yule 1975), and recent prospective research has tended to confirm the accuracy of such parental recollections. In two longitudinal studies, phonological differences among 3½-year-olds (Bryant et al. 1989) and 2½-year-olds (Scarborough 1990b) have been shown to predict future reading achievement. In the latter study, it was also observed that substantial syntactic deficits were exhibited by 30-month-olds who became disabled readers more than five years later. Although the relation of early phonological differences to subsequent reading abilities in both studies was apparently mediated by intervening differences in language and literacy skills in the later preschool years, the association between early syntax and reading was not, suggesting that some fundamental neurolinguistic limitation may underlie language processing difficulties at widely disparate points during development. To explore further the developmental relation of early syntactic deficits to later reading disabilities, in the present study the syntactic development from age 2 to 5 years was compared for children who subsequently became disabled or normal readers.

Method

Subjects

All subjects were participants in a larger, ongoing, longitudinal study of the relation of preschool development to subsequent academic achievement. All were from lower- to upper-middle-class families residing in mainly suburban municipalities throughout central New Jersey. None had any gross neurological, hearing, or uncorrected visual problems, according to pediatric and audiological examinations and research observations between the ages of 2 and 8 years. Standard English was the only language spoken in these children's homes.

The families participating in the larger study were recruited through newspaper and radio advertisements, professional referrals, and word of mouth. Families in which someone had experienced a severe childhood reading problem were especially encouraged to respond, but other families were also invited to call. By recruiting in this manner, the intent was to overrepresent children from families with dyslexic members, thereby increasing the likelihood that a sizable group of disabled readers would be included in the sample.

The children's reading abilities were assessed at the end of Grade 2, when they were 8.0 years old ($SD = 0.4$). Based on those assessments, as previously described in detail (Scarborough 1989), children were designated as disabled readers if their reading achievement scores at Grade 2 were more than 1.5 SD lower than expected levels. In the sample of 78 families from the larger study, 24 children met this criterion. All but two of these were from "dyslexic families" in which there was at least one parent or older sibling with a reading disability. The criteria used to determine the reading status of other family members have been described elsewhere (Scarborough 1984, 1989).

In the present study, the early syntactic development of two groups will be compared: a *Dyslexic* group, consisting of the 22 disabled readers from dyslexic families, and a *Control* group of 22 normal readers from nondyslexic families, selected from the larger sample so as to resemble the Dyslexic group closely with respect to SES, IQ, and sex. Detailed information has been presented elsewhere about the procedures used to select these control subjects from the larger sample (Scarborough 1990b). Table I provides a comparison of the two groups with regard to sex ratio, socioeconomic status, IQ at various ages, and reading and math achievement. The groups differed only in reading skill ($t = 9.369$, $p < .001$).

Procedures

During the preschool phase of the project, the children were visited by a research team at ages 30, 36, 42, and 48 months, at which times various tests and naturalistic observations were conducted. In the present study, measures of receptive and expressive syntactic abilities during the preschool years were analyzed.

Sentence comprehension was evaluated at ages 36, 48, and 60 months with the 40-item receptive portion of Lee's (1971) *Northwestern Syntax Screening Test* (NSST). On each item of this test, the child is asked to indicate which of four pictured scenes corresponds to a sentence spoken by the examiner.

Two measures of expressive syntax were derived from natural language samples collected during mother-child play sessions at each age. All maternal and child utterances during play were transcribed from

Table I
Dyslexic and Control groups whose early syntactic abilities were studied.

	Dyslexic	Control
Number of Children	22	22
Boys:Girls	12:10	10:12
Socioeconomic Status[a]	3.0 (1.0)	2.8 (0.8)
WJPB Reading Cluster[b]	479.6 (7.8)	502.1 (7.2)
McCarthy GCI at 36 mos[c]	106.9 (13.2)	109.6 (12.1)
McCarthy GCI at 48 mos[c]	110.9 (13.4)	118.4 (15.1)
McCarthy GCI at 60 mos[c]	113.0 (11.3)	115.9 (10.6)
WISC-R Full-Scale IQ at Grade 2[d]	110.2 (9.8)	114.8 (10.2)
Math Achievement[e]	75.4 (19.5)	83.4 (23.9)

Note: Standard deviations are shown in parentheses.
[a]Five-point scale, on which 1 is highest, based on parental education and occupational prestige (Hollingshead and Redlich 1958).
[b]Woodcock-Johnson Psychoeducational Battery (Woodcock and Johnson 1977).
[c]McCarthy Scales of Children's Abilities (McCarthy 1972).
[d]Wechsler Intelligence Scale for Children—Revised (Wechsler 1974).
[e]Percentile on school-administered nationally standardized test.

videotaped observations.[1] The *Index of Productive Syntax* (IPSyn) and *mean length of utterance* (MLU) were derived from 100-utterance corpora within these transcripts. Unintelligible, imitative, and self-repetitive utterances were not included in these corpora, and routine productions (such as counting and singing) were also excluded. The IPSyn, a measure of the grammatical complexity of a natural language sample, is computed by crediting the occurrence of up to two dissimilar tokens of 56 types of syntactic and morphological forms that are typically acquired during the preschool years (Scarborough 1990a). MLU in morphemes was computed using conventional guidelines for counting morphemes (Brown 1973), except that some compounds were considered multimorphemic when there was evidence of their components being combined productively elsewhere in the corpus. Interscorer reliability was excellent for both expressive syntax measures: $r = .981$ for IPSyn and $r = .984$ for MLU.[2]

Results

The temporal stability and interdependence of the preschool language measures were first examined. Correlations between successive measurements of sentence comprehension (NSST), grammatical complexity (IPSyn), and utterance length (MLU) are shown in the first column of Table II. For all three measures, individual differences were generally quite stable from age to age over the preschool years. The table also provides correlations among measures taken concurrently during the course of the study. The two measures of expressive syntax were closely related at all ages, although less strongly at 60 months than earlier. Performance on the NSST-Receptive, however, was not consistently correlated with expressive language proficiency, suggesting that different aspects of syntactic proficiency were tapped by the receptive and expressive measures used in this study.

Receptive and expressive syntactic abilities of the Dyslexic and Control groups at each age are shown in Figure 1. Separate analyses of variance were carried out with NSST, IPSyn, and MLU in turn as the dependent variable, age as the within-subjects repeated measure, and

---

[1]All transcripts were reviewed by a second transcriber prior to analyses. In addition, 12.9 percent of the play sessions were independently transcribed by two observers, who were found to agree in their representations of 85 percent to 99 percent ($M = 92.2$ percent) of the identifiable morphemes produced by the children.

[2]Two coders independently scored 11.5 percent of the transcripts (including those of both dyslexic and nondyslexic children at all ages). Percentage of coding judgments in agreement ranged from 91.2 percent to 100 percent ($M = 97.8$ percent) for IPSyn and from 91.5 percent to 99.5 percent ($M = 97.5$ percent) for MLU.

Table II
Correlations among language measures: temporal stability and
interdependence.

| Measure | Age (Months) | Next Available Reassessment | Concurrent Assessment | |
			NSST	IPSyn
NSST	36	.61***		
NSST	48	.51***		
NSST	60	—		
IPSyn	30	.71***	—	
IPSyn	36	.54***	.37*	
IPSyn	42	.51***	—	
IPSyn	48	.31*	.28	
IPSyn	60	—	.27	
MLU	30	.47**	—	.88***
MLU	36	.33*	.18	.74***
MLU	42	.27	—	.70***
MLU	48	.45**	.01	.71***
MLU	60	—	.04	.54***

*$p < .05$ **$p < .01$ ***$p < .001$

group as the between-subjects variable.[3,4] As summarized in Table III, main effects of age and group were found in each analysis. A group × age interaction was also obtained for IPSyn, but not for MLU or NSST. Nevertheless, as shown in Table IV, comparisons between group means at each age revealed a similar developmental pattern for all measures. That is, there were substantial differences between the Dyslexic and Control groups from age 30 to 48 months, but negligeable differences at 60 months. Because IPSyn appeared to be the most sensitive measure of outcome-related differences in early syntactic proficiency, only this measure was examined in subsequent prediction analyses.

---

[3]In the Dyslexic group, two subjects did not join the project until age 36 months, and no visit was conducted for one child at age 48 months because his family temporarily lost contact with the project. Missing scores were imputed using multiple regression analyses based on available data for these three subjects. In the Control group, the expressive syntax measures could not be derived for two subjects at age 60 months: one child produced only 19 scorable utterances during the play session, and the other persisted in producing primarily "baby talk" (much to her mother's surprise and consternation) throughout the observation. Since language production measures at age 60 months were not strongly correlated with any other measures (see Table II), these missing data could not be imputed, and were thus replaced by the Control group means when necessary. In addition, one dyslexic and one control subject refused to take the NSST at age 36 months; these scores were imputed from available scores at 48 months.

[4]Multivariate (profile analysis) solutions were in all cases similar to the reported univariate test results.

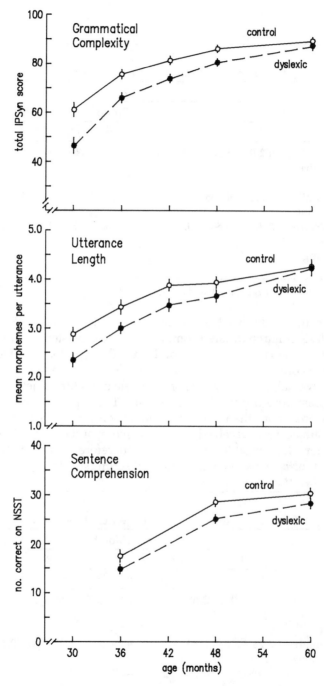

Figure 1. Preschool development of expressive grammatical complexity, utterance length, and sentence comprehension skills of children who became disabled vs. normal readers at Grade 2. Vertical bars extend 1 SE above and below each mean.

Table III
Summary of analysis of variance results.

Dependent Variable	Age			Group			Group × Age		
	F	df	p	F	df	p	F	df	p
Index of Productive Syntax	162.09	4,168	.001	24.36	1,42	.001	5.85	4,168	.001
Mean Length of Utterance	66.46	4,168	.001	9.79	1,42	.01	1.61	4,168	n.s.
Northwestern Syntax Screening Test*	209.62	2,84	.001	6.32	1,42	.02	0.35	2,84	n.s.

*Administered at ages 36, 48, and 60 months only.

As can be seen in Table V, between the ages of 30 and 48 months the dyslexic children differed somewhat in the consistency with which they exhibited expressive syntax problems, the criterion for which was an IPSyn score that was at least one *SD* below the mean of the control group. Over all, 19 (86 percent) of the dyslexic children met this criterion at least once during this period, and 17 (77 percent) earned low IPSyn scores more than once; in contrast, only 8 (36 percent) of the control subjects ever received such a low score, and only 5 (23 percent) did so more than once. Not surprisingly, therefore, when IPSyn scores at these four ages were entered into a discriminant analysis, the out-

Table IV
Summary of tests of group differences at each age.

Measure	Age (Months)									
	30		36		42		48		60	
	t	p	t	p	t	p	t	p	t	p
Index of Productive Syntax	3.94	.001	3.58	.001	4.25	.001	3.14	.01	1.12	n.s.
Mean Length of Utterance	3.26	.01	2.54	.02	2.48	.02	1.91	.04	0.13	n.s.
Northwestern Syntax Screening Test*	—	—	1.73	.05	—	—	2.95	.01	1.50	n.s.

*Administered at ages 36, 48, and 60 months only.

Table V
Syntactic deficits of individual subjects. Observations for which IPSyn scores were at least 1 *SD* below the Control group mean at that age are marked with an *x*. Subjects are ordered from the poorest (D1) to the best (C22) reader at Grade 2.

A. Dyslexic Group						B. Control Group					
	Age (months)						Age (months)				
Subject	30	36	42	48	60	Subject	30	36	42	48	60
D1	x		x	x		C1					
D2						C2	x	x	x	x	x
D3	x	x				C3					
D4	x	x				C4		x	x	x	
D5			x	x	x	C5					
D6	x	x	x			C6	x	x	x	x	
D7			x	x		C7					
D8			x	x		C8					
D9	x	x				C9	x	x			
D10			x			C10					
D11	x	x	x	x		C11					
D12	x	x	x	x		C12					
D13						C13			x	x	
D14			x	x	x	C14				x	x
D15	x	x		x		C15					x
D16	x	x	x	x		C16					
D17						C17					
D18	x					C18		x			
D19	x	x	x	x	x	C19					
D20	x	x	x	x		C20					
D21		x	x	x		C21					
D22		x		x		C22			x		
Total	12	12	13	13	3		3	5	5	5	3
Percent	55	55	59	59	14		14	23	23	23	14

come classifications of 34 of the 44 subjects (77.3 percent) were correctly predicted on the basis of early syntactic proficiency [Wilks' lambda = 0.608, $F(4,39) = 6.278$, $p < .001$]. Subjects identified in Table V as D2, D13, D17, D18, D22, C2, C4, C6, C9, and C13 were the ones erroneously classified in the analysis.

As noted earlier, previous analyses had shown that reading abilities were predicted by "readiness" skills (including phonological awareness, letter identification, letter-sound knowledge, and object naming) at age 60 months (Scarborough 1989), and that syntactic differences at age 30 months were predictive of Grade 2 outcomes even when variance attributable to these differences at 60 months was statistically controlled (Scarborough 1990b). In the present study, therefore, IPSyn scores at ages 36, 42, and 48 months were similarly analyzed in series of ANCOVAs with the readiness scores as covariates. Unique variance in reading outcomes was accounted for by syntactic differences at age 36 months [$F(1,40) = 4.432$, $p < .05$] and at age 42 months [$F(1,40) = 11.445$, $p < .01$], but not at 48 months [$F(1,40) = 3.293$, $p < .08$].

Finally, as can be seen in Table V, in which the subjects have been ranked according to their reading scores at Grade 2, the severity of early syntactic deficits was not closely related to the severity of later reading problems within the Dyslexic group. Hence, correlations of reading scores with preschool NSST, IPSyn, and MLU scores for the Dyslexic group were generally weak (median $r = .01$, range -.21 to .41). Similarly, readiness scores at age 60 months were not predictive of reading abilities at Grade 2 within the Dyslexic group alone ($r = .13$ to .17). This result is consistent with previous prospective findings of more successful prediction of superior *vs.* average reading, than of disabled *vs.* normal reading, by late preschool phonological awareness skills (e.g., Bradley and Bryant 1985; Mann 1984).

Discussion

The results suggest that many dyslexic children exhibit substantial and persistent deficits in their comprehension of sentences and in the length and syntactic complexity of their spoken utterances throughout much of the preschool period. Syntactic problems were evident between 2½ and 4 years of age, a period during which great strides are normally made in the acquisition of rules for combining morphemes, words, phrases, and clauses in grammatically complete and correct ways. As can be seen in the figure, on average the expressive syntax development of the Dyslexic group was roughly about six months delayed, relative to the Control group of similar socioeconomic status, sex, and IQ.

By the time the children were five years old (at which age most had not yet entered kindergarten), these difficulties in comprehending and producing syntactic structures were no longer evident. Does this mean that the children had fully recovered from their early difficulty in acquiring syntax and thus could be expected to have no further problems of this sort? That is certainly one interpretation of the findings, but the conclusion that these children had caught up permanently to their age-mates does not coincide well with previous research results, particularly the many observations of syntactic deficits in older dyslexic children.

At least two other accounts of the findings merit consideration.

First, the results of the present study may have been constrained by the ways that syntax was assessed. It is quite possible that the measures used may be insufficiently sensitive to potential syntactic and morphological differences among 5-year-olds. This is of particular concern regarding the expressive language measures, since neither IPSyn nor MLU has been validated as a measure of syntactic proficiency beyond the age of four. Second, it is also possible that both groups may have reached a temporary plateau in the course of language development, such that the convergence of their growth curves at 60 months merely represented an "illusory recovery" from developmental deficits that could reemerge at a later time (Scarborough and Dobrich 1990). On the basis of available evidence, it is difficult to draw any firm conclusion regarding the attenuation of observed group differences at the end of the preschool period.

What is reasonably clear, nevertheless, is that by the time dyslexic children enter school, any syntactic problems that may persist (and that might be detectible by using other measures) are probably not readily apparent during ordinary conversation and are unlikely to impede either their understanding of the relatively simple sentences found in primers or their ability to understand and be understood orally by their teachers. What, then, is the relation of their earlier syntactic problems to the development of their reading disabilities? Although poor early syntax predicted poor late-preschool readiness skills, which in turn predicted poor reading, the ANCOVA results suggest that the relation between early syntax and later reading was not merely mediated by intervening differences in phonological processing and letter knowledge. In other words, simply to amend the "phonological hypothesis"— by proposing that syntactic deficits are a precursor to the phonological problems that are actually most responsible for reading disabilities— would not account entirely for the findings.

Instead, it may be more appropriate to say that many children with dyslexia do not simply have a reading disorder, but are also affected by a broader condition that emerges even before the issue of literacy arises in a child's life (Catts 1989; Kamhi and Catts, 1989; Scarborough 1990b; Vellutino 1987). This hypothesized condition may contribute to the occurrence of different observable weaknesses at different ages: first, syntax problems; then, weaknesses in phonological awareness, naming, and preliteracy skills; and finally, difficulties with reading and spelling (as well as with oral language) during the school years and beyond. Furthermore, one might presume there to be an underlying, and probably congenital, neurocognitive limitation associated with this condition, and that each "symptom" arises whenever a developmental challenge facing the child requires facility in some aspect of verbal-cognitive processing that is limited in dyslexic individuals. For example, symbol manipulation and abstract rule learning are two possible processes that, if impaired or inefficient, might make it difficult for a child to acquire syntactic rules, phonological awareness, and phoneme-grapheme correspondences. (There are certainly other plausible hypotheses also, and as more is learned about early and later characteristics of dyslexic children, it is hoped that the range of such possibilities can be narrowed.)

Within this theoretical framework, the observed noncorrespondence between the degree of severity of successive symptoms can be accounted for quite readily. It is hypothesized that the appearance of each symptom is primarily determined by the underlying condition itself which impedes the mastery of each developmental challenge (from syntax acquisition to literacy) encountered by the dyslexic child. The degree to which that condition is manifest, however, may also depend on other factors. The amount and quality of support received from parents and teachers, for instance, may affect the child's ability to overcome difficulties in learning. In addition, dyslexic children with greater intrinsic motivation to learn may be more successful in conquering these developmental challenges despite their underlying limitation, while children with less determination to succeed may avoid (and be permitted to avoid) facing developmental tasks that are most difficult for them.

In other words, if dyslexia is associated not just with reading disabilities, but also with a more fundamental and pervasive underlying limitation that interacts with other factors affecting learning and development, then some affected children may not exhibit early syntax problems, some may not exhibit later phonological awareness problems, and (as suggested by Kamhi and Catts 1989) some may not even exhibit severe reading problems. Other individuals may exhibit every symptom, but not to the same degree. Such variation, it should be noted, would not represent etiologically distinct "subtypes" unless there were evidence that the nature of the underlying limitation—rather than the occurrence or severity of symptoms—differs from child to child.

Finally, even if learning to read does not require the application of acquired knowledge about complex syntax, it probably does require similar kinds of verbal-cognitive processes as were required for the acquisition of syntax earlier in life. The system of decoding rules to be learned by the beginning reader resembles the syntactic rule system with respect to the manipulation of abstract elements, the prevalence of "exceptions" to rules, the inclusion of order-dependent and context-contingent relations among elements, and so forth. Some or all such aspects of these kinds of developmental challenges, whenever they are encountered in life, pose greater difficulty for a child with dyslexia.

References

Bishop, D. V. M. and Adams, C. 1990. A prospective study of the relationship between specific language impairment, phonological disorders and reading retardation. *Journal of Child Psychology and Psychiatry* 31:1027–1050.

Bowey, J. A. and Patel, R. K. 1988. Metalinguistic ability and early reading achievement. *Applied Psycholinguistics* 9:367–383.

Bradley, L. and Bryant, P. 1985. *Rhyme and Reason in Reading and Spelling.* International Academy for Research in Learning Disabilities Monograph Series, No. 1. Ann Arbor, MI: University of Michigan Press.

Brady, S. A. and Fowler, A. E. 1988. Phonological precursors to reading acquisition. *In* R. L. Masland and M. W. Masland (eds.). *Preschool Prevention of Reading Failure.* Parkton, MD: York Press.

Brown, R. 1973. *A First Language: The early stages.* Cambridge, MA: Cambridge University Press.

Bryant, P. E., Bradley, L., Maclean, M., and Crossland, J. 1989. Nursery rhymes, phonological skills and reading. *Journal of Chld Language* 16:407–428.

Butler, S. R., Marsh, H. W., Sheppard, M. J., and Sheppard, J. L. 1985. Seven-year longitudinal study of the early prediction of reading achievement. *Journal of Educational Psychology* 77:349–361.

Byrne, B. 1981. Deficient syntactic control in poor readers: Is a weak phonetic memory code responsible? *Applied Psycholinguistics* 2:210–212.

Catts, H. W. 1989. Defining dyslexia as a developmental language disorder. *Annals of Dyslexia* 39:50–64.

Feagans, L. and Short, E. J. 1984. Develpmental differences in the comprehension and production of narratives by reading-disabled and normally achieving children. *Child Development* 55:1727–1736.

Fletcher, J. M., Satz, P., and Scholes, R. J. 1981. Developmental changes in the linguistic correlates of reading achievement. *Brain and Language* 13:78–90.

Hollingshead, A. B. and Redlich, F. C. 1958. *Social Class and Mental Illness.* New York: Wiley.

Ingram, T. T. S., Mason, A. W., and Blackburn, I. 1970. A retrospective study of 82 children with reading disability. *Developmental Medicine and Child Neurology* 12:271–283.

Jansky, J. and deHirsch, K. 1972. *Preventing Reading Failure.* New York: Harper.

Jorm, A. F. and Share, D. L. 1983. Phonological recoding and reading acquisition. *Applied Psycholinguistics* 4:104–147.

Kamhi, A. G. and Catts, H. W. (eds.). 1989. *Reading Disabilities: A developmental language perspective.* Boston: College Hill Press.

Lee, L. L. 1971. *Northwestern Syntax Screening Test.* Evanston, IL: Northwestern University Press.

Leong, C. K. 1989. Productive knowledge of derivational rules in poor readers. *Annals of Dyslexia* 39:94–115.

Liberman, I. Y. and Shankweiler, D. 1980. Speech, the alphabet and teaching to read. *In* L. B. Resnick and P. A. Weaver (eds.). *Theory and Practice of Early Reading.* Hillsdale, NJ: Erlbaum.

Lyle, J. G. 1970. Certain antenatal, perinatal, and developmental variables and reading retardation. *Child Development* 41:481–491.

Mann, V. A. 1984. Longitudinal prediction and prevention of early reading difficulty. *Annals of Dyslexia* 43:117–136.

Mann, V. A. and Ditunno, P. 1990. Phonological deficiencies: Effective predictors of future reading problems. *In* G. Pavlides (ed.). *Dyslexia: A neuropsychological and learning perspective.* New York: Wiley.

McCarthy, D. 1972. *McCarthy Scales of Children's Abilities*. New York: Psychological Corporation.

Morice, R. and Slaghuis, W. 1985. Language performance and reading ability at 8 years of age. *Applied Psycholinguistics* 6:141–161.

Orton, S. T. 1937. *Reading, Writing, and Speech Problems in Children*. New York: Norton.

Rutter, M. and Yule, W. 1975. The concept of specific reading retardation. *Journal of Child Psychology and Psychiatry* 16:181–197.

Scarborough, H. S. 1984. Continuity between childhood dyslexia and adult reading. *British Journal of Psychology* 75:329–348.

Scarborough, H. S. 1989. Prediction of reading disability from familial and individual differences. *Journal of Educational Psychology* 81:101–108.

Scarborough, H. S. 1990a. Index of productive syntax. *Applied Psycholinguistics* 11:1–22.

Scarborough, H. S. 1990b. Very early language deficits in dyslexic children. *Child Development* 61:1728–1743.

Scarborough, H. S. and Dobrich, W. 1990. Development of children with early language delay. *Journal of Speech and Hearing Research* 33:70–83.

Share, D. L., Jorm, A. F., Maclean, R., and Matthews, R. 1984. Sources of individual differences in reading acquisition. *Journal of Educational Psychology* 76:1309–1324.

Share, D. L. and Silva, P. A. 1987. Language deficits and specific reading retardation: Cause or effect? *British Journal of Disorders of Communication* 22:219–226.

Siegel, L. S. and Ryan, E. B. 1984. Reading disability as a language disorder. *Remedial and Special Education* 5:28–33.

Stanovich, K. E. 1986. Matthew effects in reading: Some consequences of individual differences in the acquisition of literacy. *Reading Research Quarterly* 21:360–406.

Stanovich, K. E. 1988. Explaining the differences between the dyslexic and the garden-variety poor reader: The phonological-core variable-difference model. *Journal of Learning Disabilities* 12:590–612.

Stuart, M. and Coltheart, M. 1988. Does reading develop in a sequence of stages. *Cognition* 30:139–181.

Vellutino, F. R. 1987. Dyslexia. *Scientific American* 256:34–41.

Wechsler, D. 1974. *Wechsler Intelligence Scale for Children—Revised*. New York: Psychological Corporation.

Woodcock, R. W. and Johnson, M. B. 1977. *Woodcock-Johnson Psycho-educational Battery*. Boston: Teaching Resources Corporation.

Linguistic Profiles of Dyslexic and Good Readers

Nathlie A. Badian
Frank H. Duffy
Heidelise Als
Gloria B. McAnulty

The Children's Hospital, Boston
and
Harvard Medical School

Linguistic profiles of 60 boys with average intelligence were examined at kindergarten, grade 2, and grade 4. The subjects were 7 dyslexic, 7 mildly dyslexic, 30 average, and 16 good readers, defined in terms of the discrepancy between standardized reading and intelligence scores. Across the three ages, reader groups did not differ in language comprehension, but did differ in confrontation and rapid automatized naming (RAN), three syntactic measures, and verbal memory. Group strengths and weaknesses were, with few exceptions apparent in kindergarten and maintained throughout. The kindergarten tasks which most effectively predicted reading group membership at grade 4 were giving letter sounds, and rapid naming; these predicted 4th grade reading group at close to 100 percent accuracy. The study, together with a further comparison of average and high IQ good readers, provides an interesting contrast between the role of RAN and Confrontation naming in reading.

The early focus of research and remediation on visual perceptual deficits as the underlying cause of reading disability or dyslexia was laid to rest by Vellutino (1979) who carefully reviewed the available evi-

This work was supported in part by NIHCD grants RO1HD18761 to F. H. Duffy, RO1HD18654 to H. Als, and the Mental Retardation Grant P30HD18655 to C. F. Barlow.
Mailing address for correspondence: N. A. Badian, 101 Monroe Road, Quincy, MA 02169.

Annals of Dyslexia, Vol. 41, 1991.
ISSN 0736-9387

dence and stressed the role of verbal abilities in dyslexia. Vellutino's verbal deficit theory of dyslexia suggests that poor readers have difficulty in using semantic, syntactic, and/or phonological codes to store and retrieve information (Vellutino 1983). More recently researchers have proposed that general linguistic skills (e.g., semantics) are important components of the concepts of intelligence, and that reading disability is independent of intelligence (Siegel 1989; Stanovich 1988a, 1988b). The cause of dyslexia is perceived as a specific phonological deficit, rather than as a general linguistic deficiency (Liberman and Shankweiler 1985; Siegel 1989; Stanovich 1988a, 1988b; Wagner and Torgesen 1987; Williams 1984).

In their extensive review Wagner and Torgesen (1987) examine three bodies of research on the relationship of phonological skills to reading, which, they point out, have developed in relative isolation: (1) phonological awareness (awareness of and access to the phonology or sound system of one's language); (2) phonological recoding for lexical access (getting from a written word to its lexical referent by recoding written symbols into a sound-based system); and (3) phonetic recoding to maintain information in working memory. Although there is evidence for a general phonological ability, Wagner and Torgesen (1987) provide support for distinguishing between phonological awareness and phonological recoding in working memory and present a strong case for a causal role of phonological awareness in learning to read.

Stanovich (1988a, 1988b) stresses that measures of phonological awareness tap skills which differ radically from the standard intelligence and reading readiness tasks. He points out that, although almost all poor readers have a phonological deficit, the dyslexic has only phonological deficits, whereas the "garden variety" poor reader has global weaknesses. It has been proposed that dyslexia should be defined by performance on a measure of phonological skill and, more specifically, by pseudoword reading (Siegel 1989), which Wagner and Torgesen (1987) classify as a task of phonological recoding for lexical access. Genetic research suggests that the phonological recoding deficit of reading-disabled children (tested by reading of pseudowords) is highly heritable, whereas a deficit in orthographic coding is not (Olson et al. 1989). There is also evidence that the reading process and phonological awareness are reciprocal (Perfetti et al. 1987). That is, learning to read itself improves phonological awareness. The concept that the acquisition of reading provides experiences that enrich other aspects of cognitive development has been stressed by Stanovich (1986).

According to Wagner and Torgesen (1987), the question that remains to be answered is not whether phonological skills are related to reading, but which of these skills (e.g., awareness, recoding in lexical access, recoding in working memory) are causally related to which aspects of reading. Longitudinal studies, which examine the relationship of the tasks administered to preschool children to their later reading achievement, can be an important source of information as to the causes of dyslexia. Some recent predictive batteries which embody the research findings that phonological skills play a major (or even causal) role in reading acquisition show promise (e.g., Jorm et al. 1986; Mann 1984; Share et al. 1984; Wolf 1984).

Jorm and his colleagues, who followed 453 Australian children over the first three school years, found that children with a reading disability were not deficient on general linguistic tasks (e.g., semantical and syntactical), but only on a limited number of school entry tasks, including tests of letter knowledge, phonological awareness (phoneme segmentation), times and errors for naming pictures and colors, sentence memory, and finger localization (Benton 1959). Jorm argued that finger localization may be a phonological task because it requires children to learn verbal labels for fingers.

Another longitudinal study (Badian et al. 1990), which had some success in differentiating dyslexic from normal readers, did not include a measure of phonological awareness in its large battery of kindergarten tests. This omission is unfortunate in light of the strong evidence for a causal role for phonological awareness in reading acquisition. As in the Jorm study, the kindergarten tasks included sentence memory, rapid naming, letter knowledge, and finger localization. The kindergarten measures which were 98 percent accurate in differentiating dyslexics from normal readers at grade 4 were giving letter sounds, rapid naming of numbers, and finger localization. Rapid naming tasks assess phonological recoding for lexical access. Wagner and Torgesen (1987) found support for the importance of phonological recoding in reading, but little evidence of a causal relationship.

Purpose of Study

This study is based on the Badian et al. (1990) research. The general purpose was to examine linguistic profiles of children at three points in time. Specific questions asked were: (1) Do groups of children who differ in reading capabilities at grade 4 (i.e., dyslexic, mildly dyslexic, average, and good readers) differ on tasks of general linguistic ability at grades K, 2, and 4, or only on specific tasks? (2) Within the limitations of the study (e.g., no phonological awareness measure was included), what types of kindergarten linguistic tasks most effectively predict reading capability group membership at grade 4? (3) Do linguistic profiles of good, average, mildly dyslexic, and dyslexic readers change in the early school years, as reading is being acquired?

A second minor study is included: A comparison of good readers of average intelligence with children similar in reading skills, but of superior intelligence. The purpose of this inquiry was to shed more light on the relationship of linguistic skills to the acquisition of reading (Question #1).

Method

Study 1

Subjects   The subjects of this study are a subset of a total study population of 163 boys followed from kindergarten through grade 4 (Badian et al. 1990). Subjects in the sample lived in middle- to upper-middle-class suburban communities in the Boston area. All spoke English as their primary language, and all were white. None had a history of seizures, neurological or emotional problems, or serious vision or hearing impairment. Verbal or Performance IQ was at least 90 on both the Wechsler Preschool and Primary Scale of Intelligence (WPPSI) (Wechsler 1963) at 6 years, and the Wechsler Intelligence Scale for Children-Revised (WISC-R) (Wechsler 1974) at 8 years.

Reading group membership was defined by the relationship between each subject's mean fourth grade reading standard score (based on measures, described later, of word reading, reading comprehension, spelling, oral reading, and reading rate) and predicted reading, obtained by regression on Full Scale IQ. Full Scale IQ was selected as the basis for the regression because Performance IQ, as well as Verbal, contributed significantly (p. 03) to fourth grade reading comprehension. Reading group criteria were:

Dyslexic
Mean reading >15 points less than predicted level, and >1.5 standard deviations below the normative mean of 100 (i.e., <77.5).

Mildly Dyslexic
Mean reading >11 points below predicted level, and <95.

Good Readers
Mean reading >11 points above predicted level.

Average Readers
Mean reading <5 points different from predicted level. Each average reader was individually matched, within 5 points, to a dyslexic, mildly dyslexic, or good reader, on predicted reading level.

Of the 163 boys in the study population, eight met the dyslexic, and eight the mildly dyslexic, criteria, and 19 met the criteria for good readers. One dyslexic, one mildly dyslexic, and three good readers were omitted, because they did not receive the complete battery of grade 4 tests. Thus, the study sample consisted of seven dyslexic and seven mildly dyslexic boys, 16 good readers, and the 30 average readers who served as a control group. Predicted reading level of the 60 subjects ranged from 90 to 114.5. Mean ages at testing (K, G.2, G.4), predicted and actual mean fourth grade reading standard scores, and WISC-R Verbal, Performance, and Full Scale IQs are shown in Table I.

Procedures

To answer questions #1 and #3 listed in the introduction, reading capability groups were compared on language tests administered at the three grade levels and on reading tests given in grades 2 and 4. Because the four groups differed significantly in predicted reading level, regressed on Full Scale IQ (F = 4.25 [3,56], p. 009), Full scale IQ was controlled in analyses of variance and in post-hoc tests (Fisher's LSD) used to determine the significance (p < .05) of between-group differences. Although the groups differed significantly in Performance IQ (F = 4.46 [3,56], p. 0071) and in Full Scale IQ (F = 4.24, p. 009), they did not differ in Verbal IQ (F = 2.14, p. 1049).

To answer question #2, discriminant function analyses were performed to establish which kindergarten language variables were most effective in predicting fourth grade reading group membership.

For some comparisons, good and average readers were combined to form a group of "normal readers" (n = 46). This was done to compare some of the findings with those of Wolf (Wolf 1984; Wolf and Goodglass 1986). The mean second grade Gray Oral Reading Test score (Gray 1967) of the normal readers was grade 3.1 (SD 1.4), which was almost identical with that of Wolf's average (= "average-to-able") readers (3.1, SD 1.3) at second grade.

Language Measures Language measures were selected to test a broad range of skills, including comprehension, vocabulary, syntactical knowledge, naming (confrontation and rapid continuous), and verbal short-term memory. Because of the large number of variables and the small size of the sample, it was not possible to factor analyze the variables to help cluster them. Hence, in the analysis of results and the discussion, conceptual groupings of the variables were made. Three variables, which did not readily fit into any other group, were placed in a visual-verbal association category because they all involved learning sounds or words to associate with visual stimuli. The measures are listed below. Grade levels at which tests were given are in parentheses. Less-known tests are described. Unless otherwise stated, standard scores based on age were used.

Table I

Means and Standard Deviations (in parentheses) of Groups for Chronological Age at Each Grade, Predicted and Actual Reading Standard Scores at Grade 4, and WISC-R IQs

| | Groups | | | | | |
Variable	Dyslexic (D) n = 7	Mildly Dyslexic (M) n = 7	Average Readers (A) n = 30	Good Readers (G) n = 16	Total N = 60	Range
Age (years): K	6.2 (0.2)	6.1 (0.3)	6.1 (0.3)	6.3 (0.3)	6.1 (0.3)	5.3–6.6
Age (years): G.2	7.8 (0.3)	7.9 (0.3)	7.8 (0.3)	7.9 (0.3)	7.8 (0.3)	7.3–8.4
Age (years): G.4	9.8 (0.1)	9.8 (0.1)	9.9 (0.1)	9.9 (0.1)	9.9 (0.1)	9.7–10.3
Predicted Reading	96.7 (4.1)	107.5 (5.6)	101.6 (6.2)	100.5 (5.7)	101.5 (6.3)	90.1–114.5
Actual Reading	67.7 (5.1)	90.9 (2.0)	101.9 (6.7)	114.7 (7.4)	100.0 (15.3)	62.4–131
WISC-R VIQ*	97.4 (5.5)	110.9 (9.3)	106.8 (10.8)	107.8 (12.5)	106.4 (11.0)	87–145
WISC-R PIQ*	99.9 (10.1)	116.7 (10.8)	103.9 (10.9)	100.1 (10.0)	103.9 (11.5)	80–132
WISC-R FSIQ*	98.3 (6.5)	115.1 (8.7)	105.9 (9.7)	104.3 (8.9)	105.7 (9.8)	88–126

*Wechsler Intelligence Scale for Children-Revised, Verbal, Performance, and Full Scale IQ.

Language Comprehension
    Comprehension (Wechsler 1963) (K).
    Comprehension (Wechsler 1974) (G.2).
Vocabulary
    Vocabulary (Wechsler 1963) (K).
    Vocabulary (Wechsler 1974) (G.2).
    Peabody Picture Vocabulary Test-Revised (PPVT-R), Form L
        (Dunn and Dunn 1981) (K, G.2, G.4).
Syntactical Knowledge
    Grammatic Closure (Kirk, McCarthy, and Kirk 1968) (K,
        G.2, G.4).
    Syntactic Comprehension (Menyuk 1963) (G.4). Score:
        Number correct.
    Carrow Elicited Language Inventory (CELI) (Carrow 1976)
        (G.2): The child repeats sentences after the examiner.
        Score: Number of errors.
Naming
    Boston Naming Test (BNT) (Kaplan, Goodglass, and Wein-
        traub 1983) (K, G.2, G.4). Score: Number of pictures
        named.
    Rapid Automatized Naming (RAN) (Denckla and Rudel
        1974): Colors, Numbers, Objects (K); Colors, Num-
        bers, Objects, Letters (G.2). Score: Time (in seconds) to
        name the items on each chart.
Verbal Memory: Sentences
    Sentences (Wechsler 1963) (K).
    Sentence Imitation (Newcomer and Hammill 1982) (G.2).
    Sentence Repetition (Spreen and Benton 1969) (G.4). Score:
        Number correct.
Verbal Memory: Digits and Words
    Aston Test of Auditory Sequential Memory (Digit Span)
        (Newton and Thomson 1982) (K). Score: Number of se-
        quences correct.
    Digit Span (Wechsler 1974) (G.2).
    Number Repetition (Kaufman and Kaufman 1983) (G.4).
    Word Order (Kaufman and Kaufman 1983) (G.4).
Visual-Verbal Association
    Sounds (K): The child gives the sound of each letter, pre-
        sented in upper case form. Score: Number correct.
    Finger Localization (Benton 1959) (K, G.2, G.4). Score:
        Number correct.
    Paired Associates Test (Vellutino et al. 1975) (K, G.4): The
        child pairs three-letter oral nonsense syllables with

nonsense script. A simplified version was used at the kindergarten level. Score: Number correct.

Reading Measures.   Reading tests were selected to measure word reading, pseudoword reading, reading comprehension, spelling, and oral reading accuracy and rate. Pseudoword reading (Word Attack) was not included at grade 4 because many subjects in the study population obtained perfect or near-perfect scores at second grade.

Grade 2 (Grade equivalent scores)
>   Woodcock Reading Mastery Tests, Form B (Woodcock 1973): Word Identification, Word Attack.
>   Basic Achievement Skills Individual Screener (BASIS) (Psychological Corporation 1983): Reading (comprehension), Spelling.
>   Gray Oral Reading Tests (GORT), Form A (Gray 1967).

Grade 4 (Standard scores)
>   Kaufman Test of Educational Achievement (K.TEA) (Kaufman and Kaufman 1985): Reading Decoding, Reading Comprehension, Spelling.
>   Gray Oral Reading Tests-Revised (GORT-R), Form A (Wiederholt and Bryant 1986): Passage score.
>   Rate: Time taken (in seconds) to read Passage #3 (entry level for grades 3–4) orally, regardless of accuracy.

Passage scores (M 10, SD 3) and Rate were converted to standard scores (M 100 SD 15), with the Rate scores normalized, to make them consistent with the K.TEA standard scores.

A mean grade equivalent score was obtained for the five measures at grade 2, and a mean standard score at grade 4. Grade equivalent scores were used at grade 2, because the GORT provides only grade equivalent scores. At grade 4 the GORT-R gives only standard scores.

Results

Differences of Reading Capability Groups on Linguistic Tasks at Each Grade

One-way multivariate analysis of variance (MANOVA) on the language tests at each grade level showed that the four groups differed: K: $F = 3.76$ (39,140), p. 0000; G.2: $F = 1.97$ (39,140), p. 0022; G.4: $F = 2.18$ (27,147), p. 0017. Univariate group differences, mean scores and standard deviations of groups, and post-hoc analyses of between-group differences are shown in Tables II–IV.

Table II

Means and Standard Deviations (in parentheses) of Groups on Kindergarten Language Tests

Variable	Dyslexic (D)	Mildly Dyslexic (M)	Average Readers (A)	Good Readers (G)	$F_{(3,55)}$*	p	Post-Hoc Tests*
Comprehension	11.1 (2.7)	12.1 (2.1)	10.8 (3.1)	12.1 (2.5)	0.85	.4703	
Vocabulary	10.6 (1.8)	12.9 (0.9)	11.3 (1.9)	11.7 (2.1)	0.66	.5828	
PPVT-R**	98.6 (13.5)	110.0 (10.8)	104.4 (10.7)	113.6 (6.6)	4.84	.0047	G > M = A = D
Boston Naming	22.6 (7.1)	27.3 (3.7)	25.5 (5.3)	28.5 (3.8)	2.37	.0804	G > A = D
RAN Numbers**	120.4 (31.4)	74.9 (22.6)	63.4 (21.6)	49.3 (15.4)	17.41	.0000	G > A = M > D
RAN Colors	98.9 (22.6)	84.3 (23.0)	69.9 (18.9)	64.4 (21.5)	5.60	.0020	G = A > M = D
RAN Objects	123.0 (45.8)	93.9 (23.8)	95.5 (31.1)	82.4 (31.1)	2.42	.0756	G > D
Grammatic Clos.	39.3 (3.7)	39.1 (4.7)	42.4 (5.2)	45.0 (6.1)	4.60	.0061	G = A > M
Sentences	10.1 (4.4)	9.6 (1.6)	9.9 (2.5)	11.3 (2.1)	2.04	.1186	
Digit Span	21.7 (8.5)	19.0 (3.5)	24.2 (8.0)	27.3 (10.7)	3.45	.0227	G = A = D > M
Sounds	4.1 (3.5)	11.7 (5.1)	17.8 (5.0)	19.8 (3.7)	23.02	.0000	G = A > M > D
Finger Localiz.	31.7 (4.4)	34.3 (2.8)	37.2 (4.6)	39.4 (2.4)	7.37	.0003	G = A > M = D
Paired Assoc.	13.0 (8.2)	19.0 (4.2)	18.7 (6.8)	19.9 (5.5)	1.53	.2169	

*With Full Scale IQ as a covariate. **PPVT-R = Peabody Picture Vocabulary Test-Revised; RAN = Rapid Automatized Naming. RAN scores are times in seconds to complete task.

Table III
Means and Standard Deviations (in parentheses) of Groups on Grade 2 Language Tests

Variable	Dyslexic (D)	Mildly Dyslexic (M)	Average Readers (A)	Good Readers (G)	$F(3,55)$*	p	Post-Hoc Tests*
Comprehension	11.9 (1.9)	13.0 (2.3)	11.3 (2.2)	10.8 (2.7)	1.61	.1985	
Vocabulary	9.0 (1.3)	12.3 (1.7)	11.4 (2.4)	12.3 (3.2)	2.37	.0808	G > D
PPVT-R**	101.4 (13.1)	110.0 (7.1)	104.1 (11.9)	110.6 (7.7)	2.16	.1033	
Boston Naming	32.6 (6.3)	36.7 (2.9)	34.7 (5.7)	38.1 (2.8)	2.77	.0502	G > A = D
RAN Numbers**	48.7 (19.8)	35.0 (5.7)	35.0 (10.2)	28.2 (8.2)	5.35	.0026	G > A > D
RAN Colors	64.7 (20.5)	55.3 (11.0)	52.7 (12.6)	49.2 (11.9)	2.17	.1015	
RAN Objects	91.7 (39.0)	75.9 (25.1)	68.5 (14.9)	58.3 (12.8)	4.77	.0050	G > M = D,A > D
RAN Letters	54.4 (19.6)	38.0 (10.9)	33.3 (7.4)	27.4 (7.3)	12.06	.0000	G > A = M > D
Grammatic Clos.	36.1 (4.5)	39.9 (2.3)	39.7 (5.1)	41.9 (3.5)	2.99	.0385	G > A = M = D
Sentence Imit.	9.9 (3.7)	9.4 (1.6)	10.0 (2.1)	11.5 (1.7)	3.29	.0291	G > A = M
Digit Span	9.9 (2.1)	7.6 (2.5)	9.5 (2.2)	10.9 (2.9)	6.41	.0008	G > A > M,D > M
CELI** (errors)	9.0 (8.6)	8.3 (4.9)	4.6 (3.8)	2.4 (3.1)	5.47	.0023	G > M = D,A > M
Finger Localiz.	47.0 (6.4)	49.6 (3.7)	50.3 (4.7)	50.3 (4.7)	0.67	.5729	

*With Full Scale IQ as a covariate. **PPVT-R = Peabody Picture Vocabulary Test-Revised; RAN = Rapid Automatized Naming; CELI = Carrow Elicited Language Inventory. RAN scores are times in seconds.

Table IV

Means and Standard Deviations (in parentheses) of Groups on Grade 4 Language Tests

| | | Groups | | | | | |
Variable	Dyslexic (D)	Mildly Dyslexic (M)	Average Readers (A)	Good Readers (G)	$F_{(3,55)}$*	p	Post-Hoc Tests*
Syntactic Compreh.	11.9 (1.9)	11.6 (1.6)	11.3 (1.6)	12.8 (1.6)	3.96	.0125	G > M = A
PPVT-R**	99.1 (6.8)	105.9 (5.0)	102.3 (10.4)	109.5 (7.1)	3.46	.0222	G > A = D
Boston Naming	37.3 (4.7)	42.7 (3.0)	41.3 (4.9)	44.2 (3.0)	3.98	.0123	G > A = D
Grammatic Closure	34.0 (4.3)	37.4 (4.7)	37.9 (5.2)	40.3 (3.2)	3.20	.0304	G > M = D
Number Repetition	8.1 (4.0)	8.1 (1.2)	10.7 (3.0)	11.6 (3.1)	5.17	.0032	G > M = D,A > M
Sentence Repetit.	11.9 (1.6)	12.4 (0.8)	12.5 (1.4)	13.7 (1.9)	3.30	.0269	G > A = M = D
Word Order	8.7 (2.7)	9.1 (3.2)	11.1 (2.3)	11.7 (2.9)	3.16	.0317	G > M = D,A > M
Finger Localiz.	51.7 (4.9)	56.9 (3.5)	54.3 (3.6)	53.1 (3.6)	1.08	.3669	
Paired Assoc.	26.1 (10.0)	32.6 (6.9)	35.2 (7.1)	38.6 (2.5)	6.18	.0011	G > M = D,A > D

*With Full Scale IQ as a covariate. **PPVT-R = Peabody Picture Vocabulary Test-Revised.

The groups differed significantly on seven of the thirteen kindergarten tests (PPVT-R, RAN Numbers and Colors, Grammatic Closure, Digit Span, Sounds, Finger Localization). Differences on the Boston Naming Test and RAN Objects approached significance. When the groups were compared on Sounds with scores on naming upper case letters controlled, they still differed significantly (F = 6.90 [3,55], p. 0005). There were significant differences on eight of the 13 second-grade tests (Boston Naming Test, Grammatic Closure, RAN Numbers, Objects, and Letters, Sentence Imitation, Digit Span, CELI), and Vocabulary approached significance. At grade 4 the groups differed on all but one (Finger Localization) of the nine tests.

Group Differences on Reading Tests

Scores of the four groups on reading tests at each grade (G.2, G.4) are shown in Table V. The mean reading grade equivalent score of the sample at second grade was 3.5 (SD 1.5), and at fourth grade the mean standard reading score was 100.0 (SD 15.3). Mean expected grade placement was 2.67 (SD 0.1) at second grade (group range: 2.63 to 2.7), and 4.62 (SD 0.3) at fourth grade (group range: 4.6 to 4.68). Although the group membership was determined by fourth grade mean reading scores, there were highly significant differences (with Full Scale IQ controlled) between groups on each second grade test, as well as at grade 4.

Kindergarten Linguistic Tasks Predicting Grade 4 Reading Group Membership

Discriminant function analyses were performed on the kindergarten language tests, to identify the variables most effective in predicting reading group membership at grade 4. The results are shown in Table VI.

It was possible to differentiate dyslexic from good readers, mildly dyslexic from good readers, and mildly dyslexic from dyslexic readers with 100 percent accuracy. There was also a high rate of success (95 percent–97 percent) in differentiating both dyslexic and mildly dyslexic subjects from average readers. However, average and good readers were discriminated with only 76 percent accuracy. Sounds appeared in all six comparisons, and RAN Numbers in four.

Comparison of Normal and Dyslexic Readers on Naming Tests

Combined good and average (normal) readers were compared with dyslexics on the Boston Naming Test (BNT) and on the Rapid Automatized Naming (RAN) tests. With Full Scale IQ controlled, they did not differ on the BNT at kindergarten or second grade, but dyslexics were lower at grade 4 (F = 4.97 [1,50], p. 0303). Dyslexics were lower on

Table V

Means and Standard Deviation (in parentheses) of Groups on Grade 2 and Grade 4 Reading Tests

			Groups				
Variable	Dyslexic (D)	Mildly Dyslexic (M)	Average Readers (A)	Good Readers (G)	$F_{(3,55)}$*	p	Post-Hoc Tests*
*Grade 2***							
Word Identification	1.5 (0.3)	2.6 (0.4)	3.2 (0.6)	4.7 (1.1)	53.72	.0000	G > A > M = D
Word Attack	2.0 (0.4)	2.6 (0.6)	5.0 (2.8)	8.4 (3.6)	18.25	.0000	G > A > M = D
BASIS Reading	1.4 (0.4)	2.8 (0.6)	3.3 (0.9)	4.3 (1.1)	29.59	.0000	G > A > M = D
GORT	1.3 (0.2)	1.8 (0.2)	2.7 (1.1)	4.0 (1.4)	26.85	.0000	G > A > M = D
Spelling	1.3 (0.2)	2.2 (0.3)	3.0 (0.9)	4.4 (1.4)	26.04	.0000	G > A > M = D
Mean Reading	1.5 (0.2)	2.4 (0.3)	3.4 (1.0)	5.2 (1.4)	46.90	.0000	G > A > M = D
*Grade 4***							
Reading Decoding	79.3 (3.3)	92.4 (4.5)	108.1 (9.1)	122.2 (9.7)	73.66	.0000	G > A > M = D
Reading Compreh.	77.7 (1.6)	98.0 (3.1)	103.2 (10.8)	117.8 (11.6)	51.55	.0000	G > A > M = D
GORT-R Passage	65.7 (12.1)	84.3 (4.5)	91.0 (6.7)	105.3 (15.1)	41.04	.0000	G > A > M = D
GORT-R Rate	40.6 (28.9)	91.7 (4.9)	101.8 (4.2)	106.4 (2.9)	73.64	.0000	G = A > M > D
Spelling	75.1 (5.4)	88.0 (4.1)	105.4 (10.9)	121.9 (12.1)	63.00	.0000	G > A > M = D
Mean Reading	67.7 (5.1)	90.7 (2.0)	101.9 (6.7)	114.7 (7.4)	252.63	.0000	G > A > M > D

*With Full Scale IQ as a covariate. **Grade 2: Grade equivalent scores; Grade 4: Standard scores (M 100, SD 15). GORT = Gray Oral Reading Test; GORT-R = Gray Oral Reading Test-Revised.

233

Table VI

Best Combinations of Kindergarten Linguistic Variables to Predict Fourth Grade Reading Capability Group Membership, Listed in Order of Entry into Discriminant Function Analyses

	Reading Group Comparisons					
	Dyslexic vs Good	Dyslexic vs Average	Dyslexic vs Mildly Dyslexic	Mildly Dyslexic vs Good	Mildly Dyslexic vs Average	Average vs Good
Variables in Equation	Sounds RAN Numbers	Sounds RAN Numbers	Sounds RAN Numbers Paired Assoc. Finger Loc.	Sounds Finger Loc. RAN Objects	Sounds Vocabulary Gramm. Closure RAN Colors PPVT-R Sentences	PPVT-R Sounds Sentences RAN Numbers
Percent Classified	100.0	97.3	100.0	100.0	94.6	76.1

Abbreviations: RAN = Rapid Automatized Naming; PPVT-R = Peabody Picture Vocabulary Test-Revised; Paired Assoc. = Paired Associates; Finger Loc. = Finger Localization; Gramm. Closure = Grammatic Closure.

the RAN subtests at each grade level (K: Numbers, F = 42.06, p. 0000; Colors, F = 10.73, p. 0019; Objects, F = 5.17, p. 0273. G.2: Numbers, F = 9.79, p. 0029; Colors, F = 5.15, p. 0276; Objects, F = 9.96, p. 0027; Letters, F = 28.62, p. 0000). Normal readers and dyslexics were also compared on the BNT and RAN with Vocabulary and the PPVT-R controlled. These results are given in the Discussion section.

Correlations will be given, when relevant, in the Discussion section.

Study 2: Comparison of Good Readers of Average and Superior Intelligence

Subjects. From the study population were drawn the nine boys of superior intelligence (Superior IQ good readers) whose mean fourth grade reading was within five points of predicted level and matched the reading scores of the seven top scoring good readers of Study 1 (Average IQ good readers). WISC-R Verbal, Performance, and Full Scale IQs, predicted and actual fourth grade reading standard scores, mean second grade reading, and reading subtest scores at grade 2 and 4 are given in Table VII.

Procedures and Results

The two groups were compared on the linguistic and reading tests by means of a nonparametric procedure (Mann-Whitney Two-Sample Test).

As expected, in view of their much higher Verbal IQ, the superior IQ good readers surpassed the average IQ good readers on Vocabulary at each grade (K: p. 0262; G.2: p. 0390) and on Comprehension at grade 2 (p. 0199). The difference on the PPVT-R approached significance at each grade (p. 05 to .06). The superior IQ group was also significantly higher on the Boston Naming Test at each grade (K: p. 0129; G.2: p. 0300; G.4: p. 0390), and on the kindergarten Paired Associates (p. 0343). The average IQ group was significantly higher on RAN Numbers at each grade (K: p. 0262; G.2: p. 0262). The two groups did not differ on any other language test at any grade.

Mean reading scores were similar at grade 2, as well as at grade 4. Both groups were superb at reading pseudowords tested at grade 2. Both groups were superior in reading comprehension, but at grade 4 the superior IQ group was significantly higher (p. 0343). The two groups did not differ on any other reading test, although there were highly significant differences on the three IQ measures.

Table VII

Mean Verbal, Performance, and Full Scale IQs, and Second and Fourth Grade Reading Scores of Average IQ and Superior IQ Good Readers

| | Variable | Groups | | | |
| | | Average IQ Good Readers | | Superior IQ Good Readers | |
		Mean	Range	Mean	Range
WISC-R	Verbal IQ	114.1	97–145	137.7	120–145
	Performance IQ	105.9	93–120	126.1	109–138
	Full Scale IQ	111.1	100–126	135.7	128–145
*G.4 Reading**	Predicted Mean	105.0	97.8–114.5	120.7	115.8–126.6
	Actual Mean	121.6	116.4–131	122.7	117.8–129.6
	Reading Decoding	127.0	115–135	127.6	117–136
	Reading Comprehension	126.1	118–131	133.2	123–150
	GORT-R Passage	119.3	105–135	121.1	105–135
	GORT-R Rate	108.0	107–110	106.9	104–110
	Spelling	127.4	110–151	124.8	115–137
*G.2 Reading***	Mean Reading	6.0	3.8–8.5	5.6	3.8–7.3
	Word Identification	5.4	3.9–7.4	5.1	4.4–6.0
	Word Attack	10.1	4.7–12.9	9.3	4.1–12.9
	BASIS Reading	4.9	3.9–5.9	5.1	4.1–6.3
	GORT	4.6	3.0–7.7	3.9	2.2–5.8
	Spelling	5.0	3.0–8.4	4.8	4.0–6.2

*Standard scores; **Grade equivalent scores. WISC-R = Wechsler Intelligence Scale for Children-Revised; GORT(R) = Gray Oral Reading Test (Revised).

Discussion

In this section the discussion will focus primarily on the results of the main study of the linguistic skills of dyslexic, mildly dyslexic, average, and good readers, but the results from the second study of good readers of average and superior IQ will be included, when relevant.

Language Comprehension

The four reading groups did not differ on the two Wechsler Comprehension subtests (Wechsler 1963, 1974), given at kindergarten and second grade. As the groups also did not differ on WISC-R Verbal IQ, it can be assumed that the dyslexic subjects did not have a general language comprehension deficit.

Vocabulary

Good readers showed a superiority in receptive vocabulary (PPVT-R: Dunn and Dunn 1981), especially in relation to average readers and dyslexics, whom they surpassed significantly at kindergarten and grade 4. They were superior to the mildly dyslexic subjects only at the kindergarten level.

By contrast, the only difference in expressive vocabulary (defining words) (Wechsler 1963, 1974), tested at kindergarten and grade 2, was that good readers were superior to dyslexics at grade 2. By this time the dyslexics were three years behind good readers in reading skills, and their lower expressive vocabulary could be a consequence of their reading deficit (Share and Silva 1987; Stanovich 1986).

Although average IQ good readers were inferior to the superior IQ good readers in expressive vocabulary, the two groups differed only marginally in receptive vocabulary. This finding suggests that the average IQ group's strong phonological awareness and ability to store phonological information provided them with knowledge of words, which was greater than their ability to define them.

Syntactical Knowledge

The Carrow Elicited Language Inventory (CELI) (Carrow 1976) is included in this section, rather than with tests of sentence memory, because it is designed specifically to test knowledge of syntax. As it was administered only at grade 2, changes over time cannot be observed. Good readers were highest and superior to both the mildly dyslexic and dyslexic subjects, and the average readers were superior to the mildly dyslexic group. The good readers were highest at each grade level on Grammatic Closure (Kirk, McCarthy, and Kirk 1968) and significantly higher than mildly dyslexic subjects at each grade, dyslexics at grades 2 and 4, and average readers at grade 2.

Syntactic Comprehension (Menyuk 1963) was given only at grade 4. On this test the child must answer an oral question about a sentence which contains an embedded clause. Good readers were superior to mildly dyslexic and average readers (though not to dyslexics). As storing word strings in working memory is important for such tasks as following convoluted syntax (Wagner and Torgesen 1987), and as the good readers were superior in sentence memory, Syntactic Comprehension was examined with Sentence Repetition scores controlled, as well as Full Scale IQ. With sentence memory controlled, the group difference only approached significance (p. 06).

The superiority of the good readers on syntactical tasks and the lack of difference on these tasks between the subset of average IQ good readers and superior IQ good readers attests to the phonological sensitivity of good readers to the nuances of spoken language.

Naming

Dyslexic children have been shown to be poorer than normal readers in both speed of naming continuous stimuli (Denckla and Rudel 1976; Felton and Wood 1989; Wolf, Bally, and Morris 1986), and in confrontation naming or lexical retrieval of single words (Felton and Wood 1989; Katz 1986; Murphy, Pollatsek, and Well 1988; Wolf and Goodglass 1986). Rapid stimulus naming predicts later reading, and particularly word reading (Wolf 1986), while confrontation naming predicts reading comprehension (Wolf and Goodglass 1986).

Rapid Automatized Naming (RAN) tests (Denckla and Rudel 1974), given at kindergarten and second grade, were excellent differentiators of reading groups in this study. Rank order on five of the seven RAN subtests administered were: good readers > average readers > mildly dyslexic > dyslexic, mirroring ranks on reading tests. The kindergarten RAN Numbers vied with Sounds in having the highest correlation with second and fourth grade reading (Mean grade 4 reading: $r = -.690$, p. 0000). The partial correlation with Full Scale IQ controlled was almost identical ($r = -.687$), indicating that intelligence plays a negligible role in rapid naming skills. At second grade RAN Numbers was also a good differentiator of groups, but was surpassed by RAN Letters, which was not given in kindergarten. That skill in rapid naming of symbols is closely linked with reading proficiency, though not with intelligence, is also shown by the superiority of the average IQ good readers (IQ not controlled) on RAN Numbers over boys of much higher intelligence (superior IQ good readers), whom they equalled in mean reading scores.

The Boston Naming Test (BNT) (Kaplan, Goodglass, and Weintraub 1983) given as a test of confrontation naming at each grade was a weak group differentiator (p. .05 to .08) at kindergarten and second grade, but stronger at grade 4. At each grade, good readers were superior to average and dyslexic readers, but there were no other between-group differences. These results differ from Wolf's findings that severely impaired readers were significantly lower than average readers in kindergarten and grade 1 (Wolf and Goodglass 1986). Results were similar when the dyslexic readers of this study were compared with combined good and average (normal) readers, who matched Wolf's average readers in oral reading at grade 2. Dyslexics were lower than normal readers at grade 4, but not in kindergarten or grade 2. This late-onset deficit (9.9 years) on the BNT in the dyslexics of this study could be a consequence of their poor reading and may also reflect increasing importance of comprehension in distinguishing more and less skilled readers.

Wolf and Goodglass (1986) concluded that lexical retrieval, not vocabulary knowledge, was the main source of difference between their impaired and average readers. To test the contribution of vocabulary knowledge to naming tests, the dyslexics and normal readers of this study were compared on the BNT and RAN at kindergarten and second grade, with receptive and expressive vocabulary scores controlled (but not Full Scale IQ). F ratios for group differences on the BNT decreased to near zero (K: 0.47; G.2: 0.055), but RAN subtests were little affected. The finding (Wolf and Goodglass 1986) that confrontation naming is a good predictor of reading comprehension may be explained by the shared variance of the BNT and vocabulary knowledge. Indeed a concern about the BNT is that it may become a vocabulary test with young children. In this study the correlation of the kindergarten BNT with grade 4 reading comprehension was .490 (p. 0001), accounting for 24 percent of the variance. With vocabulary knowledge controlled, the percentage of variance in reading comprehension accounted for by the BNT was less than 7 percent (r = .260, p. .0484).

Comprehension and vocabulary are closely linked, and that it is probably this linkage that is the basis of the relationship of the BNT with reading comprehension, was observed in Study 2. Comprehension and Vocabulary were among the few linguistic tasks on which average IQ good readers were lower than superior IQ good readers, and the only reading subtest on which they were lower was grade 4 reading comprehension. The implication is that their greater vocabulary knowledge gave the superior IQ good readers an edge in reading comprehension.

Verbal Memory

It has been suggested that both developmental and individual differences in verbal memory span are related to the efficacy of phonological processes, and that the short-term memory deficit of poor readers is specific to tasks requiring phonetic coding (Brady 1986). Torgesen (1988) concluded that variable attention span and difficulties in sequencing information or perceiving temporal order could be ruled out as explanations for the memory problems of the learning-disabled children he studied.

In this study good readers were superior on the verbal memory tests. The mildly dyslexic group was characterized by poor performance on verbal memory tests at all grades, in relation to good and average readers, irrespective of whether the stimuli were sentences, digits or single words. The mildly dyslexic subjects were also surpassed by the dyslexics on digit span in kindergarten and second grade. Only at fourth grade did the dyslexics show a consistent deficit on memory tasks, and only by comparison with good readers. The variability in memory performance among dyslexics is difficult to explain.

Visual-Verbal Association

The best kindergarten discriminator of good and average readers from the two dyslexic groups was Sounds. Even when differences in naming upper case letters were controlled, normal readers were still significantly superior to the two dyslexic groups, who did not differ. Difficulty in learning grapheme-phoneme correspondences is likely to be due to a deficit in phonological awareness and/or to problems with phonological recoding of graphic symbols.

On the kindergarten Finger Localization test (Benton 1959), good and average readers were superior to both dyslexic groups, who did not differ. To do well on this task children must phonologically encode (by name or number) the finger(s) touched by the examiner, maintain the label(s) in working memory and then associate the label(s) with the fingers on a diagram of the two hands. The kindergarten Finger Localization had a significant partial correlation with fourth grade reading ($r = .521$, p. 0000). Benton (1984) proposed that the kindergarten Finger Localization is a significant predictor of later reading (Jorm et al. 1986; Lindgren 1978; Satz et al. 1978) because it makes demands on a number of capacities, including the use of verbal labels to mediate thought. There is little evidence of a relationship between finger localization and reading ability once children reach school age (Benton 1984), and this was true of this study. At grades 2 and 4, reading groups did not differ on Finger Localization.

Developmental changes in the reverse direction were observed for the Paired Associates Test (Vellutino et al. 1975). At the kindergarten level the overall group analysis was nonsignificant, but the fourth grade Paired Associates was a highly significant group discriminator, with good readers superior to both dyslexic groups, and average readers superior to dyslexics. From his analysis of errors Vellutino concluded that normal readers were more likely than poor readers to code nonsense syllables phonetically. However, difficulty in maintaining phonological information in working memory may also contribute to the inferior performance of poor readers.

Conclusions

Linguistic profiles of boys who differed in fourth grade reading ability were examined at the kindergarten, second grade, and fourth grade levels. A limitation of the study was that no test of phonological awareness was given, although there is evidence that phonological awareness plays a causal role in learning to read (Wagner and Torgesen 1987).

One question for which the study sought an answer was whether the reading capability groups differed on tasks of general linguistic ability or only on specific tasks. The four reading groups did not differ in language comprehension, nor in Verbal IQ. Thus, the differences in reading skills were not associated with a generalized language factor. Tasks on which the reading groups differed involved mainly confrontation naming, rapid naming, syntactical knowledge, verbal short-term memory, and visual-verbal association. Good readers were consistently best on most of these tasks, and the dyslexic and mildly dyslexic were usually poorest. Average readers were generally inferior to good readers in confrontation naming, on some rapid naming tasks, and in verbal short-term memory.

A second question asked what types of kindergarten linguistic tasks most effectively predict reading capability group membership at grade 4. In spite of the omission of a phonological awareness task, it was possible to predict individual fourth-grade reading group membership with a high degree of accuracy. In the six between-group comparisons, accuracy of specific kindergarten tasks in defining reading group membership was 95 percent or higher in all but one comparison (average vs good readers). The success was due primarily to Sounds (giving grapheme-phoneme correspondences) and rapid naming (RAN) tests, and RAN Numbers in particular. Differential ability of children in giving letter sounds may reflect differences in phonological awareness and/or phonological recoding ability. The fact that there was still a highly significant (p. 0005) difference between groups on Sounds when letter naming ability was controlled, shows that knowledge of letter sounds taps a skill that only partly overlaps with giving letter names. Rapid naming tasks assess phonological recoding for lexical access. In their review Wagner and Torgesen (1987) were unable to find evidence for a causal relationship of phonological recoding to reading, although they admit the possibility of such a relationship. The finding in this study that rapid naming not only differentiated dyslexics from average and good readers (and sometimes also from the mildly dyslexic), but also appeared to be a major contributing factor to the equal reading ability of average IQ good readers with that of boys who were 24 points higher in Verbal and Full Scale IQ, suggests that the skills underlying rapid naming tasks are closely, and possibly causally, related to reading, although not to intelligence.

A third question asked in this study was whether linquistic profiles of different reading capability groups change in the early school years. The answer to this question was limited by the fact that not all tasks, or types of tasks, were given at each of the three levels. Subject to this limitation, the study showed relatively few changes in group profiles between kindergarten and grade 4. The strengths observed in good readers as fourth graders (e.g., receptive vocabulary, confrontation naming, short-term verbal memory, syntactical knowledge) were already apparent in kindergarten, and their rapid naming ability was superior at both grades when it was tested (K, G.2). It must be assumed that the good readers possessed linguistic strengths which facilitated reading acquisition. In view of their sensitivity to spoken language, it is very probable that these good readers also had excellent phonological awareness. There was some evidence for late-onset deficits in dyslexics, which may have been due to failure in reading. For example, they were poorer than combined average and good readers in confrontation naming only at grade 4. In this study, vocabulary knowledge accounted for most of the variance in confrontation naming. Consistent deficits in verbal short-term memory characterized mainly the mildly dyslexic group, but by fourth grade the dyslexics also showed a weakness in short-term memory. Why this should be so is not known. Finger localization was a task in which developmental changes in the opposite direction were observed. That is, it was only in kindergarten that groups differed, with both dyslexic groups inferior to average and good readers. There is some evidence that finger localization may involve phonological coding (Jorm et al. 1986).

To sum up, the findings of this study confirm those of other researchers (e.g. Stanovich 1988a, 1988b) that dyslexia (and conversely good reading) has little or no relationship to the types of verbal cognitive tasks which are included in the standard intelligence tests. Rather, within its limitations, this study found that the deficits underlying dyslexia are specific and primarily in the "phonological core" (Stanovich 1988a). Much remains to be learned about the phonological system. However, because no measure of phonological awareness was given, this study can throw no light on the relationship of phonological awareness to other skills, such as phonological recoding for lexical access, which Wagner and Torgesen (1987) subsume under the title of phonological processing tasks.

References

Badian, N. A., McAnulty, G. B., Duffy, F. H., and Als, H. 1990. Prediction of dyslexia in kindergarten boys. *Annals of Dyslexia* 40:152–167.

Benton, A. L. 1959. *Right-left Discrimination and Finger Localization: Development and Pathology.* New York: Hoeber-Harper.

Benton, A. L. 1984. Dyslexia and spatial thinking. *Annals of Dyslexia* 34:69–85.

Brady, S. 1986. Short-term memory, phonological processing, and reading ability. *Annals of Dyslexia* 36:138–153.

Carrow, E. 1976, *Carrow Elicited Language Inventory.* Austin, Texas: Learning Concepts.

Denckla, M. B. and Rudel, R. 1974. Rapid "automatized" naming of pictured objects, colors, letters and numbers by normal children. *Cortex* 10:186–202.

Denckla, M. B. and Rudel, R. 1976. Rapid automatized naming (R.A.N.): Dyslexia differentiated from other learning disabilities. *Neuropsychologia* 14:471–479.

Dunn, L. M. and Dunn, L. M. 1981. *Peabody Picture Vocabulary Test-Revised.* Circle Pines, Minnesota: American Guidance Service.

Felton, R. H. and Wood, F. B. 1989. Cognitive deficits in reading disability and attention deficit disorder. *Journal of Learning Disabilities* 22:3–13, 22.

Gray, W. S. 1967. *Gray Oral Reading Tests.* Indianapolis: Bobbs-Merrill.

Jorm, A. F., Share, D. L., MacLean, R., and Matthews, D. 1986. Cognitive factors at school-entry predictive of specific reading retardation and general reading backwardness: A research note. *Journal of Child Psychology and Psychiatry and Allied Disciplines* 27:45–54.

Kaplan, E., Goodglass, H., and Weintraub, S. 1983. *Boston Naming Test.* Philadelphia: Lea and Febiger.

Katz, R. B. 1986. Phonological deficiencies in children with reading disability: Evidence from an object naming task. *Cognition* 22:225–257.

Kaufman, A. S. and Kaufman, N. L. 1983. *Kaufman Assessment Battery for Children.* Circle Pines, Minnesota: American Guidance Service.

Kaufman, A. S. and Kaufman, N. L. 1985. *Kaufman Test of Educational Achievement, Comprehensive Form.* Circle Pines, Minnesota: American Guidance Service.

Kirk, S. A., McCarthy, J. J., and Kirk, W. 1968. *Illinois Test of Psycholinguistic Abilities.* Urbana, Illinois: University of Illinois Press.

Liberman, I. Y. and Shankweiler, D. 1985. Phonology and the problems of learning to read and write. *Remedial and Special Education* 6:8–17.

Lindgren, S. D. 1978. Finger localization and the prediction of reading disability. *Cortex* 14:87–101.

Mann, V. A. 1984. Longitudinal prediction and prevention of early reading difficulty. *Annals of Dyslexia* 34:117–136.

Menyuk, P. 1963. Syntactic structures in the language of children. *Child Development* 34:407–422.

Murphy, L. A., Pollatsek, A., and Well, A. D. 1988. Developmental dyslexia and word retrieval deficits. *Brain and Language* 35:1–23.

Newcomer, P. L. and Hammill, D. D. 1982. *Test of Language Development: Primary.* Austin, Texas: Pro-Ed.

Newton, M. and Thomson, M. 1982. *Aston Index Revised.* Cambridge, England: LDA.

Olson, R., Wise, B., Conners, F., Rack, J., and Fulker, D. 1989. Specific deficits in component reading and language skills: Genetic and environmental influences. *Journal of Learning Disabilities* 22:339–348.

Perfetti, C. A., Beck, I., Bell, L., and Hughes, C. 1987. Phonemic knowledge and learning to read are reciprocal: A longitudinal study of first grade children. *Merrill-Palmer Quarterly* 33:283–319.

Psychological Corporation 1983. *Basic Achievement Skills Individual Screener.* New York: Harcourt Brace Jovanovich.

Satz, P., Taylor, H. G., Friel, J., and Fletcher, J. 1978. Some developmental and predictive precursors of reading disabilities: A six year follow-up. In A. L. Benton and D. Pearl (eds.). *Dyslexia: An Appraisal of Current Knowledge.* New York: Oxford University Press.

Share, D. L., Jorm, A. F., MacLean, R., and Matthews, R. 1984. Sources of individual differences in reading acquisition. *Journal of Educational Psychology* 76:1309–1324.

Share, D. L. amd Silva, P. A. 1987. Language deficits and specific reading retardation: Cause or effect? *British Journal of Disorders of Communication* 22:219–226.

Siegel, L. S. 1989. IQ is irrelevant to the definition of learning disabilities. *Journal of Learning Disabilities* 22:469–478, 486.

Spreen, O. and Benton, A. L. 1969. *Neurosensory Center Comprehensive Examination for Aphasia.* Victoria, British Columbia: Neuropsychology Laboratory, University of Victoria.

Stanovich, K. E. 1986. Matthew effects in reading: Some consequences of individual differences in the acquisition of literacy. *Reading Research Quarterly* 26:360–407.

Stanovich, K. E. 1988a. Explaining the differences between the dyslexic and the garden-variety poor reader: The phonological-core variable-difference model. *Journal of Learning Disabilities* 21:590–604.

Stanovich, K. E. 1988b. The right and wrong places to look for the cognitive locus of reading disability. *Annals of Dyslexia* 38:154–177.

Torgesen, J. K. 1988. Studies of children with learning disabilities who perform poorly on memory span tasks. *Journal of Learning Disabilities* 21:605–612.

Vellutino, F. 1979. *Dyslexia: Theory and research.* Cambridge, Mass.: MIT Press.

Vellutino, F. R. 1983. Childhood dyslexia: A language disorder. In H. R. Myklebust (ed.). *Progress in Learning Disabilities,* Vol. V. New York: Grune and Stratton.

Vellutino, F. R., Steger, J. A., Harding, C. J., and Phillips, F. 1975. Verbal versus non verbal paired-associates learning in poor and normal readers. *Neuropsychologia* 13:75–82.

Wagner, R. K. and Torgesen, J. K. 1987. The nature of phonological processing and its causal role in the acquisition of reading skills. *Psychological Bulletin* 101:192–212.

Wechsler, D. 1963. *Wechsler Preschool and Primary Scale of Intelligence.* New York: Psychological Corporation.

Wechsler, D. 1974. *Wechsler Intelligence Scale for Children-Revised.* New York: Psychological Corporation.

Wiederholt, J. L. and Bryant, B. R. 1986. *Gray Oral Reading Tests: Revised.* Los Angeles: Western Psychological Services.

Williams, J. P. 1984. Phonemic analysis and how it relates to reading. *Journal of Learning Disabilities* 17:240–245.

Wolf, M. 1984. Naming, reading, and the dyslexias: A longitudinal overview. *Annals of Dyslexia* 34:87–115.

Wolf, M. 1986. Rapid alternating stimulus naming in the developmental dyslexias. *Brain and Language* 27:360–379.

Wolf, M., Bally, H., and Morris, R. 1986. Automaticity, retrieval processes, and reading: A longitudinal study in average and impaired readers. *Child Development* 57:988–1000.

Wolf, M. and Goodglass, H. 1986. Dyslexia, dysnomia, and lexical retrieval: A longitudinal investigation. *Brain and Language* 28:154–168.

Woodcock, R. W. 1973. *Woodcock Reading Mastery Tests.* Circle Pines, Minnesota: American Guidance Service.

Gestalt Imagery: A Critical Factor in Language Comprehension

Nanci Bell

Lindamood-Bell Learning Processes
San Luis Obispo, California

Gestalt imagery—the ability to create imaged wholes—is a critical factor in oral and written language comprehension. Despite good decoding, good vocabulary, and adequate background experiences, many individuals experience weak gestalt imagery, thus processing "parts" rather than "wholes," from verbal stimuli, spoken or written. This contributes to a Language Comprehension Disorder that may be accompanied by a commonality of symptoms: weak reading comprehension, weak oral language comprehension, weak oral language expression, weak written language expression, difficulty following directions, and a weak sense of humor. Sequential stimulation using an inquiry technique develops gestalt imagery and results in significant improvement in reading comprehension.

For years educators have studied reading and discussed and disputed reading efficiency in terms of primary strategies, such as the "context effect" and vocabulary, phonological segmentation and word attack, and word recognition. Yet, none of these strategies guarantees the critical skill of language comprehension.

Language comprehension is the ability to connect to and interpret both *oral* and *written* language. It is the ability to recall facts, get the main idea, make an inference, draw a conclusion, predict/extend, and evaluate. It is the ability to *reason* from language that is heard and language that is read. It is cognition.

Annals of Dyslexia, Vol. 41, 1991.
ISSN 0736-9387

Unfortunately, my clinical research suggests the existence of a specific Language Comprehension Disorder. This comprehension disorder underlies the reading process and goes beyond use of context, phonological processing, word recognition, vocabulary, prior knowledge, and background experience. It is a disorder in the comprehension of both oral and written language. It may be separate from a decoding disorder. It may be separate from a phonological processing disorder. It may be separate from a vocabulary disorder. However, it can be diagnosed and it has a cause and symptoms. It is a serious cause for concern in the field of reading.

The Imaged Gestalt

A Language Comprehension Disorder is based in the sensory system and is a weakness in creating a *gestalt*. Gestalt is defined as a complex organized unit or whole that is more than the sum of its parts. The whole may have attributes that require a certain function for each part in the whole; these attributes are not deducible from analysis of the parts in isolation. In the case of a language comprehension disorder, the weakness in creating a gestalt interferes with the *connection to* and *interpretation* of incoming language.

For many individuals gestalts are not easily or successfully processed. Instead, "parts," bits and pieces, facts and details, dates and names are processed but not the entirety of the concept. Individuals describe the phenomena as, "the words go in one ear and out the other." A high school student commented on his reading, "It is words man . . . just words." A university graduate described listening to a lecture, "It is like the language was written on a blackboard and someone was going behind and erasing it, and I only got parts"—not the gestalt.

And the gestalt is the issue. The only reason to read or listen to language—take in verbal stimuli—is to get meaning, to comprehend, to interpret, to reason. The gestalt is a prerequisite to interpretation and reasoning. For example, the main idea cannot be discerned if only a few "parts" have been grasped. An adequate inference cannot be determined or an accurate conclusion drawn from "parts." The gestalt is the entity from which the interpretive skills of identifying the main idea, inferring, concluding, predicting, extending, and evaluating can be processed. It enables the reader or listener to bring meaning—deep structure—to what is read or heard. It is an integral part of cognition.

The critical nature of the gestalt then requires us to answer the question: How does one create the gestalt? An answer: The gestalt is created by the visualization of a whole. *Gestalt imagery is the ability to create an imaged whole.* "Readers or listeners construct mental models of the situation a writer or speaker is describing. This is the basis of language comprehension" (Bower and Morrow 1990). Kosslyn (1983), "A number of great thinkers, most notably Albert Einstein, professed to rely heavily on imagery in their work. Consider these words of Einstein: 'The psychical entities which seem to serve as elements of thought are certain signs and more or less clear images which can be "voluntarily" reproduced . . . this combinatory play seems to be the essential feature in productive thought—before there is any connection with logical construction of words or other kinds of signs which can be communicated to others.' "

Imaging is a sensory link. Gestalt imagery connects us to incoming language and links us to and from prior knowledge, accesses background experiences, establishes vocabulary, and creates and stores information in both long term and short term memory. Researchers in reading and imagery have produced direct evidence linking reading and mental imagery and have studied the relationship of imagery to prior knowledge and thinking processes (Kosslyn 1983; Levin 1973, 1981; Marks 1972; Paivio 1971, 1986; Peters and Levin 1986; Pressley 1976; Richardson 1969; Sadoski 1983; Sheehan 1972; Stemmler 1969; Tierney and Cunningham 1984). Vivid gestalt imaging may even be considered a "vicarious experience."

My clinical research, identifying imagery as critical and basic to language comprehension, began almost ten years ago with a remark made by a college student. He had extraordinary language recall and interpretation and described his processing as, "I make movies when I read." He verbalized creating mental images and using the images for recall, interpretation, and reasoning. Further inquiry with individuals noted that good comprehenders reported good imaging and poor comprehenders reported weak imaging. And, more important, exploratory stimulation of imagery resulted in substantial gains in comprehension.

Historical Perspective

Though empirical research can be convincing, there is considerable evidence in the fields of both cognitive psychology and reading that support imagery as a critical factor in language comprehension. Thus, before proceeding further, it is important to note some of the historical perspective regarding the relationship between imagery and cognition.

Imagery as related to memory has been discussed since Aristotle. He stated, "It is impossible even to think without a mental picture . . . memory or remembering is a state induced by mental images related as a likeness to that of which it is an image" (1972). Moving to modern times, Jean Piaget (1936, cited by Bleasdale 1983) wrote in favor of a perceptual base to memory. According to Piaget, knowledge structures, or schemata, are acquired when the infant actively manipulates, touches, and interacts with the environment. As objects are manipulated, sensory-motor schemata are developed and changed to accommodate new information. Over time, schemata become internalized in the form of imaged thought. Piaget stated, "It is clear that imaginal representations are not formed with the same facility in each case, and that there is therefore a hierarchy of image levels, which may correspond to stages of development . . . The evolution of images is a kind of intermediate between that of the perceptions and that of the intelligence."

Proceeding chronologically to examine some of the more interesting research and historical commentary, Arnheim (1966) wrote, "Thinking is concerned with the objects and events of the world we know . . . When the objects are not physically present, they are represented indirectly by what we remember and know about them. In what shape do memory and knowledge deliver the needed facts? In the shape of memory images, we answer most simply. Experiences deposit images." He quoted the psychologist Edward B. Titchener, ". . . my mind, in its ordinary operations, is a fairly complete picture gallery,— not of finished paintings, but of impressionist notes. Whenever I read or hear that somebody has done something modestly, or gravely, or proudly, or humbly, or courteously, I see a visual hint of the modesty or pride or humility." The *visual hint* may be a means of processing abstract material. Continuing in the sixties, Allan Paivio (1969), who has written extensively on imagery and cognition, stated, "As every psychologist knows, imagery once played a prominent role in the interpretation of associative meaning, mediation, and memory. It was widely regarded as the mental representative of meaning—or of concrete meaning at least. William James, for example, suggested that the static meaning of concrete words consists of sensory images awakened [1890]."

The seventies brought further illumination from Paivio (1971). He had been attempting to demonstrate the way in which imagery can affect the acquisition, transformation, or retrieval of different classes of information. His dual coding theory for cognition defines imagery (usually visual imagery) as one of two types of cognitive code. The other type is verbal code. Paivio suggested that linguistic competence and performance are based on a substrate of imagery. Imagery includes not only static representations of objects, but also dynamic representations of action sequences and relationships between objects and events. Pribram (1971) stated, "Recently the importance of the Image concept has started to be recognized: cognitive psychologists analyzing the process of verbal learning have been faced with a variety of Imaging processes which demand neurological underpinnings. . . . Neurological research, as well as insights derived from the information-processing sciences, have helped make understandable the machinery which gives rise to this elusive ghost-making process." He further hypothesized that "*all* thinking has, in addition to sign and symbol manipulation, a holographic component." Also in the seventies, Kosslyn (1976) conducted a developmental study on the effects and role of imagery in retrieving information from long-term memory. In two blocks of trials, first graders, fourth graders, and adults were asked to determine whether or not various animals are characterized by various properties, first upon the consultation of a visual image and then without imagery. He reported that imagery provided more opportunity for retrieval.

The eighties gave us additional evidence when Linden and Wittrock (1981) stated, "Reading comprehension is the generation of meaning for written language. . . . We found that reading comprehension can be facilitated by several different procedures that emphasize attention to the text and to the construction of verbal or imaginal elaborations." In a study with fourth graders, compared with a control group of students given the same time to learn with the same reading teacher, he noted, "the generation of verbal and imaginal relations or associations between the text and experience increased comprehension approximately by fifty percent." Further research was conducted by Oliver (1982) with three experiments to determine if an instructional set for visual imagery would facilitate reading comprehension in elementary school children. He concluded, "These findings indicate that teachers should try to help children develop the metacognitive skill of visual imagery as a strategy for improving comprehension. . . . Visualization enhances comprehension."

And finally, 1989 provided the research of Long, Winograd, and Bridge. They summarized their findings regarding imagery and reading: "Our results suggest that imagery may be involved in the reading process in a number of ways. First, imagery may increase the capacity of working memory during reading by assimilating details and propositions into chunks which are carried along during reading. Second, imagery seems to be involved in making comparisons or analogies— that is, in matching schematic and textual information. Third, imagery seems to function as an organizational tool for coding and storing meaning gained from the reading."

Symptoms of Gestalt Imagery Weakness

Although imagery has been viewed with prominence in learning theory, two problems exist: 1) the ability to image gestalts has been assumed, and 2) gestalt imagery is not readily available to many individuals. First, we do appear to have assumed imagery processing, or else we would have placed imagery in the curriculum to develop language comprehension in the classroom. Second, many individuals have weak gestalt imagery that creates a commonality of symptoms, ranging from mild to severe. Individuals often display one or all of the following symptoms, with poor reading comprehension as the most evident.

For example, as stated earlier, during and after reading (either aloud or silently), individuals experience only processing "parts" of what has been read. Thus, they often reread material numerous times in order to understand it. They experience difficulty accessing and integrating old information with new, and although their vocabulary may be very good for isolated words, they have difficulty bringing the words together to form imaged gestalts.

Anecdotal references often serve to clarify theory. The following individuals all experienced difficulty imaging gestalts. A college graduate with good decoding and above average intelligence, attempting to enter medical school, described his comprehension disability as "not having a cognitive tool kit. . . . I opened up my cognitive tool kit and there was something missing. Others seemed to do this [comprehend] very easily. I could never understand how they did it and why I couldn't. . . . . About 20 percent of what I took in stayed and about 80 percent went out or was just parts." Another college student, again with good vocabulary and good decoding, but on academic probation described, "There wasn't one thing I could do right. I didn't remember anything I read. It was very frustrating. I read each sentence three times and then went on to the next sentence and read it three times. It didn't make any sense put together . . . if I read the information enough times I could remember it for maybe 30 seconds and then I had no clue."

Another common symptom is *weak oral language comprehension* and the same "parts to whole" problem exists. Individuals connect to parts in a conversation, parts in a lecture, parts in a movie, and parts in their thinking processes. They have difficulty responding relevantly and thinking logically. They often ask and reask the same question and may be labeled as poor listeners or inattentive. A teacher said that she always sat in the front row in a college class or at a professional conference in order to "try and keep the information from going past me." A husband complained because his wife, who was a college graduate, asked and reasked the same question. Unaware of her repetition, she simply rephrased the same question a little differently each time. He explained that she didn't grasp the essence of his answer or of conversation in general.

The oral language comprehension weakness is often accompanied by an *oral language expression weakness.* Individuals experience difficulty organizing their verbalization, expressing themselves easily and fluently, or they are verbal but scattered, relating information out of sequence. For example, a student on academic probation, with severely impaired reading comprehension, frequently interjected irrelevant comments in conversation. His comments were disjointed both unto themselves and to the topic. Consequently, he was often viewed as mentally disabled. After gestalt imagery stimulation was nearly completed, he explained that previously he had desperately wanted to participate in conversation but was only able to comment on the "parts" he was able to grasp, so, he blurted out irrelevant comments.

Weak written language expression is often another symptom. Though spelling and punctuation skills appear intact, writing may lack preciseness, organization, and specifics, and be described as several essays, rather than a coherent whole written to the topic. Additional symptoms include *difficulty following directions, difficulty judging cause and effect,* and a *weak sense of humor.*

Causes and Contributors

The causes of gestalt imagery—language comprehension—disorder are puzzling. Perhaps it is a hereditary factor, since usually one or both parents present a similar deficiency. Perhaps a genetic basis for weak gestalt imagery will eventually be isolated. Perhaps with the advent of more sophisticated brain measurements a specific brain etiology will be determined. Perhaps comprehension has been assumed because the focus in the field of reading has been on decoding, and more recently on the context effect.

Or, perhaps a cause is lack of stimulation, an atrophying effect. Old-time radio and record stories created auditory stimuli that promoted imagery. Currently, however, leisure time is spent engaging in a pastime that offers images rather than stimulates images. Television viewing not only provides images but also consumes what may have been reading time, storytelling time, and language interaction time—time that stimulated imagery.

Whatever the cause, gestalt imaging ability appears to be a function unto itself. Although impaired phonological processing and decoding, weak oral vocabulary, and reduced prior knowledge and background of experiences may contribute to weak imaging, these factors alone do not appear to be causal. As stated earlier, many individuals with good vocabulary for isolated words *are not able* to comprehend efficiently. Many individuals with wide experiences and good educations *are not able* to comprehend efficiently. Many good decoders *are not able* to comprehend efficiently. In contrast, many poor decoders *are* able to comprehend efficiently. If concepts or content are presented to them orally, they appear brilliant in their ability to interpret and reason.

Although perhaps not causal, weak decoding can be a primary contributor to weak gestalt imagery. An individual can have good imagery and good comprehension *only* if he or she can decode enough words critical to the integration and processing of the gestalt. A few decoding errors may cause ridiculous images, and necessitate rereading for contextual cues and correction. However, a severe phonological processing disorder, causing numerous decoding errors (difficulty with surface structure), may cause enough image distortion to interfere with comprehension.

Weak vocabulary may interfere with gestalt imagery if the unknown words are critical to the whole. If not critical to the gestalt, the imaged concept—context—may serve to stimulate vocabulary development. It is not clear which problem existed first—poor vocabulary or poor gestalt imagery—though it is evident that stimulating images for vocabulary aids in the storage and retrieval of meaning for isolated words. Smith, Stahl, and Neil (1987), after a study with 142 university students, state, "The significant difference that occurred between the definition only and the definition and sentence and imagery groups supports Paivio's dual coding theory. In accord with Paivio's theory the visual image did provide an additional memory trace that improved long term memory for the vocabulary items in the study. This finding mirrors research spanning the years as far back as Kirkpatrick in 1894."

Prior knowledge and background experience also may interfere with comprehension and imaging. But, techniques to access prior knowledge such as first discussing material with children, first setting the scene, and first teaching vocabulary do not necessarily stimulate independent comprehension. The *individual* will need to be able to set the scene by decoding, imaging, and interacting with stored images so as to have deep structure available for meaning. The individual will need to have imaging ability to hold and integrate vocabulary with incoming language and images—creating a gestalt.

Development of Gestalt Imagery

Nonentities can be created from theories that start and become unwieldy and often inaccurate as they spin. Thus, the firm earth of experimental data is often comforting and reassuring. My data comes from clinical interaction and empirical research with individuals of all ages. After years of trial and error, and the weeding out of irrelevancy, a process of sequential stimulation emerged. The result is that development of gestalt imagery is possible and produces significant improvement in language comprehension.

Many individuals need more than just a cue or reminder to image. For these individuals gestalt imagery can be developed by direct stimulation, requiring specific questioning. The gestalt of the stimulation is: verbalization of given pictures, verbalization of images for a single word, and verbalization of imaged gestalts for sentences, paragraphs, and pages of content. The specific steps are:

1. Picture to Picture
   The individual describes given pictures. Structure Words of *what, size, color, number, shape, where, when, background, movement, mood,* and *perspective* are introduced to provide descriptive elements. By questioning with "choice and contrast," the teacher stimulates a detailed verbal description of a given picture. The goal is to develop fluent, detailed verbalizing from a given picture prior to requiring detailed verbalizing of an image.

2. Word Imaging
   The individual describes his or her own image with assistance of the structure words and specific questioning of choice and contrast. The procedure moves from the "personal image" level to the "known noun" level that stimulates detailed imagery for a familiar, high-imagery word such as clown, doll, Indian, cowboy, etc. The goal is to develop detailed visualizing and verbalizing of a word prior to requiring detailed visualizing and verbalizing of sentences.

3. Sentence Imaging
   The individual images and describes—visualizes and verbalizes—a sentence using a previously imaged noun. The teacher creates the simple sentence, presents the sentence to the individual orally, and questions with choice and contrast to stimulate imagery.

4. Sentence by Sentence Imaging
   The stimulation is now directed at assisting the individual with

the creation of an *imaged gestalt*. The procedure begins recep-
tively, from a short self-contained paragraph, with each sentence read orally to the individual. The individual visualizes
and verbalizes each sentence and places a three-inch colored
square to note the imaged sentence. Each sentence of the paragraph is visualized and verbalized. At the completion of the
paragraph, with approximately four colored squares representing the sentences, the individual gives a "picture summary" by
touching and describing his/her images for each square. Following this, he or she gives a "word summary" by collecting
the colored squares and sequentially summarizing the paragraph, using specific images to assist with retrieval.

5. Sentence by Sentence with Interpretation
   As the Sentence by Sentence process is developing an imaged
   gestalt, the stimulation extends to interpretation and critical
   thinking. The imaged gestalt is used as the cognitive base for
   higher order thinking skills of main idea, inference, conclusion, prediction, and evaluation.

6. Multiple Sentence Imaging, Paragraph Imaging, Paragraph by
   Paragraph Imaging
   The succeeding steps extend the language from which the individual visualizes and verbalizes, and interprets. The material
   becomes longer and denser with the individual decoding or orally receiving the language input. The process requires the individual to visualize gestalts, verbalize summaries, and interpret from both oral and written language.

The Visualizing/Verbalizing process that has been exploratory now
appears to be compatible in scope to the dual coding theory, Paivio
(1971). "The most general assumption in dual coding theory is that
there are two classes of phenomena handled cognitively by separate
subsystems, one specialized for the representation and processing of
information concerning nonverbal objects and events, the other specialized for dealing with language." The nonverbal (symbolic) subsys-
tem is referred to as the imagery system because its critical functions
include the analysis of scenes and the generation of mental images.
The language-specialized system is referred to as the verbal system,
Paivio (1986). "Human cognition is unique in that it has become specialized for dealing simultaneously with language and with nonverbal
objects and events. Moreover, the language system is peculiar in that it
deals directly with linguistic input and output (in the form of speech or
writing) while at the same time serving a symbolic function with re-

spect to nonverbal objects, events, and behaviors. Any representational theory must accommodate this functional duality."

Clinical Data

My focus has been in the area of clinical diagnosis and treatment, offered individually, to students of all ages. The primary focus of treatment is to develop language comprehension, or phonological processing, or a combination of both. This results in interesting individual case studies showing marked improvement in language processing. One example is the filling of one college graduate's cognitive tool kit. Before clinical treatment to develop gestalt imagery—language comprehension, he had twice taken the MCAT (Medical College Admissions Test) and received a score of four on the reading comprehension subtest. Since the average was eight, he said, "No medical schools will consider me." After ten weeks of intensive treatment, he was performing at the 98th percentile in reading comprehension on the Gray Oral Reading Test Revised. When he retook the MCAT he received a score of ten in reading comprehension, performing above average.

Although the following results are based on clinical study, there necessarily was no control group. Therefore, the results should be considered tentative, a basis for additional controlled studies. In 1989, 45 individuals received clinical intervention—intensive therapy consisting of four hours of daily individual treatment—for whom the focus of treatment was *only* gestalt imagery—language comprehension stimulation. Each individual was diagnosed to determine receptive oral vocabulary (Peabody Picture Vocabulary Test), expressive oral vocabulary (Detroit Tests of Learning Aptitude, Verbal Opposites), phoneme segmentation ability (Lindamood Auditory Conceptualization Test), word attack (Woodcock Reading Mastery Tests), word recognition (Slosson Oral Reading Test), oral paragraph comprehension (Gray Oral Reading Test, Revised), and silent reading comprehension (Descriptive Tests of Language Skills of the College Board, Reading Comprehension subtest). The 45 individuals ranged in age from nine to 57 years old and included 22 males and 23 females: 18 were in grades K–8; 13 were in grades 9–12; 5 were in college; and nine were adults, primarily college graduates. Although performing poorly in reading comprehension, it is important to note their performance on other diagnostic tests. For example, the Peabody Picture Vocabulary Test indicated that 80 percent had age-level or above receptive oral vocabulary skills. The Detroit Test of Learning Aptitude, Verbal Opposites subtest, indicated that 71 percent had age-level or above expressive oral vocabulary skills.

The Lindamood Auditory Conceptualization Test indicated that 88 percent had excellent phoneme segmentation ability. The Woodcock Word Attack Test indicated that 83 percent had above grade level word attack skills. The comprehension disorder clearly appears to be isolated from the above factors.

Since attention had been given to each individual rather than to a group, the 45 were not all given the same pre- and posttests. However, the following will report on the individuals who were given the same pre- and posttest from which statistical evidence can be evaluated. The average time in individual treatment was 47.26 hours, with a range from 16 to 110 hours.

Seventeen individuals, ranging in age from 11 to 57 years old, were administered the Gray Oral Reading Test Revised. The percentile mean for the pre GORT-R Test was 43.94. The percentile mean for the post GORT-R Test was 75.55. This repeated measure showed highly significant effect for the group, $p < .001$.

Sixteen individuals, ranging in age from 15 to 52 years old, were administered the Descriptive Tests of Language Skills of the College Board, Reading Comprehension subtest. The percentile mean for the pre College Board was 56.06. The percentile mean for the post College Board was 71.29. Again, this repeated measure showed highly significant results for the group, $p < .001$.

Twenty-seven individuals, ranging in age from 11 to 59 years old, were administered the Detroit Tests of Learning Aptitude, Oral Directions subtest. The mental age level average for the pre Oral Directions subtest was 11.80 and the mental age level average for the post Oral Directions subtest was 14.33. The overall average gain in mental age was 2.53 years.

Chance Program

Motivation and interest can interfere with comprehension and active focus, but individuals with good comprehension appear to have access to automaticity in gestalt imaging. They appear to comprehend readily, with ease. However, many individuals with a Language Comprehension Disorder may be mislabeled lazy, unmotivated, inattentive, and not interested. Graceland College in Iowa, a private liberal arts college, was considering a "motivation tract" for college students at risk, many on academic probation. In 1988 a study was conducted resulting in the Chance Program. Diagnostic testing indicated that a high percentage of students being considered for the motivation track, scored low on reading comprehension measurements. Thus a number of these students entered into a trial voluntary program, entitled the Chance Program, and were given direct stimulation to develop gestalt imagery while continuing to attend their regular classes.

Diagnostic tests measuring oral vocabulary, phoneme segmentation, word attack, word recognition and paragraph comprehension were administered to the 16 Chance Program students. The testing indicated good phoneme segmentation, good spelling, good word recognition, good word attack, low vocabulary, and *poor reading comprehension*. The mean beginning scores on the Nelson-Denny Reading Test, vocabulary and reading comprehension, were lower for the 16 students in the Chance Program as compared with Nelson-Denny scores taken from a sample of 120 students randomly selected from the study body. For example, in vocabulary and reading comprehension, the mean percentile rankings for the Chance Program students were 13.8 and 13.3, respectively. The mean percentile rankings in vocabulary and reading comprehension for the 120 students of the student body were 41.1 and 44.8, respectively.

After treatment to stimulate gestalt imagery, the Chance Program students demonstrated a significant gain in reading comprehension. On the Descriptive Tests of Language Skills of the College Board, Reading Comprehension subtest, the mean percentile ranking improved from the 29.8 percentile to the 51.6 percentile. On the Nelson-Denny Vocabulary, the mean percentile ranking improved from the 13.8 percentile to the 22.1 percentile. On the Nelson-Denny Reading Comprehension, the mean percentile ranking improved from the 13.3 percentile to the 33.1 percentile.

The gains made on the Nelson-Denny Comprehension Test were highly significant, $p < 001$. The gains made on the Nelson-Denny Vocabulary Test were significant, $p < .05$. The gains noted on the Descriptive Tests of Language Skills of the College Board, Reading Comprehension subtest were also significant, $p < .05$.

Of further interest, the grade point average (G.P.A.) for the students who received gestalt imagery treatment in the Chance Program improved from an average of 2.31 to 2.76. This is an 11 percent increase in G.P.A. and is more significant considering that 14 of the 16 students also had an increase in graded semester hours, from an average of 10.95 to 14.0. Because of the noted gains in comprehension and G.P.A., the status of the Chance Program changed from that of a pilot study to that of a part of the curriculum at Graceland College.

Paivio (1986) said, "The dual coding interpretation is straightforward. The concrete descriptive tasks require a high degree of referential exchange between the verbal and imagery systems." The Chance Program data, our case studies, and statistical data are a *beginning* statement that sequential steps of visualizing and verbalizing stimulate imaged gestalts and language comprehension.

Summary

Reading is cognition. Gestalt imagery contributes to the cognitive process of comprehending oral and written language. The imaging factor, discussed for many years in the field of cognitive psychology, appears to be automatic for many individuals and has, perhaps, been assumed to be present for all. This assumed factor, as well as the focus on decoding, the lack of good oral and written comprehension tests, a culture addicted to television viewing, and the continuing dispute over context, phonological processing, and sight word instruction has left comprehension without *direct* stimulation. Instructional procedures to develop comprehension have been in the format of reading and/or listening and answering questions—a format that *tests* comprehension rather than *teaches* comprehension.

Of late, because of the psycholinguists' cry for meaning and deep structure, the field of reading has been turning away from excessive concern over surface structure. However, increasing vocabulary and stimulating background knowledge or use of context clues does not guarantee comprehension development.

With specific attention to the integration of imagery and verbalization, it is possible to develop an imaged gestalt from which interpretation and reasoning can be processed. "According to the dual coding theory, meaning consists of the relations between external stimuli and the verbal and nonverbal representational activity they initiate in the individual," Paivio (1986).

It is my hope that this initial inquiry will serve to generate further discussion and research focusing on the diagnosis and development of the imaged gestalt and language comprehension.

References

Aristotle. 1972. *Aristotle on Memory.* Providence, Rhode Island: Brown University Press.
Arnheim, R. 1966. Image and thought. *In* G. Kepes (ed.). *Sign, Image, Symbol.* New York: George Braziller, Inc.
Bell, N. 1986. *Visualizing and Verbalizing for Language Comprehension and Thinking.* Paso Robles, California: Academy of Reading Publications.
Bleasdale, F. 1983. Paivio's Dual-Coding Model of Meaning Revisited. *In* J. C. Yuille (ed.). *Imagery, Memory and Cognition: Essays in honor of Allan Paivio.* New Jersey: Lawrence Erlbaum Associates.

Bower, G. H. and Morrow, D. G. 1990. Mental models in narrative comprehension. *Science:* Jan: 44–48.

Kosslyn, S. M. 1976. Using imagery to retrieve semantic information: A developmental study. *Child Development* 47:434–444.

Kosslyn, S. M. 1983. *Ghosts in the Minds Machine.* New York: W. W. Norton.

Levin, J. R. 1973. Inducing comprehension in poor readers. *Journal of Educational Psychology* 65:19–24.

Levin, J. R. 1981. On functions of pictures in prose. *In* F. Pirozzolo and M. Wittrock (eds.). *Neuropsychological and Cognitive Processes in Reading.* New York: Academic Press.

Linden, M. A. and Wittrock, M. C. 1981. The teaching of reading comprehension according to the model of generative learning. *Reading Research Quarterly* 17:44–57.

Long, S. A., and Winograd, P. N., and Bridge, C. A. 1989. The effects of reader and text characteristics on reports of imagery during and after reading. *Reading Research Quarterly* 19(3):353–372.

Marks, D. F. 1972. Vividness of visual imagery and effect on function. *In* P. Sheehan (ed.). *The Function and Nature of Imagery.* New York: Academic Press.

Oliver, M. E. 1982. Improving comprehension with mental imagery. Paper read at the Annual Meeting of the Washington Organization for Reading Development of the International Reading Association, Seattle, Washington, March 1982.

Paivio, A. 1969. Mental imagery in associative learning and memory. *Psychological Review* 76:241–263.

Paivio, A. 1971. *Imagery and Verbal Processes.* New York: Holt, Rinehart, and Winston. Reprinted 1979. Hillsdale NJ: Lawrence Erlbaum Associates.

Paivio, A. 1986. *Mental Representations: A dual coding approach.* New York: Oxford University Press.

Peters, E. E. and Levin, J. R. 1986. Effects of a mnemonic imagery strategy on good and poor readers' prose recall. *Reading Research Quarterly* 21:179–192.

Piaget, J. and Inhelder, B. 1971. *Imagery and the Child.* New York: Basic Books, Inc.

Pirozzolo, F. and Wittrock, M. 1981. *Neuropsychological and Cognitive Processes in Reading.* New York: Academic Press, Inc.

Pressley, G. M. 1976. Mental imagery helps eight-year-olds remember what they read. *Journal of Educational Psychology* 68: 355–359.

Pribram, K. 1971. *Languages of the Brain: Experimental paradoxes and principles in neuropsychology.* New York: Brandon House, Inc.

Richardson, A. 1969. *Mental Imagery.* London: Routledge and Kegan Paul.

Rollins, M. 1989. *Mental Imagery: On the limits of cognitive science.* New Haven, Connecticut: Yale University Press.

Sadoski, M. 1983. An exploratory study of the relationship between reported imagery and the comprehension and recall of a story. *Reading Research Quarterly* 19(1):110–123.

Sheehan, P. W. (ed.). 1972. *The Function and Nature of Imagery.* New York: Academic Press.

Smith, B. D., Stahl, N., and Neil, J. 1987. The effect of imagery instruction on vocabulary development. *Journal of College Reading and Learning* 20:131–137.

Stemmler, A. 1969. Reading of highly creative versus highly intelligent secondary students. *Reading and Realism* 13:821–831.

Tierney, R. J. and Cunningham, J. W. 1984. Research on teaching reading comprehension. *In* P. D. Pearson (ed.). *Handbook of Reading Research.* New York: Longman.

Index